REVIVALTIME

PULPIT

SERMON BOOK
NUMBER NINE
C. M. WARD

ASSEMBLIES OF GOD NATIONAL RADIO  DEPARTMENT SPRINGFIELD, MISSOURI

PRINTED IN U.S.A

CONTENTS

Listed alphabetically

CONTENTS

Listed chronologically according to the date preached on the
Revivaltime broadcast service.

FOREWORD

A *Revivaltime* listener recently wrote, "We take our small recorder and record the broadcast. It's surprising *how much more* you can receive from hearing it a second or third time." That's the reason for this volume of C. M. Ward's radio messages. They can and should be read over and over again.

We want to preserve and propagate these wonderful gospel messages. Each sermon is so impregnated with meaning that it is impossible to absorb it all in hearing it on the radio broadcast.

These sermons are printed here just as they were preached on *Revivaltime* in 1964. In fact, as you read them you will suddenly feel the anointing and compassion with which they were written and preached. God has endowed Evangelist C. M. Ward with an unusual ability to relate the Scriptures to the common needs of mankind.

With his frequent interjection of "mister," "neighbor," "lady," or "sir," you realize he is speaking to you. He invites those who will kneel beside him at the altar to remember that though it's one of the longest altars in the world, it's one of the easiest to reach—where your knee touches is your altar and where your life can be changed.

LEE SHULTZ
Secretary of Radio
Assemblies of God

THE BROADCAST MINISTRY

New levels of accomplishment were achieved by *Revivaltime* this year. Every phase of the Radio Department's outreach was strengthened.

Station coverage increased to an average of more than 450 releases, including 59 from key foreign stations. Literature distribution pushed past the 5 million mark, and more persons received personal counsel from Evangelist C. M. Ward than ever before. Across the nation an upsurge of church interest in the broadcast ministry was evident.

Behind the success of the broadcast ministry is an experienced, dedicated production and promotions team. The Reverend Bartlett Peterson serves as executive director of the department and as a narrator of *Revivaltime*. The Reverend Lee Shultz is secretary of the Radio Department and producer-narrator of *Revivaltime*.

The Reverend C. T. Beem is office manager and directs the broadcast service. The Reverend Stanley V. Michael serves as field representative, and the Reverend F. Wildon Colbaugh is publicity director.

Music for each broadcast service is provided by the 40-voice student choir from Central Bible College, Springfield, Missouri. The choir is directed by Cyril McLellan, and features Denise Power as soloist.

Since going on the ABC network in 1953, Radio Speaker C. M. Ward's vast listening congregation has continually expanded until it reaches the far corners of the earth. Millions of persons listen each week as the dynamic evangelist preaches in a most challenging fashion the whole Word of God.

Thousands of Radio friends have responded to the broadcast ministry, and many have been led to Christ. An increasing number of young Christians, reached through *Revivaltime's* ministry, are finding their places as pastors, teachers, and active laymen in local Assemblies throughout the nation.

BACKWARD — INWARD — UPWARD
FORWARD — OUTWARD

Text: *"This do ye."*

1 *Corinthians* 11:25.

THERE is no question about the *command*. You cannot be a Christian and scorn the Lord's Supper. This is a testimony that Christ demands to be given before the world. It is *His table,* and He does not approve of empty seats. The shed Blood and the broken Body are God's victory, and the Lord's Supper is *a victory celebration.*

1. At the table THINK BACKWARD. Someone died for us. Recently in Los Angeles I met and fellowshiped a friend whom I have known for many years, "First Mate Bob" of The Haven of Rest ministry. I never weary hearing his testimony.

In 1934, at three o'clock in the morning, on a San Diego, Calif., dock, this man was a lonely alcoholic, *a fugitive from God.* He was wandering aimlessly. The faces of his Christian wife and four children kept appearing again and again upon the screen of his consciousness. His soul sickened under wave after wave of self-condemnation.

A nearby piling seemed to say, "Sit here. Rest your aching feet." The cardboard he had put in the bottom of his shoes to reinforce the soles had long ceased to serve the purpose. The clanging of a ship's bell aroused him, and he realized it was four o'clock.

The cold had penetrated, and memories would not be stilled. He thought of *an old-fashioned altar* where he had knelt and prayed as a boy at home. Snatches of *gospel songs* his mother had taught him returned. He felt again the *prayers* his wife had offered for him.

"First Mate Bob" had been a businessman, and a successful one, in the radio industry. He had been the executive manager of two Southern California radio stations. Liquor had taken its toll. His home and marriage were wrecked, and he was near the end of a dead-end street.

Sunrise seemed only the beginning of another dreary day. "Suddenly," he testifies, "I realized this was Sunday morning. People would be going to Sunday school and church. Church! How long had it been since I sat in church?"

At that moment a glimmer of *hope* entered his mind. He decided to find help. A convenient gasoline station washroom afforded the means of making himself as presentable as possible. He decided to go to church.

This is how "First Mate Bob" recalls that morning. These are his own words:

"I entered the church, listened to the organ, the choir, the sermon, and finally the benediction. No mention was made of a Saviour who could rescue a lost soul. The whole meeting was cold, formal, and ritualistic. No one even offered a smile or a handshake. I was stunned!

"Heartbroken, I returned to the cheap room where I had been staying. My eyes focused on a book. It was a Gideon Bible. In desperation I opened its pages, placed it upon a chair and knelt before it. I poured out my heart to God, acknowledging my guilt and declaring my faith in Jesus Christ to save my soul. *Then and there I passed from death unto life.*"

Before the day was over he had hitchhiked back to Los Angeles to tell his wife that he was a new man and to ask for her forgiveness and faith. He remembers that he greeted her with the words, "Thelma, I have found Christ, and He's real to me at last."

Tears of joy moistened her cheeks, and she replied, "Thank God, my prayers are answered after twelve long years."

The rest is a story from that moment to this day of service for Jesus Christ. Yes, sir, we look back to Calvary! "He was wounded for our transgressions." He fought our battles against alcohol, lust, greed, embezzlement, hatred, narcotics, revenge, and profanity. He was *wounded*. The marks are there. He "bare our sins in his own body on the tree" (1 Peter 2:24).

When you lift the cup and partake of the bread, you are saying, "Thank You, Lord, for taking my place upon the Cross and bearing away my sin in Thy body."

2. At the table THINK INWARD. Do you come "unworthily" or carelessly? "Wherefore whosoever shall eat this bread, and drink this cup of the Lord, unworthily, shall be guilty of the body and blood of the Lord" (1 Corinthians 11:27). *That is a serious charge.*

The apostle says, "But let a man examine himself." What questions should you put to yourself? I believe there are two. *One,* ask yourself, "Am I truly trusting only in Christ for salvation?" Any other attitude is *unworthy* of the Lord's Supper.

Two, ask yourself, "Am I seeking to live obediently, with a conscience to please Jesus Christ in all things?" Only a hypocrite will profess one thing and live another. "So let him eat of that bread, and drink of that cup." The *cup* and *bread* are no ordinary cup and bread.

Paul adds: "For he that eateth and drinketh unworthily, eateth and drinketh damnation to himself" (1 Corinthians 11:29). It is a bad thing to *pretend* at the Lord's Supper.

Let me say this at once. *The purpose of the inward thought is to bring us to the table, and not to keep us away from the table.* The supper is for needy people. I am glad the Word says, "Let a man examine himself, and so let him eat" (1 Corinthians 11:28). It does not say, "and so let him stay away." *Bring your failure and your defeat to the table.* Christ will share His victory with you.

3. At the table THINK UPWARD. There is an interesting fact expressed in these well-known verses. Paul says, "For I have received of the Lord that which also I delivered unto you" (1 Corinthians 11:23). *How could Paul receive any message*

directly from Jesus Christ if Jesus Christ were dead and buried?
Only a risen, living Christ could correspond with the apostle.

Calvary is not a shrine. It is not a national park. It is not a
monument. It is like the fountain that flows from the rock in
the midst of the Confederate Prison at Andersonville in the
state of Georgia.

One hundred years ago in that prison stockade, parched Union
prisoners called to God for water to slake their tormenting
thirst on a hot, fetid summer night. God smote a great granite
boulder within the prison grounds with lightning and thunder,
and immediately there gushed forth cool, pure water. It has
never ceased to flow from that day to this. It is there for
every visitor to see. Calvary is like that.

> Grace is flowing from Calvary,
> Grace as fathomless as the sea,
> Grace for time and eternity,
> Grace *enough* for me.

A living Lord greets us at His table.

4. At the table THINK FORWARD. "For as often as ye eat
this bread, and drink this cup, ye do shew the Lord's death till
He come" (1 Corinthians 11 :26). Frances Havergal wrote:

> Thou art coming! At thy table
>   We are witnesses for this,
> While remembering hearts Thou
>   meetest,
>
> In communion clearest, sweetest,
>   Earnest of our coming bliss;
> Showing not Thy death alone,
>   And Thy love exceeding great,
> But Thy coming and Thy throne,
>   All for which we long and wait!

The ungodly have no future. The sinner must live for the moment only. *It affects his character.* It makes him reckless. The Christian can say, "Even so, come, Lord Jesus!" Calvary is a pledge of Olivet.

The same Bible that has foretold the whole history of Israel before it ever happened—their enslavement in Egypt for 400 years, their captivity in Babylon for 70 years, their restoration under Cyrus, the Persian, the birth of the Messiah at Bethlehem, His rejection, crucifixion and resurrection, the destruction of Jerusalem, the worldwide dispersion, and the miracle of regathering in our generation—*is the same Bible that says over and over again that Jesus Christ will return.*

If all these prophecies have been literally fulfilled, is it not logical to conclude that the rest of the divine plan will be fulfilled?

Brigadier General F. D. Frost has brought this to our attention:

"A generation is approximately forty years. It is forty years since the Balfour declaration (making Palestine a National Home for the Jewish people) was confirmed by the League of Nations. It is seven times seven generations since Christ's birth, and seven times seven generations of prophetic years (360 days) from the birth of the Church at Pentecost. We are warned against fixing *dates,* but we are definitely told to watch for *signs."*

I raise the cup to His coming! I eat the bread in faith that I will see Him face to face.

5. Finally, at the table THINK OUTWARD. "Wherefore, my brethren, when ye come together to eat, tarry one for another" (1 Corinthians 11:33). The Lord's Supper is a meal of communion, *of fellowship.*

Mister, there are a lot of saved people. I constantly meet them in the most unexpected places and working at unusual tasks. The other morning I met a Pentecostal banker on board the jet flying from Boston to New York.

A university football coach stood up recently to declare his faith in the Lord Jesus Christ. Royal Brougham, veteran sports editor of Seattle's *Post-Intelligencer,* will testify of what Jesus means to him at any time.

You meet them everywhere. You and I are surrounded by "so great a cloud of witnesses." I ask you, sir, if such a crowd of folk are serving God and trusting in His Son, Jesus Christ, *why are you not doing the same?*

No, I have no claim on Jesus Christ that anyone else does not have! I have no priority. I have no special position or place at His table. There is no rank at the table. *We are all one.*

There is no room for me to feel superior. And there is no room for me to feel *inferior.* It took the same death and resurrection to save me as it took to save Martin Luther and John Wesley.

The table is for sinners saved by grace only! I thank God for every other Christian. I thank God for every Christian home. I thank God for every evangelical message that is preached. I thank God for every full-gospel, radio preacher. I am glad for this big family of the redeemed.

There is still room at the table! *There is a place for you.* Let faith lead you to that place.

FIFTEEN YEARS

Text: *"O Lord, by these things men live, and in all these things is the life of my spirit."*

Isaiah 38:16

THESE are the words of Hezekiah after his miraculous restoration from sickness, *when fifteen years had been added to his life.* God put this incident and this example into His Word for a purpose. The Bible says, "Now all these things happened unto them for ensamples: *and they are written for our admonition"* (1 Corinthians 10:11).

Have we a right to ask God to lengthen our lives upon earth? Sooner or later everyone asks that question. Do some people die prematurely? I believe the story of Hezekiah answers these questions.

During his terrible sickness Hezekiah expresses these thoughts. I am going to paraphrase them to you from the Old Testament Hebrew text of Isaiah 38:10-14. He says:

"In the cutting off of my days I shall go to the gates of the grave, *and be deprived of the residue of my years.* No more shall I see God in the land of the living; I shall behold no more the inhabitants of the world. Mine earthly dwelling is plucked up and removed from me as a shepherd's tent; and my life is cut off as a weaver's thread. *He is wearing me away with pining sickness; from morning to night he is making an end of me.* Mine eyes fail with looking upward. O Lord, I am oppressed; I am weighed down with my sorrows. Do thou—O do *thou,* undertake for me."

Hezekiah had lived under terrible pressures. Sennacherib, the bully of Assyria, had threatened him with extinction. Fortunately God had provided Hezekiah a good pastor, *Isaiah.* Here is the incident as your Bible reports it:

"In those days was Hezekiah sick unto death. And the prophet Isaiah . . . came to him, and said unto him, Thus saith the Lord, Set thine house in order; for thou shalt die, and not live. Then he turned his face to the wall, and prayed unto the Lord, saying, I beseech thee, O Lord, remember now how I have walked before thee in truth and with a perfect heart, and have done that which is good in thy sight. And Hezekiah wept sore.

"And it came to pass, afore Isaiah was gone out into the middle court, that the word of the Lord came to him, saying, Turn again, and tell Hezekiah the captain of my people, Thus saith the Lord, the God of David thy father, I have heard thy prayer, I have seen thy tears: behold, I will heal thee: on the third day thou shalt go up unto the house of the Lord.

"And I will add unto thy days fifteen years; and I will deliver thee and this city out of the hand of the king of Assyria; and I will defend this city for mine own sake, and for my servant David's sake" (2 Kings 20:1-6).

That was a great gift! *There is not enough wealth in all the world to buy* fifteen years of time. Who determines when enough is enough? What is time for? Can we do any better with the next fifteen years than we have done with the last fifteen? *What was the reaction of this man?*

The usual digest out of such an experience is this. Our afflictions are intended for spiritual profit. *Hezekiah's reflection is quite different.* He says that this tunnel experience emphasized to him the brevity of his days. We never seem to have enough time to get done what we ought to get done.

I do not suppose teen-agers ever feel this way. They wish time would hurry. They cannot wait. No one can hurry time. No one can slow it. No one can stop it. God alone is Master of time. He made this plain to Hezekiah.

"And Hezekiah said unto Isaiah, What shall be the sign that the Lord will heal me, and that I shall go up into the house of the Lord the third day? And Isaiah said, This sign shalt thou have of the Lord, that the Lord will do the thing that he hath spoken; shall the shadow go forward ten degrees, or go back ten degrees?

"And Hezekiah answered, It is a light thing for the shadow to go down ten degrees: nay, but let the shadow return backward ten degrees. And Isaiah the prophet cried unto the Lord: and he brought the shadow ten degrees backward by which it had gone down in the dial of Ahaz" (2 Kings 20:8-11).

For so many in this audience, time is running out. Your step has slackened. Your cheek is furrowed. Your spirit is sobered. Your pulse is slower. The warning bell is ringing. God's witness has come to you and is saying, "Set thine house in order." *You hardly know where to start or what to do first.*

One thing you know. You cannot determine time any more than you can lengthen a second or shorten an hour. The steady, never-varying beat tells you, in language bolder than any sermon can ever tell you, *that eternity is inescapable.*

There seems to be just enough time to get an education, sort out the lessons, and move on. *What is the purpose of this brief space between the two eternities?* Is there something all important that must be done? If so, what is it? *What right did men like Joshua and Hezekiah have to make time stand still?* Am I on probation? Is there a test that I must pass between the cradle and the coffin that determines my worth in another world? Hezekiah's experience gives me a peek into these things.

Is this world the place for completion? I think of words I pondered a long time ago in school days:

> "To will is ours, but not to execute.
> We map our future like some unknown coast,
> And say, Here is a harbor, there a rock.
> The one we will attain, the other shun!
> And we do neither! Some chance gale springs up,
> And bears us far o'er some unfathomed sea.
> Our efforts all are vain; at length we yield
> To winds and waves that laugh at man's control.
> ... Upon each beckoning scheme
> No sooner do we fix our hope, than still
> Time bears us on, leaving each still undone,
> Adjourned forever!"

The best of us can simply say: "The time of my departure is at hand. I have fought a good fight, I have finished my course, I have kept the faith: *henceforth ...*" (2 Timothy 4:6-8). If there is no "henceforth," no "tomorrow," time is an enigma, a universal frustration.

If we were allowed to dawdle, we could all slump into a

dreamlike, pandoric existence. To the contrary, nothing comes easily except sin. "All things," says Solomon, "are full of labor." Time does not allow a postponement.

If we are going to enjoy anything this earth affords, we have to reach for it. That is why God has put salvation in this bracket of time. The offer can be terminated, as far as you are concerned, without notice. *You are just a breath away from hell at any moment.* If a good man like Hezekiah cries out in despair, what must be the flashing thoughts of a sinner in that final second? The next automobile crash may have your name written on it.

Yes, sir, time crowds you! It makes you sit up and take notice whether you want to or not. If the changes of the world were the incidents only of centuries, instead of from one network newscast to another; if the trials and sorrows of our short life were spread out over thousands of years; if friends were cut down and graves opened only at long distant periods, *it would be easy to forget that earth is not our final home.*

Time acts as discipline. The cemeteries get larger. My Christmas card list becomes shorter.

The abruptness of his life brought Hezekiah face to face with the eternal value of every second of time. Perhaps some doctor will face you with a similar message this week, "Thou shalt die, and not live." Will you look back over the years already allotted to you? This good man could say, "I have walked before thee in truth and with a perfect heart, and have done that which is good in thy sight" (Isaiah 38:3). Can you say that?

Yet Hezekiah wept in anguish! *Why?* Because there was so much more he wanted to accomplish, so many more victories to be won in God's Name. *And how will you feel with a wasted life?* Would you dare ask God for more time? I will tell you this, when you believe God has a job for you to do on earth, you can believe He will provide enough time for you to do that job.

Examination day is ahead, sir. No one can say, "I will stay this long on earth. I will finish this task. I will complete this plan." Look around you! There is a new car in the garage, with less than a thousand miles on it, that he will never drive again. There are clothes in the closet that she purchased less than a month ago that she will never wear again. There is a chair in the committee room that he will never fill again.

God posts ten thousand messengers to remind us that our life "is even a vapour, that appeareth for a little time, and then vanisheth away" (James 4:14).

God intends this parenthesis between eternities to be meaningful, *to be serious business.* He commits to us something that is amazing, something that really matters. It is not just paper work. Eternity will reveal those final results. In all that work, it is true, God shows us our position, surrounds us with motives, and offers us His truth, His sympathy, and the aid of the Holy Spirit. *But there He leaves us.*

He will not do our work for us. The warfare is ours, and only we can fight it. The seed we now sow we are sure to reap, and He is leaving to us whether it shall be a harvest of glory or of death.

Will we be any more ready to leave fifteen years from now than we are at this moment? What is to follow death depends, not on the act of dying, *but on the life lived before we come to it.* I need to live that life NOW, not fifteen years from now.

Did Hezekiah do any better under a guarantee of fifteen years, with prosperity and deliverance from a Hitler-like oppressor, than he did when he was living moment by moment? *The record says, no, he did not.* Nor would we!

I am afraid that were we to have an eternal estimate in writing, a guarantee of so many years to the day, that we would all live with an eye to settling accounts like the dying thief, *at the last hour.* Mister, God does not run this time capsule on presumption. He runs it on faith. The only wise person is that man or woman who says like Paul, "I am ready."

I want to say one more thing to you. *Fifteen years, and then another fifteen years will never satisfy you.* It will take an eternity in God's presence. A nibble here and a nibble there is like one forever dying of famine but never dead. Here in this world, I grant you, you may keep from utter starvation by feeding on the husks of time and sense, or in part slake your thirst at the impure fountains of sin, though it be like salt water that will destroy. But when the fifteen years are past, when you find that even these streams have dried *and there are no more husks,* what then? What will you do with your desires? Where and how will you satisfy them? *That is what becomes the unquenchable flame and the undying worm to you.*

Soon, my friend, the results of your term on earth will be posted. If there are rewards, there will be punishments. If there are to be words, "Well done," there will be words, "Depart from me." I think of those many examinations I took in school. It was within my power to change my answer until the final second before time was called, and I handed my folded paper to the examiner.

My life is like that. I can govern the answer until that moment. Then the results are recorded forever. No one can change them.

------◄◆►------

THE HEREAFTER

Text: *"What I do thou knowest not now; but thou shalt know hereafter."*

John 13:7

IN his famous poem, "The Charge of the Light Brigade," Lord Tennyson says:

> "Theirs not to make reply,
> Theirs not to reason why,
> Theirs but to do and die:
> Into the valley of death rode the six hundred."

Is life like that? Must we absolutely trust the Superior Intelligence and never ask questions? If so, there must be *a hereafter.* My text talks about one.

I have listened to these words when I have had to lean upon them for strength:

> "I do not know why oft 'round me
> My hopes all shattered seem to be;
> God's perfect plan I cannot see,
> But some day I'll understand.
>
> "Some day He'll make it plain to me,
> Some day when I His face shall see;
> Some day from tears I shall be free,
> For some day I shall understand."

Is there one world of *faith* and another one of *knowledge,* where "we shall *know"?* God does not always wait for that next world for explanations. The "hereafter" came in this life for Job. *He knew the answer to his trust long before the undertaker came for him.*

So did Jacob! Before the light came, Jacob walked for years in the shadow of a great sorrow, the mysterious disappearance of his favorite son, Joseph. *God allows these evidences to strengthen our faith.*

Abraham asks, "Shall not the Judge of all the earth do right?" (Genesis 18:25).

What is the alternative? Ask yourself that question! *It must be one or the other.* What alternative do you present, sir, when you rule out God and the hereafter?

There has been only one indispensable man. He is "the Man" Christ Jesus. There would be no history, no dispensation, no meaning without Him. *Yet every man's life is part of the great plan of God.* But this plan of God is so great that you cannot judge of it by one event or even by one life.

You and I are in no position to make the complaint, "If there were a God, then this could not have happened." I am as foolish to say that as I should be to go into a vast building yard full of materials—brick, stone, timber, steel, conduit, cement, glass, tile, and ten thousand other items—and say, as I look at the assortment, "Where is the giant skyscraper?" *I am not the architect.*

In the text the Son of God was speaking to Peter. Peter lived enough years to come to grips with the plan of God for his life. *There was a time when he wanted to throw it all away.* He wanted to curse and plunge. He wanted to deny that God had anything to do with his life. His dreams were badly damaged. His plans were sidetracked. His self-will had bumped into Calvary. *He wanted to quit.*

In his torment, he wanted to fling himself into a post-crucifixion mardi gras. He was not ready for eternity, for a final blackout like his erstwhile brother minister, Judas; *but he was sick with disillusionment.* How could right triumph in the face of dirty politics such as he had witnessed at Pilate's forum? He was not the first. Nor has he been the last.

Job's wife reached the point of "what is the use?" A wife and mother—and as fine a woman as she no doubt was—must have been rocked and shocked to have ever said to her husband, "Curse God and die."

Naomi knew despondency. Her tragedy almost keeps company with Job's. Death lodged in her family circle; first her husband, and then her two sons. *And what death began famine finished.* She came back to Bethlehem spiritually bankrupt. Her only strength was her bitterness. "Call me Mara," she said, "for the Almighty hath dealt very bitterly with me" (Ruth 1:20).

Friend, there is a *hereafter!* There was one for Peter. He, who shunned to have his feet washed and to learn by example of service the true path to greatness, is a leader within two months, turning the militant city of Jerusalem upside down with his preaching.

There was a hereafter for Naomi. Let me read it to you from the Book of Ruth:

"And Naomi took the child, and laid it in her bosom, and became nurse unto it. And the women her neighbors gave it a name, saying, There is a son born to Naomi; and they called his name Obed; *he is the father of Jesse, the father of David"* (Ruth 4:17).

And there is a hereafter for you!

Yes, you and I live in a world of mystery. *We cannot change that.* The physical world about us, the world of nature, has revealed very few of its secrets. Think of the generations that lived without the knowledge or benefits or responsibilities of radio, television, space travel, automobiles, and the utilities of this moment.

How little they knew! How cramped and small the world must have seemed! Has our generation exhausted Nature's secrets? What big, new things are reserved for our grandchildren? *What about this constant unfolding?* Do you want to deny it because you cannot explain it?

Now look at your life, sir! It comes shrouded in mystery. *Yet there are clues.* Think of times when you sensed there was a pattern. Deep within you there is a consciousness of a plan. Have you come to grips with it? *Have you made a commitment to it?*

The struggle that makes your life unhappy is the struggle between yourself and God. God has a "hereafter" for your life. You say, "Preacher, why do I have to have someone tell me what to do? Is that fair? Why can I not live my own life the way I please, and let the other fellow live his life the way he pleases? And when it is over, why can we not simply check out and be forgotten?" A lot of people have asked those same questions.

First of all, mister, whether we like it or not, *there is a supremacy in this universe.* When God endowed man with a free will, He made him the supreme work of the universe;

but at the same time, He rendered possible the thwarting of His own will.

The price of freedom is the risk of rebellion. Sinner, I say this to you kindly but firmly. When you look at what a mess you have made of your own life through sin, what would happen to this universe if there were no God to decide, without appeal, what is right and what is wrong?

By acts of creation and redemption God has the right to use your life and my life, and to fit our lives into His plan. He does not need to ask us, but He does, *and He makes that request in so many different ways.*

How could the boy, Samuel, know? How could the poverty-stricken peasant, Gideon, know? How could the ignorant, rude fishermen, James and John, the sons of Zebedee, know? *How can any man know the uses to which God means to put him or the glory to which He means to exalt him, even in this world; how much less than in the world to come!*

You have to trust Him, my friend. There is no other way. And the disposition of my life can either help redeem or wreck the lives of others. One dropped stitch can start a run that can ruin the whole garment.

The testimony of every Christian has been this. The nearer they approach the world to come the more they realize that God's guidelines—which they could not understand at the time— *have been for their benefit.* That is a testimony worth examining before you turn your back on God, sinner.

Jesus said on another occasion to His disciples, "I have yet many things to say unto you, but ye cannot bear them now" (John 16:12).

A child in the third grade can be swamped with arithmetic that is suitable for the sixth grade. God does not burden us with all the answers in our youth. There is a burden, a responsibility, sufficient for the day. *God asks you to trust Him.* You trust your banker. You trust your doctor. Why is it you do not trust your God?

The very economy of marriage, man's most intimate relationship upon earth, depends upon this axis. *The husband has the right to the wife's right thoughts toward him, as well as her right affections toward him.* Does he need to give constant explanations for his conduct? Not if the marriage is to continue to be a happy one. Marriage can only survive on the basis of trust.

Now, if God explained this sickness or that bankruptcy, this bereavement or that sorrow, there could be no exercise of faith, and the law of the whole economy under which we are placed would be completely reversed. *Salvation can only survive on the basis of faith, never on the basis of explanation.* Simply believe Calvary was for you!

As there is God and there is faith, there is a hereafter, a heaven, *an eternity.* There are answers. "But thou shalt know hereafter." Moses did. Luke reports that on the Mount of Transfiguration, Moses with Elias appeared "and spake" to Jesus "of his decease which he should accomplish at Jerusalem" (Luke 9:31).

The long years of exile and the long years of migrant, wilderness life were all explained. *Long since, Moses had realized the part God had asked him to play in the drama of redemption.* It gave meaning to the steps he had taken in Pharaoh's court and the abuse he had suffered from the people he had tried to save. They all had meaning, eternal meaning, in Calvary.

> "There are so many hills to climb upward,
> I often am longing for rest;
> But He who appoints me my pathway,
> Knows just what is needful and best.
> I know in His Word He hath promised
> That my strength 'it shall be as my day';
> And the toils of the road will seem nothing,
> When I get to the end of the way."

Two worlds meet in every man. That is the mystery you feel so often in your soul. And when the soul is renewed from sin, the spiritual apprehension is clearer, the spiritual longing stronger. Steadily the longing for the bigger world of full knowledge increases while a desire to remain lessens. *Only sin makes you afraid of eternity.* You do not want to face the answers.

I believe this. God longs for that moment when He can make it plain to us. I think this obscurity is as great a hardship upon God as upon us. It exposes Him to constant misinterpretation and suspicion. *He longs for our perfect trust.*

Have you rebelled? Are you out of step with your God? Do you walk in darkness? Then already the "hereafter" torments you. Hell has already begun. It can be different, sir! Turn your heart toward God in trust. Then it will be sunrise tomorrow.

WHAT SHALL I WEAR?

Text: *"Take Aaron and Eleazar his son, and bring them up unto mount Hor: and strip Aaron of his garments, and put them upon Eleazar his son: and Aaron shall be gathered unto his people, and shall die there. And Moses did as the Lord commanded: and they went up into mount Hor in the sight of all the congregation. And Moses stripped Aaron of his garments, and put them upon Eleazar his son; and Aaron died there in the top of the mount: and Moses and Eleazar came down from the mount."*

Numbers 20 :25-28

THERE are no baggage checks into the next world. I have stood at the lip of the grave and said these words so many times: "We brought nothing into this world, *and it is certain we can take nothing out.*" What do those words mean? Do we enter the next world as we entered this world?

Look at the scene described in this text! Only the eye of God is on this little group. Moses, the younger but as God's prophet, now the more honorable brother, begins to take the mitre from the elder brother's brow, the breastplate from his bosom, the ephod from his shoulders, and the white surplice from his body and puts them all on Eleazar. *Increasingly poorer and humbler becomes the dying man, until he stands there at last, externally like every other mortal.*

I pray that God will stamp our memories with this picture. Kings and emperors die this way. Generals and champions die this way. Bishops and businessmen die this way. *We all leave the same way.* There is only one exit.

This world is filled with honors and titles, achievements and distinctions. We wear our ribbons and medals, display our degrees and successes with pride. We grow accustomed to privilege and echelon. *More and more, we depend upon them to open doors.* We become persuaded that we have earned our way and that what we have acquired is permanent. Then comes this moment of truth. It is always there. *It is waiting for each of us.* Someone right behind us is waiting to take our place. We must let go. Authority and station must pass to the next generation. *Where do we go, and how?*

I ask you. Are you coming to that hour with the mitre of human wisdom? What cap are you wearing? Does it speak of engineering or of medicine or of philosophy or of business administration?

More than once you have moved through the corridors of undergraduates. On your head is that symbol that assures your right to fellowship among doctors and professors. You have earned it, but one day you must lay it down. *It has opened many a door for you down here, but it cannot open a single door for you up there.*

I ask you, are you coming to that hour with the breastplate of human ambition? What place have you scrapped and clawed for? What ribbons, what insignia do you wear across your chest? What varsity do you claim? What campus is your alma mater? What team reckons you in its starting line-up? How many letters have you won? Are you the big man in the fraternity? Your pin can be recognized around the world, but in the next world there are different letters.

I ask you, are you coming to that hour with the surplice of good works? What robe are you wearing? How many initiations do you boast? People look at you in the annual parade. Your group is among the elite and the best disciplined. Your special jacket is a sign of accomplishment. Your admission to the inner circle is the result of hours of study and practice. Your card is international, but it cannot bridge two worlds.

Stripped! It is not a pleasant thought. All of us have grown accustomed to the stage props of this world and to some percentage of playacting. *We live to impress and to be impressed.* Suddenly, it is finished. "And strip Aaron of his garments . . . and Aaron died." *Will it be any different for you?*

What is left? Look at this man whom life had crowned with many honors and who had walked in places of responsibility and authority. Despite weaknesses and sins, which are matters of record, Aaron had always, through divine mercies and discipline, returned to the Lord. He had never refused to accompany Moses to the vacillating Pharaoh. With prayer he had upheld his brother's hand in the battle with the Amalekites.

After the destruction of Korah and his band, when the people murmured against him and Moses and the plague broke out among them and thousands perished, he, like a true priest, with the atoning censer in hand, flung himself into the breach. It was a great moment. He interceded for a rebellious people. He stood between the living and the dead until the plague was stayed. *He exposed himself.*

O, yes, mister, there was something behind the glamor and spotlessness and dignity of the robe and insignia of office! *There was heart.* There was choice. There was courage. And there were hunger and thirst after God *inside*. It was not pretense and show. It was not form and ceremony. Things like that can take you only so far. *It is what is inside that carries you across.*

Death undresses us. Clothes do not make the man or the woman. Character, what is inside, does. "The beggar died, and was carried by the angels into Abraham's bosom: the rich man also died, and was buried; and in hell he lifted up his eyes" (Luke 16:22, 23). What kind of a person are you? Shorn of your badge and rank, what are you? Have you worn one thing and believed another?

Aaron went up that mountainside a dignitary, second only to Moses in authority. He wore the regalia of the high priest. *Suddenly, he was nothing more than a man.* His dependence was the same dependence of every other soul that stands before God. He could carry with him no human merit, no privilege of office, no honor, no right of birth. *What worthiness could he submit?* These were private moments between his soul and its Maker.

The public needed to know the Aaron of mitre, breastplate, and robe. There is purpose and design for it all—every title, every distinction, every level of authority, every respect and acknowledgment. *But they are for this life only.* Keep that in mind. At the end you and I will stand stripped.

Aaron needed the Great High Priest. He needed covenants stronger than public acclaim. He needed Blood better than family connections. He needed a salvation that only Calvary can buy. No amount of learning can sufficiently cover my need. No number of trophies or awards can erase my defeats.

Aaron's life had been a stormy one. His failures were spectacular. They remind you of David. These two men had a lot in common. David came toward the terminal of his life garnished with stores and stocks of everything sufficient to build the most costly and beautiful temple of all time, but God said, "Thou shalt not build."

He, too, had to lay it all down for his son. Thank God, there was no argument! *It is a record of submission to God's will.* Leaning on a God who had called him and sustained him, Aaron, stripped of everything but that faith, stepped out calmly and confidently into eternity. David went the same way.

Yes, sir, there will be *final revision.* More than one experience in a lifetime has brought us all "down to earth," as we say. *Suddenly, we realize that we are not as good as we thought we were.* We lose face. Publicity shrinks. Crowds turn in another direction. Evaluations change. Promotions linger. We are embarrassed. Our friends pretend to look the other way.

How soon we forget! We live as though there would be no final Examiner. That is a mistake. Death strips us. Death looks for the contents.

Alfred Tennyson put it this way :

> Sunset and evening star,
> And one clear call for me!
> And may there be no moaning of the bar,
> When I put out to sea.
> Twilight and evening bell,
> And after that the dark!
> And may there be no sadness of farewell,
> When I embark;
> For though from out our bourne of Time and Place
> The flood may bear me far,
> I hope to see my Pilot face to face
> When I have crossed the bar.

You and I must bring something more than earthly trappings to that moment, no matter how honored and good they may be. As I entered this world and had to be covered with garments that I had not labored to make nor earned money to purchase, so I must enter the world to come, dependent again on being clothed by Another, whose love and sanction bid me come.

It was a long road for Aaron. He was one hundred and twenty-three when this incident took place. "And Aaron the priest went up into mount Hor at the commandment of the Lord, and died there, *in the fortieth year* after the children of Israel were come out of the land of Egypt" (Numbers 33:38).

He had seen enough in those years to have discouraged him

and to have turned him out of the way. *But he never turned back to Egypt.* He traveled the weary miles by faith. God gave him a glimpse of the Promised Land before He called him home.

This man stumbled, but he never quit. This man was bent to the views of others, but he never broke in willful rebellion with his God. Stripped, he stood ready to go—confident in the mercies that he had so often represented in the sacrifices he had offered for the people along the desert miles of their journey.

God's verdict was this, "And Aaron shall be *gathered.*" Out of this life—broken yet brilliant, with its high moments and its low moments, with its strange interludes and then moments of high resolve—a life that represents so many of us in this audience, God gathered the pieces together and quietly beckoned him into another world.

I can ask no better. The story of my life is scattered. There are pages I would expunge. There are pages that bring warming memories. I do not know what to say. I will leave it to Him. He must *gather.* He alone knows what is worthy of another world.

> "Nothing in my hand I bring;
> Simply to Thy cross I cling."

HOME

Text: *"Let not your heart be troubled: ye believe in God, believe also in me. In my Father's house are many mansions: if it were not so, I would have told you. I go to prepare a place for you."*

John 14:1, 2

WORDS that American music lovers have lifted up around the world say:

Going Home, going home
I am going home;
Quiet-like, some still day,
I am just going home.

"It's not far, just close by
Through an open door;
Work's all done:
Care laid by
Goin' to fear no more.

"Mother's expecting me:
Father's watching too;
Lots of folks gathered there
All the friends I knew
All the friends I knew,
Home, home, *I am going home.*"

Jesus put it that simply. *He said heaven meant going home.*

Jesus Christ sets Himself up as the supreme authority about heaven. "If it were not so, *I* would have told you." Is there a scientist or theologian big enough to debate that authority? He came, and He returned, and He declares, "If it were not so, *I* would have told you."

Christ places all that He claims to be on His truthfulness about heaven. The gospel rises or falls with Christ's declaration about heaven. He takes complete responsibility. So, mister, when you question the reality of heaven, you tangle with the Son of God.

I think the background upon which this text was spoken sharpens the meaning considerably. We can see the Lord with the eleven disciples pass out of Saint Stephen's gate, down the slope, across the brook Kidron, and then up the path that leads to Olivet. They pause now and again while He speaks to them His parting words and while He utters His matchless prayer to His Father.

In one of these pauses they look back toward Jerusalem and gaze upon the many-mansioned city. They behold, as a diadem upon a queen's brow, the marvelous temple, glistening white upon its summit and beautiful beyond compare in the silver splendor of the passover moon at its full.

But in its sacred precincts He had just been rejected. He had no mansion in all the city, and when He needed it, not one of the many chambers surrounding the court in the temple was placed at His disposal. That same evening He had observed the passover and instituted His own memorial supper in the house of a friend, in the guest chamber that was prepared for Him *in a spare room.*

There was no welcome for Him in His own beautiful mansion in Zion. *As there had been at the first no room for Him in the inn, so at the last there was no room for Him in the temple.* He had no place to lay His head.

Now repeat the words of the text, "In *my* Father's house are many mansions." They did not want Him here. That is certain. If there is no other world, no place for a real Christ and real believers, no welcome, no supremacy of right, the life and gospel of the Nazarene are meaningless.

As He was rejected, so would His disciples be. They would be outcast. Jerusalem would drive them forth. *Jesus left them this legacy.* "In the world ye shall have tribulation" (John 16: 33).

It was not much. Jesus said there will be trouble. The prospects were not bright for this small posse of men.

Then, as though His look rose above the temple and He saw a vision in the sky and caught sight of the city of God with its many mansions, He directed His disciples' vision beyond the temple, and the city, and the gates of death, and gave to them, and the believers of all the ages, and to us today *the vision of home.* "I go to prepare a place for you." He was on His way at that moment to pay the full price and make it possible.

Did He not know what it meant when there at Capernaum, Peter and Andrew and John and James forsook their nets and followed Him? When Peter said, "We have forsaken all" (Matthew 19:17), *did He not know how great was the sacrifice?*

Yes, He knew. He replied that whoever made such a sacrifice should receive a hundredfold in kind here and then a myriadfold in everlasting life. *He knew mankind's longing for home.*

No figure of history ever got nearer to men. He understood the heartbeat of humanity. He knew the inward cry of crippled folk and blind folk. He knew the struggle of the mute, the lame, and the sick with all manner of diseases. He was "acquainted with grief" (Isaiah 53:3).

He had been at weddings and funerals, at fasts and feasts, in huts and palaces, in cities and villages, by the seashore and on the plain, in the mountain and in the desert places; *and He knew men; and He knew the home hunger of the human heart.* He knew the homesickness of these men who stood with Him that night. "In my Father's house are many mansions ... I go to prepare *a place* for you."

The world, that night, was ready to erase them. No editor had room for them, even on the back pages. No historian pondered what place to give them in history. No Chamber of Commerce prepared to welcome them. Only the Son of God knew their value. "*I* go to prepare a place for you."

The domestic instinct is a strong one. This urge is woven into mankind. It is like thirst, hunger, and sleep. To gain a home, men endure the hardest denials and sacrifices. To preserve it, they forego all the comforts of life. To perfect it, they undergo most arduous toil. To defend it, they spill their blood. *There is no meaning to life without home.*

> "'Mid pleasures and palaces though we may roam,
> Be it ever so humble, there's no place like home;
> A charm from the skies seems to hallow us there,
> Which, seek thro' the world, is ne'er met with elsewhere.

"An exile from home, splendor dazzles in vain;
O, give me my lowly thatched cottage again;
The birds singing gayly, they came at my call:
Give me them and that peace of mind, dearer than all."

And so the word comes to a universal heart hunger of human-ity. "In my Father's house are many mansions: if it were not so, I would have told you. I go to prepare a place for you ... that where *I am* there ye may be also" (John 14:2, 3).

Sometimes we question our hymn writers, our composers, and our singers for dwelling so much on heaven. Some say it is sickly sentimentality. Ask yourself when you lose a loved one or a close friend, what it is. *I say it is natural language to repeat these words*:

"Life's day is short; I soon shall go,
To be with Him who loved me so.
I see in the distance that shining shore,
My beautiful, beautiful home."

I say that to sing songs like that is to express faith in Christ's promise and to testify to the power of Calvary. I am not ashamed to talk about heaven or to sing about heaven.

When Jesus said, "I go to prepare a place for you," the Greek word rendered in the text "place" is used for the root of our word "topography." *The very word selected by the Holy Spirit indicates a real place, something substantial.*

Jesus is saying to His disciples that though He and they are unwelcome, that though He has nowhere to entertain them in Galilee or Judea, He is going to make sure of this one thing, *a place* for them where He can make them "at home" with Him.

The physical aspect of heaven may mean something different to each of us. I think the best thing to do is to accept the simple faith which was that of P. P. Bliss, the gospel song-writer who before boarding the night train that took him to heaven by way of the fatal Ashtabula, Ohio, disaster, sang to a congregation as his farewell hymn:

"I know not the form of my mansion fair;
I know not the name that I then shall bear,
But I know that my Saviour will welcome me there,
And that will be glory for me."

That is how I feel, and I am content.

Nothing is more tender to me; nothing is more meaningful or down-to-earth than these words of Jesus, "In my Father's house." Had He spoken of God's almightiness, of His splendor, of His infinite beauty, of a warehouse of infinite resources, I would feel a remoteness. But when Jesus speaks about "My Father's house," He touches a responsive chord in every human breast. *Thank God, there is a place in that "house" for me!*

I am glad He did not leave the design of heaven to me or to any religious denomination of which you and I may be members. It is not going to be a Methodist or Baptist heaven any more than it is going to be an Assemblies of God or Presbyterian heaven.

He did not ask James, who was soon to go, or the others what their preferences were. Probably they would have made as great mistakes as would we. Did you ever wonder when you read Milton, how he would really have been satisfied through eternity with the heaven of his own conception?

We are seldom satisfied for long with a house we build or an automobile we purchase here. Heaven is a matter that the Lord has undertaken Himself. This is not a combined effort between earth and eternity. The Son of God knows us better than we know ourselves. He who knows us will interpret our longings in terms of His knowledge and love, and will "prepare a place" for us.

Leave it in His hands, sir! *You must either have faith or be a lost soul.* There is no future without Jesus. The future is in His hands and in the hands of no one else. I have seen enough men try to make heaven down here. I have seen the shambles of enough efforts to create man-made paradises. I am glad that I have an Architect from another world "preparing a place" for me.

Is it little wonder that those nearing death want these words read to them? "I go to prepare a place." I, who have lived among you and know you so well; I, who was tempted in all points like as you are and yet without sin; I, who am now about to enter Gethsemane and know its agony and drink its cup of bitterness; I, who love you so that I am about to die to save you and make this wonderful thing possible; I, your Saviour, *"go* to prepare a place for you. And if I go and prepare a place for you, I will come again, and receive you unto myself; that where I am, there ye may be also. Let not your heart be troubled, neither let it be afraid" (John 14:2, 3, 27).

Only Jesus makes it possible. There is no heaven without Him. It troubles me to see the planned avoidance of Jesus in so many of our community matters today. There is no gospel without Him. There is nothing but ethics, philosophy, and social service.

Christ, Himself, has placed the challenge. "Ye believe in God, believe *also* in me." He is your passport. He has turned paradise into a world of reward and homecoming for sinners saved by grace. Put your future in His hands! Then leave it to Him. That is what He asked eleven men to do in the shadow of Gethsemane.

———————◆▶———————

THE LORD OF HADES

Texts: *"In which also he went and preached (or, made procla-mation) unto the spirits in prison, that aforetime were dis-obedient, when the long-suffering of God waited in the days of Noah."* 1 Peter 3:19, 20 (*A.S.V.*)

"And when I saw him, I fell at his feet as one dead. And he laid his right hand upon me, saying, Fear not; I am the first and the last and the Living one; And I was dead, and behold, I am alive for evermore, and I have the keys of death and of Hades." Revelation 1:17, 18 (*A.S.V.*)

I WANT to speak to you about the Living One in this service—the Living One who in the actual words of the original text "became dead."

If Jesus Christ had not chosen to die, if He had not surrendered to death, and had it not been God's will, Jesus Christ could still be walking the streets of this world in flesh and blood as Galilee saw Him, *untouched by the marks of age and decay.* He was Life to the last pulse of His physical being. No seed of death could lurk in any recess of His holy nature. That is why He did something that He alone could do.

These two texts declare the lordship of Jesus in the world of the dead. As His *body* was master of the *grave,* so His *Spirit* was Lord of the unseen world. His soul was not left in Sheol, nor did His body see corruption. *He alone holds the keys.* There are no other solutions to death and judgment.

Every sinner asks the question, "Why doesn't God do something?" Every Christian testifies, "He has, and He is doing something—something about the devil, something about sin, something about death, and something about another world."

I. JESUS DID THIS DELIBERATELY. He "became dead." He had authority to lay down His life, and He had authority to take it up again. *He had to have this authority.* The natural and necessary thing for the "Living One" was life. Death could only come by choice. He said, "Therefore doth my Father love me, because I lay down my life, that I may take it again. No man taketh it from me, but I lay it down of myself" (John 10: 17, 18). He said, "I am the resurrection, and the life" (John 11:25).

Whenever and wherever He spoke of His death, He hastened to speak of His power to rise again, when and where He chose. He never questioned it for a moment. *Death was subject to Him.* He believed it without hesitation.

Whatever He touched leaped to life. He is Master of all the destructive forces of nature. He touches the deaf, and they hear; the blind, and they see; the mute, and they speak; the sick, and they are healed; the dead, and they arise. *He deliberately makes death the instrument of His redemptive purpose.* Jesus Christ is no mere man.

How did He "become dead"? There are those who say His death was unnecessary. They say it because they do not understand what His death implies. They say a life lived such as He lived and, at the end, a normal death would have been equally good for us. They are dead wrong.

Christ came purposely to wreck and ruin a wrong system. He knew the cost. He anticipated the bruises. He knew that the organization of rebellion would turn its rage upon Him. He knew it would destroy Him as far as it had power. *He came to challenge hell.*

His miracles and teaching were only the preliminary rounds. He stepped into the center of humanity's sin and curse. He came to destroy or be destroyed. There is no "perhaps" or "maybe" about the gospel. It is deliberate.

His death is far more than the death of the body. His death means He entered the darkest domains and left these domains in *worse shambles* than sin had ever left this planet. A martyr could not do this. A martyr is one whose life is taken from him by those whom he has no power to resist, for he surrenders but a mortal body.

Jesus was not a martyr. He never lost His power to resist. He laid it down. He "became dead." *He meant to pursue sin to its ultimate.*

II. JESUS DID THIS FOR ME. It was not necessary for Him to seek the keys of death and Hades for Himself. *It was humanity that had lost the keys.* This race could not deliver from the grave or hell. No civilization had found the solution. *Death and Hades were absolute masters.* Jesus "became dead" so that He might become alive again. No one else had accomplished it. No one knew how to accomplish it.

"Forasmuch then as the children are partakers of flesh and blood, he also himself likewise took part of the same; that through death he might destroy him that had the power of death, that is, the devil; and deliver them who through fear of death were all their lifetime subject to bondage" (Hebrews 2:14, 15).

It is a divine paradox that the Lord of life should enter these foul and wretched regions at all, but it would have been more than a paradox—it would have been the triumph of atheism—*if they had been able to detain Him*. He volunteered to go. No one else ever has.

Once there, without any outside help, He burst their bands asunder. *He came back.* He left a shattered prison. It has never been the same. They were compelled to admit into their stronghold one stronger than they. *They had no choice.* He "became death."

He says for Eternity to hear, "I was dead, and behold, I am alive for evermore." That means something to you, mister! This is the biggest chance you will ever have. Christ offers to share His victory with you. Jesus left no doubt about it. *He is in command.* No devil can argue successfully.

I am not at this time concerned about the many theological questions this Petrine passage raises. The central truth is this. In this descent and proclamation and claim, *Jesus Christ effectively establishes Himself as absolute Lord of the quick and the dead, the supreme Judge of the "spirits in detention," and the redeeming, life-giving Saviour of the godly in the world of the departed.*

There is no hope for you, sinner, when you leave this world to find further means to escape your responsibility toward Jesus Christ. He has been there before you. He has asserted His authority. When you die, you will be under His authority, whether you choose to be so or not. Who and what can challenge it? Just as His coming into our earth shook our world with new power, so His entry into Hades shook this shadowy realm with new forces. He has been there. There is no rebellion in hell, no government but His.

The lesson God taught Noah's generation is there to serve as a warning to this generation. I warn you. *"The Father judgeth no man, but hath committed all judgment unto the Son* (John 5:22). It is not a matter of respect for the Creator or the understanding of a great, loving, universal Father of the human race. It is too late for that! Your next appointment is with Jesus Christ, for better or for worse.

Only Jesus Christ has been able to do something for the world of the dead. No engineer, no statesman, no educator, no inventor has ever been able to affect a change in that world. *But Jesus did.*

He said, "Verily, verily, I say unto you, The hour is coming, *and now is,* when the dead shall hear the voice of the Son of God: and they that hear shall live" (John 5:25).

My friend, from that moment until this, that world of the dead has been *a world of life, of conscious, employed existence.* This is the meaning of the latter part of the familiar passage, "I am the resurrection, and the life: he that believeth in me, though he were dead, yet shall he live: and whosoever *liveth* and believeth in me shall never die" (John 11:25, 26). It gives meaning to the text which says, "Blessed are the dead which die in the Lord *from henceforth"* (Revelation 14:13). It is the answer to the question you ask, "What has happened to my Christian loved one?"

Jesus Christ brought a scintillating, Calvary-bought life to what the Old Testament described as *death.* He does even more for that world of the redeemed than He does for the sinner saved by grace on earth. That is why Paul said, "We are willing rather to be absent from the body, and to be at home with the Lord" (2 Corinthians 5:8 A.S.V.). He kindled a light that world never knew before.

III. JESUS HOLDS THESE KEYS FOR THE WORK OF HIS KINGDOM. *This absolute authority and domain is resident in His gospel.* None other can duplicate it. But there is no lack of effort. Voices arise from industry, entertainment, government, research, and money circles to say, "The *life* is in us." They cannot back their claims. Only the gospel can satisfy. He gives every son and daughter who trusts Him a share in His power of the keys. And that, sir, is the greatest thrill a mortal can have! That is why the experience of new birth is so immense. In that moment of trust you experience personally Christ's victory over death. Chains that bind your life are snapped.

Jesus said, "As the Father raiseth up the dead, and quickeneth them; *even so the Son quickeneth whom he will*" (John 5:21). The Christian message is this, "Christ is our life." He that believeth on Him (the person who depends entirely upon Him) has passed from death unto life. Apart from Him we can do nothing. The keys are in His hands. There is no gospel, there is no salvation, there is no heaven without Jesus. The grave cannot injure you, believer! It has no victory. It has no sting.

The thief on the cross expressed the muffled hopes of Old Testament folk, when he said, "Lord, remember me when thou comest into thy kingdom" (Luke 23:42). The future was misty. It is not that way now. The Lord of Hades changed that. He said, *"To day* shalt thou be with me in paradise" (Luke 23:43). It is instant, sir!

Every dark power knows his final doom is certain. Hell will never have a revival. Sin will never launch another attack on another world. Death and Hades shall be cast into the "lake of fire," which is the second death, and there is no redemption for that.

The gates of Hades cannot prevail against the gospel. Their power has passed into the hands of Jesus Christ. *Evil cannot win.* It is an utter impossibility. Every hour brings their final liquidation closer. *God asks you for an act of trust.*

Your salvation depends upon your personal faith in the good news: "I am the first and the last and the Living One. And I was dead, and behold, I am alive for evermore, and I have the keys of death and of Hades." That is what Calvary accomplished. Now let that victory go to work in yourself!

ELECTION

Text: *"Ye have not chosen me, but I have chosen you, and ordained you, that ye should go and bring forth fruit, and that your fruit should remain: that whatsoever ye shall ask of the Father in my name, he may give it you."*

John 15:16

DO not let these words baffle you. There are depths past finding out in the Incarnation. The Atonement offends the wisdom of this world. Many stumble at the message that man is justified freely in Christ, apart from any personal merit or moral achievement. *God does not ask you to analyze His grace. He asks you to believe His grace.*

We must learn from the angels to "desire to look into" these things and not spurn them as soon as they seem to confuse our limited logic. I believe John reported accurately the teaching of Jesus Christ. My dependence for salvation is upon that teaching. If I am lost, I will be lost believing the gospel of Jesus Christ.

Millions have rejoiced in that consciousness which came upon the disciples, and never afterwards left them, that they were the chosen vessels of divine grace. I believe in the gospel of the song which says, "When my Saviour reached down His hand for me."

In this consciousness, the consciousness that He first loved me, the greatest spiritual heroes have been made. Such consciousness is important to my spiritual well-being. I must sense that Someone loves me beyond all explanation.

I. THIS GRACE IS NOT ARBITRARY. As it is impossible for God to lie, because He is absolute Truth, even so it is impossible for Him to be arbitrary, because He is absolute Reason. *God must do right as He must be honest.* Not a wild flower grows arbitrarily in the wilderness; not a wild fowl is fledged arbitrarily among the crags.

There is always a purpose. There can be no act of God in time or eternity which is not the offspring of moral right and infinite reason. Old translations turned Paul's question into, "Hath not the potter *power* over the clay?" (Romans 9:21). But the apostle's real question is quite different. It is: "Hath not the potter a *right* over the clay?"

Does anyone question the *right* of God to save me? Does anyone question the *right* of Jesus Christ to love me? It has nothing to do at all with exclusion. I simply must know that it is happening to *me*. I must have the conviction that He loves even me. And when I have that conviction it becomes far easier to believe that a God who loves even me is "not willing that *any* should perish, but that all should come to repentance" (2 Peter 3:9).

Where can you find in your Bible an argument that says God has a "right" to save whom He will and to reject whom He will, that no one has a claim upon His grace, and that therefore no one has a right to complain at being left out? *Where do you find that?*

The only "right" that Love has is just to be *boundless love and grace.* Love that picks and excludes is not love at all. "God so loved the world, that he gave his only begotten Son, that *whosoever* believeth in him should not perish, but have everlasting life" (John 3:16).

I will tell you this, when God writes something in the book of life, you will find a first carbon copy in the life of the believer. God is not the God of the dead but of the living. There is not one record in heaven and an entirely different one of earth.

Love is moral energy. Grace is not theory. Grace is reality. When you feel that God *wants* you, it is a feeling that God wants you to be full of faith and the Holy Ghost. This reach of God does not link itself with a body of corruption, except to call it into life and service. *This is no convenient arrangement of live and let live.*

"He that hath my commandments, and keepeth them, he it is

that loveth me: and he that loveth me shall be loved of my Father" (John 14:21).

"You did not choose me, but I chose you, and appointed you, that you should go and bear fruit, and that your fruit should abide" (John 15:16, A.S.V.).

II. THIS GRACE IS EXTENDED TOWARD PEOPLE. There are theologians who would lay the election of God upon Christ, as the representative of His redeemed ones, *and not upon individual believers in their own persons.* I believe God deals directly with me.

God does not treat people like numbers or items, an inventory of moving things. I am not some insignificant, component part of a great big package. *I am not interested in a religion of generalities.* A song of our church says:

> "Thou thinkest Lord of *me*.
> What need I fear, since Thou art near,
> Thou thinkest Lord of *me*."

The New Testament calls upon you to "make your calling and election sure" (2 Peter 1:10). This is a personal matter and not a package deal. My Bible teaches that the Father chose the Son, and that when He did, He chose to redeem this planet, and that together the Father and the Son choose other sons. "And other sheep I have, which are not of this fold: them also I must bring" (John 10:16).

This positive action is always continuing. That is what makes missionary-evangelism the adventure and thrill that it is.

Other theologians suggest that the only force of our text is that God merely elects someone to a certain office or position in the kingdom. It is true that Paul was told that he was a "chosen vessel."

But Paul knew that something even greater had happened to him before he ever became aware of his ministry. He testified, "But when it was the good pleasure of God, who separated me, even from my mother's womb...to reveal his Son in me" (Galatians 1:15, A.S.V.).

There is a reach of God that saves the soul. It is a divine current that catches the sinner and calls him to be a saint. It is an electrifying power that touches mankind. It is in the world today. *Its voltage is unlimited.* It can and does save to the uttermost. It is the continuing initiative of God whereby people "bear fruit" with holy power. It cannot be done apart from His will. No man can agree to do this of himself, by himself, and through himself. If you think it can be done, sinner, try it! We can "bear fruit" because God makes it possible for us through Christ.

III. THIS GRACE HAS SPECIAL EFFECTS. No Bible student can ignore the fact that God chose the family of Israel for a special mission. Israel was chosen to stand under the brightest blaze of divine revelation. The central, spiritual energies of the self-revealing God surged around this favored people.

Paul says theirs was the law, theirs were the prophets. Of them, according to the flesh, Christ came. Human history has asked and will ask, "Why the Jew?"

History will also confirm that the righteousness and the love of God are manifested in this choice. By electing this focus and center in the midst of the nations, God kindled a central fire of worship *which nothing has been able to quench.* By concentrating upon it the glories of His spiritual presence and power, God kept His revealed truth from being dissipated.

He created and sustained a sacred center from which His light and His truth is being shed upon the whole world. Never forget that! God's designated blessing is never for selfish consumption. *It is deposited to flow outward, to reach others.*

The same thing is true respecting the choice of His disciples. These men were privileged above all others. The vast and holy energies of His immediate presence were poured upon them night and day. These Galilean fishermen could not have told you why they were thus favored, *but the purpose of it is clear.*

The Son of God took these men and created in the center of the world a Holy Ghost witness that compassed land and sea to communicate God's intention toward all men.

"Ye have not chosen me, but I have chosen you; and ordained (appointed) you, that ye should go and bear fruit, and that your fruit should remain" (John 15:16). What happy and successful appointments! That is the story which history tells, sir.

Men and women have this consciousness of "selection" in every generation. I have it. I feel that God has reached out and saved my soul, redeemed my life, and appointed me to broadcast His gospel and bear fruit for Him. I feel that the results will tell for eternity. *That gives purpose to my life.*

Mister, you will feel God's "impact" upon your life. That is what makes His supernatural salvation more than a religious philosophy or a code of ethics. *There is a love that will not let go of me.* What I do with that love is another question. One thing I know. I know my life was never meant to be *wasted.* It was meant to be *invested.*

Each focusing of divine grace is for larger extension. What God does in me is meant to affect others. So God's grace is never *exclusive.* It is always *inclusive.* Holiness does not mean a "better-than-thou" attitude. It means compassion and concern. I can be intense without being solitary. Israel made a mistake.

Israel interpreted God's election to mean God's rejection of His other nations. You can become a walled sepulcher that way. The disciples understood. *They went forth to bear fruit.* That fruit remains to this day.

God's mighty "impact" upon you does not compel salvation. The final commitment is yours, and yours alone, to make. You will never be able to say, "God did not want me." You will never be able to say, "God made me."

God does not ignore your freedom. He wants to take advantage of your freedom. Thus He *concentrates* on you.

Our fathers called it old-fashioned, Holy Ghost conviction. I believe it to be the basis of genuine salvation. To harden the heart against this is the sin of sins. There must be a penalty to those who brush aside the evident desire of God to save and use their lives.

This is my message to you. *God is not passive, simply waiting for the world to come round to Him.* God is doing something about it. He is advancing toward you. He is saying to you personally, "I *want* you."

God intends every church service to be an evangelistic meeting, where souls are saved. There is no random, haphazard dispensation. The Lord knoweth them that are His.

Every one of God's employees has been approved and assigned. I am not the forgotten man on the totem pole. Having loved His own, He loves them even to the end.

My parents used to tell me when I was a youngster that they *wanted* me. They had planned to have me. They prayed for my birth. I have always wondered what it feels like to be a child who is not wanted, who is treated as though he were in the way. I do not think anything can be worse.

God *wanted* me. Long before my spiritual birth my Heavenly Father wanted me. I am not a religious accident. *I am His choice.* That is what New Testament life means. And that is what is gripping you in this service.

FIVE STEPS GOD TAKES TOWARD EVERY SINNER

Text: *"But God, who is rich in mercy, for his great love wherewith he loved us."*

Ephesians 2:4

I AM glad to see a concern for soul winning. Congregations are meeting in study groups. Techniques are demonstrated.

Sales know-how is applied. Field work is outlined and supervised. Success is contagious with excitement. Membership and church educational records grow.

This is evangelism, *but it can also be a new form of "huckster-ism."* I want to say this plainly. I do not say that it is. I say that there is a built-in possibility that it can become no more than that. I pray to God that it never will.

The eternal soul is too priceless to ever be further corrupted by misguided enthusiasts who want that soul to be a part of their success formula.

A soul has to be *loved*. It has to be *yearned* over. It has to be *reached* and *wanted*. A soul is not easily born again. It is a miracle that affects three worlds. It is deliberate. A sovereign power wills it. Destiny is involved.

Calculations that only an Almighty God can summarize belong to such a birth. The dimensions are big, sir!

Not for one second would I discourage or would I discount one single soul-winning effort. I pray fervently that we may have more of them. *There is a part for all of us to do.* But it is a *part.*

A spiritual birth is not something that God has given out as a franchise to interested parties. *Every spiritual birth is God's concern.* It could never take place without His burden for it. That is what makes it the biggest thing to happen to anybody between the cradle and the coffin.

I am going to point out *five steps* that God takes—and that only God can take—toward any soul before a spiritual birth can take place. No technique, no program, no sales or service method can ever substitute for these five steps. *There can be no spiritual birth without them.*

I. GOD ELECTS. I know. I dealt with that in a previous service. I want to come back to it. The New Testament has so much to say about it. I have knelt many times in a hotel room and prayed earnestly before I went to preach:

"God in heaven, I affirm that Thy desire and Thy faithfulness to reach souls in this community are a million times stronger and longer than my desire and faithfulness can ever be. In Thy name and in Thy company, I go forth now to reach with Thee these souls." I pray that prayer.

All the soul winners of the New Testament believed this. Peter says, *"Elect* according to the foreknowledge of God the Father, through sanctification of the Spirit, unto obedience and sprinkling of the blood of Jesus Christ" (1 Peter 1:2).

John reports the words of Jesus, "All that the Father *giveth* me shall come to me" (John 6:37).

Paul says, "Knowing, brethren beloved, your *election* of God" (1 Thessalonians 1:4).

God takes the *initiative* toward the soul. John touches this theme again and again, "We love him, because he first loved us" (1 John 4:19). In every community this *divine compulsion* is at work. I must sense it to ever be a partner in God's redemptive work.

Soul winning starts with *caring* about someone. You can use tritely the phrase, "God loves you"; or you can use it with depths of meaning that can reach the lost with a lifeline.

God has made the lost His number one business. I ask myself on repeated occasions, "C. M. Ward, does anyone really *care* about you?"

It is a solemn thought. How much do I matter? Am I only a statistic? Am I only someone to hang a suit of clothes on, issue an automobile license to, fill out tax forms for, and give a few five-dollar flower sprays to at my funeral? How big is life anyway? How important is it? Who on earth can give me those kind of answers? No one, sir! I must feel a tug from another world.

Only God himself is capable of knowing the height, depth, length, and breadth of one soul. *Only God can know that.* The soul must be "warmed" before the seed can enter. The winter must pass. Only God can dictate the seasons. "That the purpose of God according to election might stand, not of works, but of him that calleth" (Romans 9:11).

II. GOD CALLS. "And for this cause he is the mediator of the new testament, that by means of death, for the redemption of the transgressions that were under the first testament, they which are *called* might receive the promise of eternal inheritance" (Hebrews 9:15).

Here is the picture of my soul as it develops from the Word. God not only *cares* about me; He *wants* me.

"And the Spirit and the bride say, Come ... And let him that is athirst come. And whosoever will, let him take the water of life freely" (Revelation 22:17).

Anyone who has heard the call of God in his soul will never forget it. "I am not come to call the righteous, but sinners to repentance" (Matthew 9:13).

Every gospel songwriter has known this basic fact. Song after song has been written about this tender, far-reaching call that finds a wave length right down into the center of a person's being. *"Jesus* is tenderly calling today." That is a fact, mister!

I knew He was calling me when I was in my late teens. I could have shaken off preachers' talk. I already knew enough answers for those who were questioning me about religion. I was not a candidate for a formula or a tradition. *I needed the hidden Persuader.*

Some folk tried to scare me to the altar. Other folk tried to talk me to the altar.

Jesus Christ simply said, "Come!" I knew He *wanted* me. It made His birth, ministry, death, and resurrection meaningful. I did not feel "lost" anymore. I knew instinctively that I should head where I belonged—like the birds to their sanctuary, like the fish to their native streams.

The invitation song, "Come *home;* come home!" meant something to me. "Home" did not mean some church building. Most of them are cold, uncomfortable, and foreboding to me. "Home" meant to me the heart of God. It still does.

III. GOD CONVINCES AND CONVICTS. "And Saul arose from the earth; and when his eyes were opened, he saw no man: but they led him by the hand, and brought him into Damascus. And he was there three days without sight, *and neither did eat nor drink*" (Acts 9:8, 9).

You can say that man was shaken. Talk about modern shock treatments! This man had one from another world.

Saul of Tarsus was devoted to a false set of standards. He said later, "Who was before a blasphemer, and a persecutor, and injurious: but I obtained mercy, because I did it ignorantly in unbelief" (1 Timothy 1:13). Something from another world had to intervene. It did.

God not only cares and calls, but He *stops* men and women. He stopped the sheriff of Philippi.

"Then he called for a light, and sprang in, and *came trembling,* and *fell down* before Paul and Silas, and brought them out, and said, Sirs, what must I do to be saved? And they said, Believe on the Lord Jesus Christ, and thou shalt be saved, and thy house" (Acts 16:29-31).

These are powerful and marked symptoms: "three days without sight," "neither did eat or drink," "came trembling," "fell down."

Add to those, this: "Now when they heard this, they were *pricked in their heart,* and said unto Peter and to the rest of the apostles, Men and brethren, what shall we do?" (Acts 2:37).

It all adds up to this. *God does something*. It is personal intervention. I believe the Holy Spirit, with a warrant from God the Father, puts a man under *arrest*.

IV. GOD QUICKENS. "Who *quickeneth* the dead, and calleth those things which be not as though they were" (Romans 4:17). The dictionary gives these meanings to the word quicken: to hasten, to rouse, to become alive.

God undertakes to bring response where there is no response, to bring action where there is no action. A blessed portion of the Word tells us, "But God commendeth his love toward us, in that, while we were yet sinners, Christ died for us" (Romans 5:8).

Our fellowmen practice the art of artificial respiration, the bringing back to life again of someone whose heart has stopped beating and whose pulse has ceased. This is emergency treatment to be applied within seconds or minutes at the most.

But God reaches the sinner after years of transgression, after conscience has been dulled, after self-respect is gone, after patterns of evil have been formed. *God reaches that sinner and awakens a response.* He *rouses* the sinner.

The Word says, "And you hath he quickened, who were dead in trespasses and sins. Even when we were dead in sins, hath quickened us together with Christ" (Ephesians 2:1, 5).

I thank God for this quickening power. You do not find it in ritual or ceremony. You do not find it in the mechanics of religion. You do not find it in program or training. *It is supernatural, sir.*

I know when it is present just as I know when there is oxygen in the air. It brings life. It makes a gospel song live and become a challenge. It makes a testimony penetrate, and a sinner say, "He is talking to me." It makes preaching "a sound from heaven."

Without it words are duds. Without it a church service is another item on an agenda. We are always trying to provide pep and spark and enthusiasm for the program. *It can never reach the sinner.* We must depend upon *the quickening* of God.

V. GOD WORKETH GODLY SORROW AND GIVETH REPENTANCE. "Now I rejoice, not that ye were made sorry, but that ye sorrowed to repentance: *for ye were made sorry after a godly manner,* that ye might receive damage by us in nothing. For *godly sorrow* worketh repentance to salvation not to be repented of: but the sorrow of the world worketh death" (2 Corinthians 7:9, 10).

How easily pressures and ideologies and sales techniques can damage lives! Investments are made on someone's advice that turn out badly. Governments are overturned, and national histories move in a right-about-face direction because revolutionaries advocate change. Marriages are contracted, and children are brought into this world because moods and romance were created; and later, sober moments revealed the total incompatibility of the people involved.

God intends that you must never be sorry that you became a Christian. This is a powerful line that says, "That ye might receive *damage* by us in nothing" (2 Corinthians 7:9).

This is not waking up the morning after the night before, and saying, "Now what foolish thing have I done? What have I gotten myself into? Why in the world did I do that?" Salvation is not that kind of thing at all.

There is a line in 2 Timothy 2:25, which says, "If God peradventure will give them repentance to the acknowledging of the truth." *God intends you to come, mister, with your eyes wide open.* God does not use high-pressure methods. There is no oversell.

He wants you to know what you are missing and what you are gaining. He wants you to look at cost. He wants you to look at yourself for what you are.

It is your *need* He offers to meet. It is your *destiny* He offers to settle. It is your *soul* that is being weighed in the balances. It is not our business to make people sad, to dampen the fun and pleasure in a community.

Paul told the Corinthians, "Now I rejoice, not that ye were made sorry." No, sir! It is not that at all. *Salvation is repairing the damage that sin has done in a man's life.*

These are the five steps that God takes toward every sinner. God alone can take them. He is taking them toward you. And I am so happy, because I know from observation and experience, that God saves a multitude more sinners than we ever "get saved."

SOUL WINNING IN THE HOME

Text: *"Go home ... and tell them."*

Mark 5:19

IT seems *inconsistent* to me to be concerned about some- one else when you are not concerned about your own children who are at home.

I do not know how any God-fearing father *whose own son is unsaved* can leave a church service today without either going to the altar or prayer room of that church and pouring his heart out to God. I do not know how any mother claiming salvation can keep an uninterrupted schedule today *and know that her own daughter has not yet made a decision for Christ.*

Soul winning should begin in the home. It will not take long to spread if it begins there.

God holds the parent responsible for the spiritual welfare of the child. Isaiah 38:19 says, "The father to the children shall make known the truth." Christ's command to every father who has a boy for whom the devil is bidding is, "Bring him ... to me" (Matthew 17:17).

The heart cry of every mother whose daughter is away from the Lord, should be, "Have mercy on me, ... thou Son of David; my daughter is grievously vexed with a devil" (Matthew 15:22).

God leaves this matter in no doubt. The Word says: "And ye shall teach them your children, speaking of them when thou sittest in thine house, and when thou walkest by the way, when thou liest down, and when thou risest up. And thou shalt write them upon the door posts of thine house, and upon thy gates" (Deuteronomy 11:19-21).

God says the salvation of our children should be our im- mediate and foremost concern. It should be on our minds constantly.

A parent is closer to a child than any pastor, evangelist, or

Sunday school teacher can ever hope to be. *A parent has an unequaled opportunity to observe the rise of the consciousness of sin and the coming of the child to the hour of accountability to God.* In the same manner that a father and a mother have the responsibility to adequately and seriously place the facts of life before their son and daughter, so that father and mother have a comparable responsibility to place the facts of eternity and a decision for Jesus Christ before their children. The neglect of this is appalling.

If we must clothe, feed, house, protect, and educate our children for *earthly citizenship,* we should also give them the preparation needed for *heavenly citizenship.*

Elisha's question to a mother in his generation, "Is it *well* with the child?" (2 Kings 4:26), should constantly be on the conscience of every Christ-confessing parent in this audience.

David's question about his son, "Is the young man Absalom safe?" (2 Samuel 18:29), is a question every parent should raise about the boy in their home long before he comes to the hour of his death.

Do not wait until an accident takes that boy to the hospital! Do not wait until a misdemeanor takes him to prison! *Now is the time to ask the question.*

It is a long lament that will eat the heart out of you, father, "O my son, . . . my son . . . would God I had died for thee" (2 Samuel 18:33). *Make it your duty each day to check on the spiritual safety of your son.*

How many children could say today, "My parents have never talked to me about Christ? Never once have they ever asked me face to face to seek salvation. They have sent me to Sunday school. They have taken me to church. They have left it to others. I have felt cheated. I have felt they were embarrassed. They could not face me with it."

How many children in this audience would have to make some statement like that? It should not be like that.

The secret is to start early. I believe a child of tender years can have a real experience. I believe a father and mother should aim to have their child accept Christ, make a public profession, receive water baptism, partake of communion regularly, and join the church. That should be the target, and it should not be postponed for the late teens. *It should be the target of every parent for the child as soon as that child comes to the hour of accountability.*

When you treat a child either from the pulpit or the breakfast table as though he were *in the way,* it will not be long before you realize that you have turned that boy or girl *out of the way.* Nature brings the child into this world with a confidence toward and a reliance upon the parent.

A parent is in a position to know better than anyone else the exact time a child passes from under the atoning blood into accountability to God. Every moment thereafter, Christian father, Christian mother, that your child remains unsaved, *you are gambling with death.* Every child passes from Atonement's sheltering protection into saving faith in Christ. Never forget that!

Too many parents never see the march of progress in a child's life. A father is suddenly surprised and embarrassed to see his son sprouting whiskers. A mother cannot bring herself to realize that she has a daughter old enough to date. No wonder parents miss the most important growth-point of all, the moment when the child becomes fully accountable for sin and trespass.

I will tell you this, if we bring the *souls* of our children to Christ early for salvation, we then have a noble chance to bring their *lives* and *characters* to Him for service.

God help you to hear this as I say it! No parent has any moral excuse to be a party, by neglect or indifference, to the unspeakable tragedy in the damnation of the soul and the eternal waste of the life of his child. You have a job to do, parent!

Dad, let me speak to you for a moment! You are on the

deacon board. You help to call or retire the preacher. Where was the Shunammite woman's husband when their boy grew rigid under the last convulsion? He was too busy with the crops to either bring the sick boy home, saddle the ass, or go after Elisha. *The mother had it all to do.* She got her son back from death because she brought God's power into requisition.

Where was Elkanah, Hannah's husband, when she took the child Samuel to the tabernacle for a lifetime of service to God? He was a handsome man, generous, even-tempered, sympathetic, but not overly religious. He preferred to stay at home on Wednesday night rather than to attend the midweek service.

Where was Zebedee, the father of James and John, when his wife sought places of prominence for her two boys in the kingdom of God? *No thanks to this avid fisherman that these two hair-triggered boys turned out to be blessed apostles.*

Mister, if you have enough courage to act as a deacon, you have enough courage to lead your own son to Jesus Christ. That is if you care; and if you do not care, you should not be a deacon.

At the moment your child passes from under the atoning blood into accountability to God—from that exact moment— father and mother, *your battle in the home is with sin and the devil in the life of a boy or girl.*

The Syrophenician mother knew it (Matthew 15:21-28). She determined that she would find salvation for her daughter. She faced on that girl's behalf as many difficulties as any mother faces today. She put it in plain language. She said, "My daughter is grievously vexed with a devil."

Style-conscious, society-oriented, foolish, church-member parents want to think something else today. They want to pay out good money for high-sounding medical terms that hide the plain truth that their spoiled children have a bad case of mean, ornery, sin-blight on their souls.

The woman in the Bible won a solution because she called

the symptoms by the right name, went directly to the right Person, and refused to budge until she received heaven's assurance.

Luke, a qualified physician who knew tantrums and evil possession when he saw them, tells about a distraught father (Luke 9:37-42). That man could not go to work when he saw sin's ravages that scarred his boy.

He said to the Son of God, "Look upon my son." He learned the lesson of fasting, prayer, and faith and led his son home in his right mind, delivered from the power of hell. What are you doing, sir? What are you doing, mother, *right there in the home?*

No, no, you cannot *force* children to become Christians. That will not work. Deal with your child as earnestly and yet as sensibly and calmly as you do in other matters. *But do it!*

Have confidence in the Word. Read the Bible in their presence. Let them remember that not a day passed while they were at home when they did not hear a portion of the Word of God.

Early as their birthdays come and go, give each child in the home his own beautiful copy of the Bible. Find time to pray with each child separately as well as around the family altar.

Be careful to distinguish between the *commands of Christ* and *parental obligations.* Coming to Christ and joining the church are duties to God and not to man. We must make this clear. A child must act on his own initiative. A daughter who makes a profession just to please mother and obtain further favor, has not yet grasped what it means to be a Christian.

Christian parents ought to exercise all the tact and wisdom a great God can give them in *encouraging* their children to move toward this most important decision. The tender plant can be easily bruised and set back. Watch conviction for sin run its course as you would watch and calculate a fever. *You must know when to sense a crisis.* There is a breaking point.

Jesus urged extreme care. He said that it is better to have a millstone about our necks and be cast into the sea (that means lost beyond recall) than that we should offend one of these little ones (Luke 17:2).

Do not sin against your own child! The hearts of children are responsive to the claims of Jesus Christ. Children are not hardened by sin's indulgences. They are sinners by nature, but practice in outstanding sin has not calloused their souls.

Soul winning ought to start in the home with your own children. Jesus still says, "Suffer *little children* to come unto me, and forbid them not" (Luke 18:16). He says *"little* children." That does not mean wait until they are teen-agers. That means when they are ready to read and write, when they are ready to go off to school. *Win them then!*

NUMBER ONE

Text: *"For he must reign, till he hath put all enemies under his feet."*

1 *Corinthians* 15:25

I T would take Handel's "Messiah" and the "Hallelujah Chorus" to do this text justice. *It demands a great crescendo.*

Perhaps we do not realize how Jesus reigns now. We usually contemplate this as something in the future. *In what manner and by what means does Jesus reign?*

He reigns through the uniqueness of His message. Ideas rule the world. No message ever uttered can compare with the message of divine atonement for sin. That message goes down to the deepest roots of human sin.

It has changed the cannibal. It has rebuilt the prodigal. It has subdued the rebel. It finds its way into the guilty conscience and sheds the light of pardon and peace that passes understanding.

The sinner knows no music so sweet and no power so mighty

as the message of the atoning Christ: "Behold the Lamb of God, which taketh away the sin of the world" (John 1:29).

My friend, just compare this message to the schedule of messages you hear every day, from drugs to politics. *The gospel is the king of messages.* It tells me that the God the human race expelled has returned with an offer of mercy, with a determination to save Adam's seed.

That message is far greater than the message of the pantheist who speaks of the immanence of Nature. *The gospel speaks to me about the immanence of Grace.* It tells me God has not forsaken me, that God wants to help me.

The gospel tells me there is eternal life. *Every other message stops with the grave.* The message of Jesus Christ has brought "life and immortality to light." *It is a different world since the first Easter.* It is no longer the world of myth and murkiness. Death has lost its sting. The grave has lost its victory.

He reigns because He is the only Person in history to come back. He has no rival. He is "the first fruits of them that are asleep" (1 Corinthians 15:20 A.S.V.).

It was not a phantom that appeared forty days on earth. The events are recorded, and they have withstood the investigation of twenty centuries. *God has revealed in Him the design and decision of the Throne for mankind in the new earth of tomorrow.* Man's advances in science seem insignificant compared to the resurrection glory of Jesus Christ.

He reigns by means of His continued real, although invisible, presence in the world. His personality dominates our earth. The dead do not have this grip. This is what gives His message authority. It is not philosophy taught in a classroom. It is a command.

Our world is sensitive to powerful personalities. They may be as inferior and as unworthy as Hitler or Mussolini; but they grab the headlines and the conversation, *until they pass from the scene.* Jesus Christ is headline conversation today, because He is alive. That is why He reigns.

The dividing line between faith and doubt lies in the answer to the question of whether Jesus is but a memory and an influence in the world or whether He is here in personal presence as our Lord and our God. Thomas the disciple made that his test. *When the Church fails to realize the vital presence of her Lord, she becomes weak and doubtful.* Jesus Christ is the living, present Word.

You and I have a right to ask, what is the record and *evidence* of the reign of Jesus Christ in these past twenty centuries?

The record of His reign is the record of the creation of the grandest human lives the world has ever seen. The writer to the Hebrews in the New Testament puts it this way, "Of whom the world was not worthy" (Hebrews 11:38).

They have little discernment for the finer beauties of the human spirit who cannot see that the finest type of pagan character, compared with the finest type of Christian character, is as iron to fine gold.

Place Seneca or Marcus Aurelius, with their philosophical and maxim-fed virtues, beside Paul, with the multitudinous beauties of his new life in Christ and the endless surprises of his consecration and faith and love. *There is no comparison.*

No one but Jesus Christ could have fashioned Paul. He said it himself, "It is no longer I that live, but Christ liveth in me" (Galatians 2:20 A.S.V.).

This power of Christ to create unparalleled lives has succeeded in the case of the lowest and most debased of mankind. *When philosophy has succeeded in making a reputable or admirable moral character, it has always started with a respectable subject.*

Remember that! Christ starts the same way with every man; He starts with a new birth. Every man must be born again before he can see God's kingdom.

Philosophy does not pretend to save the vicious nor lift the depraved and morally impotent out of the mire of trespass. *That* is where Jesus of Nazareth is triumphant. He has not come to call the righteous but sinners to repentance. The Son of Man is come to seek and to save that which was lost.

He is able to save to the uttermost all that come to God by Him. *Jesus Christ will take any challenge of sin.* That is where He reigns supreme.

What a glorious roll of apostles, saints, and martyrs makes the Christian generations illustrious! John says it is *a multitude* which no man can number, out of all tribes and peoples and nations and languages and tongues. *Can any power on earth match it?* His power has been the same in every generation.

What Jesus Christ did for folk in my grandfather's day He is doing for folk today. Where can philosophy produce such *a multitude* whose voices are as the sound of many waters? how often does philosophy produce a Seneca or a Plato? *There is no stock behind the few samples.* Jesus Christ does it again, and again, and again.

Now I come to a matter I beg you never to forget. *The message and operation of Jesus Christ is the one thing that has remained triumphantly unchanged throughout the generations.* It has never needed to be remodeled or updated. It is the same blessed story. *Nothing has ever been repeated so often and so long.*

Here is a message of life to men given in essence and in detail in the New Testament almost two thousand years ago. Since it was given, human theories of all kinds have undergone mammoth changes. Science has repudiated its dogmatisms again and again. Social and political ideas have changed with the centuries and are in the midst of change today.

This great, stumbling, changing world has been trying to make all things new. *It never quite finds the answer.* But God's answer has never changed. It is the same message today as when it was first proclaimed. It stands alone and unique. It makes Jesus King. No other message has had the vitality to survive.

I know that men have tried to change it. *They have not wanted it to change them; so they have tried to change the message.* Sometimes in their vain imaginings they think they have succeeded. We can afford to smile at their folly.

Mister modernist in the pulpit, you have changed nothing! We look down the vistas of past history, and we find them strewn with the remains of new gospels, up-to-date messages, which were promulgated with the same confidence as today's modern gospel.

Every attempt to change the message of Jesus Christ will meet the same fate. Whatever may happen to either heaven or earth, mister, the message of Jesus Christ to the sinner will remain unchanged forever.

Finally you say to me, "Brother Ward, what guarantee do you offer that present trends will not dethrone Jesus Christ?" Paul says, "He must reign, till he hath put all enemies under his feet" (1 Corinthians 15:25).

What are the odds that Jesus Christ will survive today's changes and attacks?

The answer is not difficult. There is no message to take its place. Man is a sinner. He is guilt-conscious. He needs salvation. Where can he obtain it? *He is a moral failure.* He must have cleansing and a new start with new life. He is separated from God and needs a Mediator to bring him into the presence of the Father.

All the boasted schemes of men for the amelioration of humanity only scratch the surface. "There is no other name under heaven given among men, whereby we must be saved" (Acts 4:12) ; *neither is there salvation in any other.*

We are a lost race without Jesus Christ. It still remains apparent: "Lord, to whom shall we go (but unto Thee)? thou hast the words of eternal life" (John 6:68). That is why Jesus Christ is King today.

I know the more superficial appeal may seem to win for a

time. But the appeal that turns the prodigal from the wasteland of lust and passion and self-love is the appeal of Father and home. *Riotous living can never survive the love of the Father.* Jesus has the offer that outlasts all other offers.

A world system offers you *husks*. God offers you *heaven*. There is a divine compulsion in this world that makes the sinner say, "I will arise and go to my Father." Nothing today can erase that longing.

Member of this audience, Jesus must reign to the end. There is purpose and plan in these centuries. He came once. He is coming again. What He has done in twenty centuries with His message and His presence, He will bring to a climax with His manifested glory.

He has pledged Himself to complete the work of redemption, "till he hath put all enemies under his feet." These enemies are gathering right now for one last Armageddon stand.

You say, "What difference can there be between the invisible and visible presence?" It is like a cloudless day with a perfectly blue sky. But suddenly, with the cool of the evening, it sometimes happens that clouds seem to spring out of space and cover the face of the sky. From where did they come?

The answer is this. They were present all day as invisible vapor, and with the cool of the evening, they suddenly condensed and became visible.

Thus the Lord is with us, although unseen to the eye of man. But with eventide He will clothe Himself with the robes of His visible glory, and all the world shall see the Son of Man coming in the clouds with power and great glory. *It will complete the triumph of His reign.*

"The kingdoms of this world ... (shall) become the kingdoms of our Lord, and of his Christ" (Revelation 11:15), and the followers of the Lamb shall become an everlasting priesthood and kingdom unto God. *Make sure now that you are among this number.*

AN UNMARKED GRAVE

Text: *"And his disciples came, and took up the body, and buried it, and went and told Jesus."*

Matthew 14:12

THE story of John the Baptist closes with a thud. A lot of folks will always ask, "Did he not quit preaching and go to meddling?" It cost him his head.

John's life flashes and dies like a meteor. Perhaps strains of Herod's drunken, lascivious ball drifted down to the dungeon. What did he think in those closing hours? As the wine flowed and the dance quickened, no guards brought the condemned man a final meal.

He could feel the venom of Herodias. Nothing could reach her soul. She had made her pact with the devil. Her plans for revenge were as sordid as her thirsting for the blood of God's people. The die had been cast. *Public opinion was at stake.*

John's preaching had thrilled Israel. Luke comments on the ascendancy of his ministry, and says, "And as the people were in expectation, and all men mused in their hearts of John, whether he were the Christ, or not" (Luke 3:15). He had touched all classes.

Then he spoke out against Herodias and the political power of the day. Was it a mistake? Is that why help from the nearby Christ did not reach him at the last moment?

It was one thing to preach to the public, "He that hath two coats, let him impart to him that hath none; and he that hath meat, let him do likewise" (Luke 3:11); and to say to tax collectors, "Exact no more than that which is appointed" (Luke 3:13); and to the military, "Do violence to no man, neither accuse any falsely; and be content with your wages" (Luke 3:14). *That kind of preaching will always have a lot of popular appeal.* Perhaps he should have stuck to that.

But he did more than talk about better standards of living, a steady economy, and settled conditions. *He called sin in high places, sin.*

Luke says, "And many other things in his exhortation preached he unto the people. But Herod the tetrarch, being reproved by him for Herodias his brother Philip's wife, and for all the evils which Herod had done, added yet this above all, that he shut up John in prison" (Luke 3:18-20).

The battle had been joined. *No armistice could be reached.* Does it ever pay to crusade?

To behead a man of God, to tell him it was orders, to bend over in the dankness and mold of the doomed, and to let the head that had arrested the attention of the multitude fall on a charger was a shameful thing to ask any soldier to do. *It was degrading to be mixed up in it.*

Only scullions and menials dragged the bloodied and hewn torso from the cell. They must have dumped it where the offal of the palace was disposed of. That leads me to this text: "And his disciples came, and took up the body, and buried it, and went and told Jesus."

Did He do more for Lazarus than He did for the "Voice in the wilderness"? What do you make of it?

Some will point to it as a graphic example to the Church to mind her own business. They will maintain that there is no place in this day for a country preacher, rawboned, out of the hills, to thunder God's dynamics. They argue that such preaching belongs to the Old Testament. *They say there is a new way to deal with hypocrisy, lust, and theft.*

They forget that John was God-sent and Spirit-filled. They overlook that John attracted crowds of all sorts, publicans, sinners, Pharisees, scribes, Sadducees, and soldiers. They came from the cities. They came from the mountains and plains. Kings and governors came to listen and went away in fear.

He was great in tenderness, lion-like in boldness, simple, pungent, convincing, and powerful like a storm from Lebanon's snowy summits. *There was no compromise in him.*

He was God's big preacher and the prophet of a new day. He was the voice of a strange and new message, repentance of sin, confession, God's Messiah Lamb ready for the sacrifice, baptism—a new ordinance carrying a new doctrine of redemption by death arched with resurrection hope—and Holy Ghost power. *He brought in a new day for dying men.* It has grown brighter ever since.

His ministry was a short one, but oh, how meaningful to the world's destiny! He overturned the traditions of centuries. He brought multitudes to the Light of life and introduced the Light of the ages to men everywhere. These are the facts. Did it end in failure? *What do you do with sin anyway?*

Is it a mistake to stick your neck out for fear of getting your head chopped off? Mister, let me tell you this about my fellow evangelist. His preaching bristled with the vital doctrines later brought out so wonderfully in the Gospels. *He defined sin*—deep-dyed, hell-deserving sin. *He called for repentance*—genuine soul-moving, heart-cleansing, life-purifying repentance. *He pointed to faith in Christ*—trustful, reliant, confident faith.

He proclaimed the deity of Jesus of Nazareth. He pegged his life on the atonement. He called Christ God's Lamb; and he pictured the victory of Calvary in the new ordinance of baptism which he introduced by God's authority.

He preached and lived in the power of the Spirit which filled him from Elizabeth's womb. He was willing to die for these things. Darkness met him head-on. It coiled and struck. He was chosen of God to introduce the Light of the world. Hell could not accept it by default.

More than one person in this audience is asking, "Is it worth it?" An unmarked grave seems a dismal ending. There does not seem to be much grandeur in going down before a cheap burlesque.

It is not Stephen dying before a fusillade of stones and saying "Behold, I see the heavens opened, and the Son of man standing on the right hand of God" (Acts 7:56).

It is not Paul finishing his course and saying, "Henceforth there is laid up for me a crown of righteousness, which the Lord, the righteous judge, shall give me at that day" (2 Timothy 4:8).

It is dying like so many have died, in the trenches, in mud and filth, alone and unattended.

Is the world any better because of it? Can you stop a Philip's wife from changing partners? Will there not always be adultery and promiscuous indulgence? *Can you police morals?* Is it not better to try to outlive it?

John did not think so. He believed that life in its eternal bearings and meaning does not consist of groceries, a catalog of clothes, headlines, special privilege, nor of space of years. *He believed it consists of doing God's will in God's place, in God's time, in God's way.*

This is the truth to remember. John's body lies in an unmarked grave, but his life, wholly given to God in soul winning in the back hills of Judea during a remote age, *is never forgotten.* It has cast a golden glory and given a radiant hope to all subsequent history. Remember this! God has already given the verdict. God says that John, simple, country Baptist preacher, *was the greatest born of woman.* Tourists see no shrine or monument. Archaeologists do not know where to dig. Students argue about John's tactics. God says he was the greatest. That is what counts. What will God say about your life?

My text says, "His disciples ... *went and told Jesus."* John's life and sacrifice find meaning in Jesus. *Without Calvary, without that center cross, John's preaching and John's uncompromising attitude would be meaningless.*

John was always willing to decrease that Christ might increase. He lived with that in view. Thank God for the thousands who have kept step with him. It has made lonely hours bearable. It has given purpose to deprivation and struggle. It has provided fortitude in hours of torture and threat. It has given this world a breed of men and women who have never blanched before devils. They have loved Jesus so much that they felt unworthy to unlatch the Redeemer's shoes but powerful enough in His name to capture the public imagination.

These are men and women whose courage is unmatched. They fear only one thing. They fear God's disapproval. They would not smile at a Herodias and tolerate her wickedness for all the gold in Fort Knox. She may flaunt her disregard for morals in high society. She may use Herod's position for unworthy ends.

But she will never get a John the Baptist to look the other way. He will call it sin in God's Name and take the consequences. *A hot and holy fire burns in such souls.*

These are investments for which this world must one day stand in judgment. Neutral you cannot be, sir! You may postpone your decision about political and social issues of this day. But you cannot postpone your decision about the death of a man, that God called the greatest, at the hands of a drunken king who wanted to gratify the desires of an enraged, adulterous woman. *God asks for your decision now.*

Salome's dance may be just another unfortunate midway act to you. It may be human nature in the raw. God says that behind such entertainment there is a calculating spirit of evil that is vile, murderous, and satanic. God promises a day of reckoning. John's trust was in Jesus. That is where the case will be settled. What is your relationship with Him?

JESUS CHRIST

Text: *"And he said unto them, Ye are from beneath; I am from above: ye are of this world; I am not of this world."*
John 8:23

MARK says that Jesus was a carpenter. All agree that Jesus was a Galilean peasant. There is no glitter in the background. *The glory is in the Man.*

This Man, in common clothes, makes claims for Himself. We say with profound reverence that if these claims were not true and could not be demonstrated they would stamp Him with insanity. There is no other choice.

These claims startled everyone. They maddened His enemies. He said, "If a man keep my saying, he shall never taste of death." They said, "Art Thou greater than our father Abraham, which is dead?" They asked, "Whom makest thou thyself?" (John 9:52, 53). Would you not have asked the same question had you been there?

He claimed to be unique. Not for a moment did He class Himself with earth's great ones, the geniuses of human genealogy. He refused to be bracketed with generals, statesmen, scientists, or preachers. "Who shall declare his generation?" (Isaiah 53:8). *He stands alone.*

"Ye are from *beneath;* I am from above." Jesus Christ claimed divine origin. He expressed this without a moment of hesitation. He came from another world as the Messenger. *He came as Lord of salvation.* "The Son of Man is come to seek and to save that which was lost" (Luke 19:10). *He claimed power unlimited,* all the power that could ever be needed to redeem the worst sinner.

"And no one hath ascended into heaven," He said, "but He that descended out of heaven, even the Son of man" (John 3:13 A.S.V.). It was not man *ascending.* It was God *descending.* He came to a Greek and Roman culture creating and building their own gods. *They associated their own sins with their own gods.* Jesus Christ says, "I am not of this world." He came to raise penitent sinners to sit with Him in heavenly places. He said, "The Son of Man hath power upon earth to forgive sins" (Luke 5:24).

He did not link Himself with celestial beings of created splendor. He talked about the glory which He had "before the world was." I say this reverently. If a man came to New York and talked like that today he would be committed. He said,

"I came out from the Father, and am come into the world:
again, I leave the world, and go unto my Father" (John 16:
28 A.S.V.).

He dared to make these claims without purse or bank account.
He had no property or academic background. He spoke these
words although He had never traveled beyond Palestinian bor-
ders. *They are the most important and far-reaching claims ever
recorded in human history.*

And what is even more amazing, these claims have been
believed. *Instead of ridicule there has been testimony.* History
has not written this Galilean peasant as some classic figure
symbolizing scorn or pity or hopeless insanity. Remember that!
These astounding claims have been believed.

There is no other figure in human history before whom we
can conceive any great souls of men worshiping and crying,
"My Lord and my God." People who have made this confession
have been judged by their achievements in every walk of life
to have been sane, lucid people—people of high intelligence.

I marvel at this. I know there are plenty who do not believe.
You may be among that number. Who are the unbelievers?
Examine your own life! Are you so good, perfect, pure, and
honest that you can look down upon Jesus Christ of Nazareth
and say, "Peasant, you are a blasphemer; you are deluded; you
are a hoax; you are an eternal bore"? Can you afford to say
that? *If not, what are you going to do with His claims?*

Do you hate Jesus because His sublime truth stabs your
life, your way of living, your darkened deeds? Does the Man
condemn your corrupt thoughts and actions? His own generation
asked, "Whence hath this man these things? What is the wisdom which is given unto this man, and what mean such mighty
works wrought by His hands?" Take a long, steady look, and
deny Him if you can!

Are you prepared to say that millions who have accepted
His claims are *deluded?* I ask you about the men who first

followed Him. They were the ordinary run of Galileans. They were not influenced by the cathedrals that have been built in His Name today. The masters had not yet painted His picture in imperishable oils. Great denominations of church members had not yet been formed. *They knew Him only from Nazareth.*

Jesus made no attempt to occupy a mysterious pedestal above them or to hold Himself majestically aloof. He did not make His dwelling in some twilight heights or in secret retreats of imagined glory. *He let them see daily and close at hand, His lowly peasant manhood, in humble and everyday circumstances in lowly places.* They ate with Him. They talked to Him familiarly. They slept with Him. Familiarity never bred contempt. They knew every mood, His joy and His tears. He was among them as one that served. *He never tried to impress.* He had nothing to hide. He never apologized for His humble means. They saw it all, every bit of it.

If there had been one factor of unreality in it, they would have discovered it. They knew one another's faults. They would have found His, had there been any. *Insincerity cannot survive under such daily scrutiny.* At the best, had it existed, it would have made them fellow conspirators. *But Christ's life had the opposite effect on them.* It made them the greatest moral and spiritual heroes of history.

The Nazarene had conquered and forced His astounding claim upon the noblest thought and deepest apprehension of the world. Can you explain it? *What has compelled this marvelous verdict?*

Jesus Christ backed these out-of-the-world claims with His life of absolute sinlessness. Mister, there is yet to arise one person to accuse Jesus Christ of the tiniest imperfection, and to substantiate it. *No one in history can equal the record.*

I have heard unbelievers try to explain it. I know what they say. Listen! The idea that that sinless life was *invented* by sinful men is one of the absurdities of fantastic speculation. Put that theory to the test, sinner! Do you know what you are saying?

Under your theory Jesus is depicted in every variety of circumstance. He breathes with vital and muscular energy. He is not withdrawn. He is not a monastic. He is never sheltered. He moves amid passion and indignation, in the midst of front-page circumstances of the most subtle and most aggressive temptations—enough to make the best of us lose our tempers or yield to a quick gain.

Remember, four different men give their close-ups of Him. One was a doctor. One was a tax-collector. One was a commercial fisherman. One was a favored son of a reasonably well-to-do widow. *There is not a chance for collusion.* They all write the same verdict, "yet without sin."

Here is something else I want you to remember. Jesus taught His disciples to pray for forgiveness for their trespasses, *but He never breathed such a prayer for Himself.* Other men, as they grew holier, became more and more conscious of their imperfections.

This is not so with Jesus. Never once does He acknowledge the slightest trace of sin-guilt. He opened Himself to the presence of the Father. In that presence He spoke with calmness and boldness. Other men go to church and speak of their sins and unworthiness to God. Jesus spoke to God of His "glory." It is an amazing record.

Look again at the carpenter! His personality outshone every personality in contrast of physical meeting, from John the Baptist to Pontius Pilate. It was not done with props and stagecraft. It was not accomplished by arranged publicity. It was not done by scriptwriters and cleverly engineered backdrops.

He spoke, and critics of speech said, "Never man spake like this Man." He cast a spell that bound the hands of His enemies until "His hour was come." His judgment was so apparently right that accusers of the woman taken in sin slunk away, and desecrators of the temple fled. *Everyone was conscious of it.* He exuded a mysterious awe. It could be so overpowering that ruffians who came to Him in the garden fell in a faint.

"I am from above . . . I am not of this world" (John 8:23).

Can anyone doubt it? His life moved on the easy plane of supernatural power. He walked on water as easily as He walked on land. He multiplied food as easily as He cast out evil spirits. He raised the dead with the same authority as He borrowed boats and beasts of burden. He found tax money as He found friends, in strange places.

He never staged these things as a seasonal buildup. They were the constant essence of His daily life. *He lived in the ease of the supernatural as we live in the harrowing demand of economic urgency.* His calmness and ease were an open rebuke to the hurry and worry of others.

Never once did He accept second, third, or fourth place. He demanded unqualified submission and homage. He was Lord. He was Master. "I am," He said, "the way, the truth, and the life" (John 14:6). It was never open to question.

One more evidence demands my attention. *He knew the very heart of God.* He knew that heart intimately and completely. The secrets of eternity were all wide open to His gaze. This was not the access of a student. This was not the calculated guess of an intuitionist. This was not the mysticism of a visionary. *He had been there.* He spoke in detail. He spoke with finality. No one has added to that knowledge in these centuries which have followed. The revelation is complete in Him. He said it Himself, "I am the light of the world" (John 8:12).

I ask you, What are you going to do about such claims? I might as well ask you, What are you going to do about the sun, about the law of gravity, and about earth's tides? Any failure to recognize the glory of Jesus Christ must be attributed to moral reasons rather than to intellectual reasons. *Sin alone can twist your decision.*

This Man makes a personal claim upon you. Here are His words: "I said therefore unto you, that ye shall die in your sins: for if ye believe not that I am He, ye shall die in your sins" (John 8:24). To know the secret of Jesus is to know the secret of God, and this secret is eternal life.

THE TWO HOPES IN
THIS WORLD

Text: *"And ye yourselves like unto men that wait for their lord, when he will return from the wedding."*

Luke 12:36

J ESUS Christ said that *to His countrymen*. It is a verse that is coming into sharp perspective.

The two hopes of this world are running *concurrently*. The first hope is called the *Messianic hope*. This is the hope of Israel. The second hope is called the *Blessed hope*. This is the hope of the Church. *Both are looking for the same Man.*

In the long centuries that have passed nothing has been able to erase these hopes. It is a major miracle. *That the coming of the Messiah and the return of the Saviour have not yet taken place is secondary to the undeniable fact that these hopes are brighter today than when they were first expressed centuries ago.* Can you explain this persistent vigor?

Every preacher in the Old Testament preached the *Messianic hope*. Every preacher in the New Testament preached the Lord's return. Through the centuries the Hebrew has faced his wailing wall or his Passover, and clutched the divine promise that his Messiah will come. Generation after generation the born-again believer has held fast to the Word of God and faced the scoffer who asks, "Where is the promise of his coming? for since the fathers fell asleep, all things continue as they were from the beginning of the creation" (2 Peter 3:4).

The Israeli race outlives its tormentors and detractors. Whether it is Pharaoh's devilish program of infanticide or Hitler's hellish scheme of liquidation, Israel moves irresistibly towards its divine destiny. The Church survives persecutions and apostasies. It has a rendezvous to keep with its Head and Bridegroom.

This is why Jesus Christ told His followers to watch Israel. *The Messianic hope and the Blessed hope are entwined.* One cannot be fulfilled without the other. Moral and corruptible darkness will turn its awful strength upon these two hopes to extinguish them forever, if that is possible. This is the setting for the end-time drama.

Our blessed Lord has given us something to see, *something to bolster faith,* as tribulation days near. Israel has been re-established as a nation. The exiles are being regathered. *Israel's hope has turned to substance.* Now the Holy Spirit would say to the believer, "Look! If the promise is being kept with Israel, when it seemed impossible that it would ever be kept, will not the promise of His second coming be kept with you?"

Two things identify this twentieth century. First, there has been a repeated outpouring of the Holy Spirit upon all flesh. Under this supernatural stimulus the message has been, "Jesus is coming soon." *It is the bridal call.* This gospel has been preached in the greatest missionary activity the world has ever known.

Second, the sudden rebirth of the Hebrew nation out of the bone piles of Europe, is the unmistakable sign that the Messiah will keep His Abrahamic and Davidic covenants with this race. *This is that century!*

Christ put His finger on the difference in faith that exists between the Hebrew and the Christian. He said of His country-men, "And ye yourselves like unto men that wait for their lord, when he will *return from the wedding*" (Luke 12:36). The born-again believer anticipates being *at the wedding.* "And at midnight there was a cry made, Behold, the bridegroom cometh; go ye out to meet him" (Matthew 25:6).

One thing is certain, if the longing of the centuries has any meaning at all, *there is going to be a celebration of the ages.* The New Testament in prophetic word describes it this way:

"Let us be glad and rejoice, and give honour to him: for the *marriage* of the Lamb is come, and his wife hath made herself ready" (Revelation 19:7). This is the picture of *union*. This is the ecumenical event in which I am interested.

Faith must have ultimate fulfillment. A physical, material Christ must be realized. The world's greatest corporate Body must be seen with its Head. Nothing else makes sense. The New Testament describes it further: "The kingdoms of this world are become the kingdoms of our Lord, and of his Christ; and he shall reign for ever and ever" (Revelation 11:15). I believe that.

Jesus says the Hebrew waits tenaciously with his *Messianic hope* for the revelation of his Lord after that *wedding*. Mister, it is not difficult to piece together. If there is ever going to be a final solution to the Jewish problem, there must *first* be a fulfillment to the Saviour's pledge, "I will come again, and receive you unto myself; that where I am, there ye may be also" (John 14:3).

I believe the infilling of the Spirit of God *seals* this pledge in the believer. "And grieve not the holy Spirit of God, whereby ye are sealed unto the day of redemption" (Ephesians 4:30).

I loved to hear my mother sing a song of trust while she was with us. "I've received *an invitation,*" she would sing, "to the marriage supper of the Lamb, and I'm going to be there." She knew, with unshakable confidence, that the Holy Spirit had brought to her a blood-bought reservation for that feast of the ages. My mother was the second person in Canada to receive the baptism of the Holy Spirit when the Holy Ghost was outpoured at the beginning of this century. *From that moment she was heading toward the wedding.*

The great combat of sin, error, and unfaithfulness that is now developing is to distort or destroy this *bridal call*. "While the bridegroom tarried, they all slumbered and slept" (Matthew 25:5). *All that miss the wedding will be left to the mercies of the apostasy.*

The apostle Paul, gifted with Holy Ghost insight, notes two directions from which satanic pressures will come in the last days. First, he directs our attention to "the *rulers* of the darkness of this world." Second, he directs our attention to "spiritual wickedness *in high places*" (Ephesians 6:12).

The rulers of the darkness of this world have taken *human form*. They are visible. Their visages are creased with utter dedication to evil. *They impose a totalitarian effort to build impenetrable walls against the light.* Look at them: Mao Tze-tung, Castro, Ho Chi Minh, Sukarno, Khrushchev!

Moscow's Communist party newspaper put it this way in recent days:

"Any religion, any belief in the supernatural, in good and evil forces, in a God Creator, is a distorted anti-scientific view of nature and society, a disregard of science, a replacement of scientific knowledge by fantastic legends. . . . Any religion transforms a human being into a slave of gods invented by himself. . . ."

Millions are condemned to this authority of darkness. They are shackled as no previous generations ever have been shackled. *Rulers watch the ramparts.* A bride for hell is being organized.

At the same time on this side of the Iron, Sugar Cane, and Bamboo Curtains, *a subtle erosion is taking place,* which the apostle describes as "spiritual wickedness in high places." Faith is being weakened by decisions that make the believer ask, "How can these things be in a nation founded by spiritual quest and whose testimony has been 'In God We Trust'?"

From where do these decisions emanate? They come from "high places." The infidelity of this day is not the contempt of the masses. It is not the beastlike brutishness of the streets of the French Revolution. No. It is not that. It is the cleverness, the contrived sales pitch, the specious reasoning of leadership that is turning from the God of our fathers, and is leaning upon human counsel and the security of science. *This is the arena of spiritual wickedness.*

Like a nutcracker, they are closing in upon the two hopes in this world—first, *the Church;* then, second, when the Church shall have been caught away beyond reach to the wedding, *Israel.* God has written His eternal truth in both of these repositories. Hell has sworn to destroy them. There can be no truce.

But the Holy Ghost is present upon earth, still convicting of sin and of righteousness and of judgment, *and testifying to the appearance of Christ.* No culmination of evil can take place until "he be taken out of the way."

That means one world resting upon one religion can never become a reality until the Holy Spirit has finished His ministry to mankind. *So the bridal call is going forth with renewed emphasis.* Leaping across denominational lines and ignoring built-in prejudices and traditions of creed and procedure, the Eliezer of eternity has been commissioned by the Father to secure a bride for His Son.

Even as the gathering of Israel's exiles is taking place before our eyes, so the gathering of true believers from every denomination is taking place at the same time. These facts are out in the open. They are so evident that they cannot be ignored. I am thrilled to be a part of this generation. The next big event is the wedding, the victory celebration of the ages.

Will you be there? What are you doing with the invitation? The Word says, "A certain man made a great supper, and bade many" (Luke 14:16). This message has pointed to that *Man* and to that *supper.*

The last invitation is going out now. I beseech you not to be among those of whom it will be said, "That none of those men which were bidden shall taste of my supper" (Luke 14:24). Yield to the Holy Ghost and let this Divine Servant lead you into all truth.

BRANDED

Text: *"I bear branded on my body the marks of Jesus."*
Galatians 6:17 (*A.S.V.*)

WE are reminded every day by those who offer us merchandise, "to buy the *brand* names of our day." This is name merchandise that has been proved by test and use. These *brand names* suggest confidence and appeal.

Paul is staking out a big claim. He says, "Look at me. I am a Christian." You cannot mistake his allegiance. He belongs to Jesus Christ. *The trademark is unmistakable.*

Of course, there were physical marks that identified Paul with Jesus Christ. He testifies: "Of the Jews five times received I forty stripes save one. Thrice was I beaten with rods, once was I stoned" (2 Corinthians 11:24, 25). The scars were deep. The marks of his steadfast devotion to Christ were branded indelibly upon him.

But there is more than that to be said. The marks of Jesus were branded on his soul. He was not a Christian only for adventure and circumstance. *He was a Christian because he wanted to be one.* He could never have endured the terrible physical torture had he not been inwardly conformed to Jesus Christ. *You have to believe to take what Paul took.* The scars were only the outward sign. The real marks were inside where it really counts.

Not many today are called upon to endure scourging and brutality. Thank God! We are branded in other ways. The world wants to see the genuine. We may plead our connection with the Church, our orthodoxy of belief, or our good works; but the world asks, "Where are the *marks?*" Paul had a personal answer to that question. Have you?

I ask first, WHAT ARE THE MARKS OF JESUS? *That is not an easy question to answer.* They cannot be confined to some mode of dress, some menu of approved foods, or some selection of occupations.

It is easy to enumerate certain qualities: coolness, courage, prudence, initiative, imagination, and magnetism. But you have not answered the question. I can find these in a great crosscut of people. *They are not confined to Christians.*

Everything depends upon how these qualities combine. For instance, he may be prudent when he ought to take risks, or he may take risks when he ought to be prudent. *No, it is far more elusive!* It is not the result of any personality program or school of sales technique. There is some subtle, intangible, indefinable quality which lies behind and permeates all these other qualities. *It is in a man's spirit.* It shows through.

It is easy to enumerate Christian virtues: love, humility, purity, strength, tenderness, sacrifice. These are qualities you know are Christian. There is nothing vague about these things. You look for them. They are easily recognized. But when you have catalogued them, you have not produced a picture of Jesus Christ. *Only God can put them together in a certain way.*

Let me illustrate! A friend of yours sits for his portrait. You look at the canvas and compare it with your friend. You cannot deny that the reproduction is correct, but there is something lacking. You cannot place your finger on the missing thing, but you know the picture does not truly express your friend. You know that at once. It just is not he.

Then he sits for another artist. This artist does not portray the features any more accurately than the former, but with insight and the skill of genius, he looks *inside* your friend and succeeds in placing on canvas the suggestion, *the message* behind the features your friend always conveys to you. And when you see the picture, you say, "Yes, that is he. You've got him." It is the *inside* that shines through. Without it you may have a cold composite put together from the police files.

You come in contact with a real Christian, and you say, "I was greatly impressed with the beauty of his *character*." But if I ask you what it was that impressed you, you do not find it easy to tell me exactly what you mean. *You are most conscious of the immediate impact that life has made upon you.* You cannot define it. It is an atmosphere, a fragrance. You can tell it as quickly as you can tell the scent of a rose.

May I say this to you, sir! The beautiful markings on flowers have not been painted by hand. Likewise, the marks of Jesus are not *moral achievements.* They are spiritual gifts. A man has to know Jesus. A man has to associate intimately with his Saviour to be permeated with the Personality of the Ages. That is how you are marked.

Second, I say, THESE MARKS ARE MARKS OF OWNER-SHIP. When the choir sings, "Now I *Belong* to Jesus," they are telling you the truth. Everyone rejoices in his independence. That is what we are fighting for. Nevertheless, the fact remains that you and I *belong.* Ball players belong to a club. The military belong to some branch of the armed forces. Husbands and wives belong to each other. Children belong to parents. Businessmen belong to corporations.

We all bear those imprints. They are far more visible than is commonly thought. If you want to know who or what is a man's master, listen to his conversation, and unconsciously he will give you the clue. Whatever the subject he is discussing, *you will soon discover his attitude toward life,* and you will know the name of his owner.

The Christian is not his own. We have been bought with a price. Christ has established claims upon us. His chains are chains of love, and they are infinitely stronger than links of steel. Just try to get away from Him, mister! You will find it is the most difficult thing you ever attempted. This is why you do not need to announce or advertise that you are a Christian. The world will know whether or not you have been with Jesus. They knew all about Peter.

If the world cannot pick you out, something is wrong. You are not the Christian the New Testament describes. In that day the ungodly said, "See how these Christians love each other !" *They were a brand distinguished and set apart.*

Third, I ask, HOW ARE THESE MARKS PRODUCED? They are branded on us. *There is a cost tag.* Conflict shapes the soul.

Contrary to the song, life is not just a bowl of cherries. It is serious business. We are not here merely to kill time as pleasantly as possible. Life is not aimless or purposeless. No, sir, I have a job to do, an assignment to complete. *A report will be issued.* One thing that is surer than death is Judgment Day. You have an appointment, friend. Your name is on the book.

The big purpose of life is to conform us to Jesus Christ. That is the image the Creator wants to produce in us. Every experience, every sorrow, every hour, and every lesson are designed for this alone. If we choose to turn into devils or into greedy monsters or into sniveling cowards, *that is not God's choice for us.*

All of us go through this world. It is the same world. That is what we have in common. It is strange the different effects it leaves on people. On some it leaves ugly scars and gaping wounds. On others it brands the very marks of Jesus.

What is this passage through time doing to you? Look at yourself as I speak to you! *Do you like what you see?*

There is a story told about Francis of Assisi. It is said that he experienced such a vision of Jesus crucified that he actually felt sharp pains mingling with his ecstasy. Stirred to the depths of his being when he perceived in his body the marks of Jesus, he anxiously sought the meaning of it all.

It may be legend. The more important thing to me is Francis' fellowship with Jesus Christ. It must have been very real and his conformity to Christ very close, before a legend could have sprung up about him. What is important to me is this. *When men thought about Francis they thought about Jesus.* Do men think that way about me? They will if I bear the identification.

Last, I must say this, THE MARKS CAN BE REPRODUCED IN EVERY ONE OF US. God is able to do it in the vilest and in the pagan farthest away. Do not for a moment say it is impossible. We are sometimes inclined to forget that Paul and all the apostles were men like ourselves, *subject to like passions.* These were not super men to begin with. We are the same material. Remember that!

I want you to examine what Christ offers us. It is not moral respectability. It is not culture or social standing. It is not top grading academically. These are men's goals. They are accepted and rewarded. *Christ offers you conformity to His glorious likeness.*

If you do not want to be like Jesus of Nazareth, the gospel has nothing to offer you. Christmas and Easter are meaningless to you. There is nothing in this evangelistic service that will interest you. There is nothing to involve your money or your time.

Real New Testament Christianity has no other message. That is the whole thing. *Be like Jesus!* Let God make you over. It starts with the New Birth.

God can do it, mister! Give Him your personal consent in this moment, and you will see the result. Men will take knowledge that you have been with Jesus. Your neighbors will say it for you, "That man is a Christian."

----◆----

BETTER THAN LIGHT AND SAFER THAN A KNOWN WAY

Text: *"In the defence and confirmation of the gospel"*
Philippians 1:7

LET me pass along to you one of the best stories that came out of World War II.

After a service, a young lieutenant stepped up to the chaplain and said, "Sir, I am an atheist. I would like to *argue* some things with you. I would like to discuss this matter of religion with you."

"No," the chaplain replied. "I do not *argue* religion. *There is nothing to argue about.* You either have it or you do not. You will not get religion, certainly not Christianity, by arguing about it."

"Well, I want to argue," the lieutenant replied. "I have a lot of arguments that I want you to face."

But the chaplain persisted. He refused to argue or even discuss. *There was nothing to discuss.* Finally, nonplussed, the lieutenant demanded to know what he meant.

"Well," said the chaplain, "I have nothing to argue, *but I have a lot to tell.* Indeed, God has sent me to tell you and everyone else here what He has to say about Himself, about us, about our need, and about what He in His love has done, when we could do nothing to save ourselves. *He had it all recorded in a book.* He wants me to tell you what He has said. If you have an hour, I will be glad to tell you. But I have no time to argue."

The hour was at last reluctantly given, and the chaplain, who understood the great secret of the gospel—that it carries within itself its own message, defense and confirmation—went on to tell the gospel as can only one who has personally experienced it. Time and again the lieutenant tried to interject, "I would like to argue that point with you, chaplain." But the chaplain persisted, "No, there is nothing to argue, nothing at all."

When he had completed the story of God's great love for sinners in Jesus Christ, he picked up a copy of a service prayer book. He turned to a simple, forthright prayer it contained and told the lieutenant: "Now, lieutenant, you go to your tent, get down on your knees, and if there is a speck of honesty in your heart, you pray that prayer from your heart. *Ask God to reveal*

Himself to you as He has in His gospel and ask Him to show you the way."

The lieutenant took the book and went home. Some time later the chaplain met him again. What a transformation he saw written on the officer's face!

"You *changed* my life, chaplain," he exclaimed. "No, you are mistaken, lieutenant; *I never changed any man's life.*" "But you did," he insisted. "No," said the chaplain, "neither your life nor any man's life have I changed."

"Well, will you autograph this book, then, chaplain?" "No, I cannot do that either. You say I changed your life. *Only God can do that.* No, I cannot autograph your book."

"Oh, I believe I understand now. Well, God changed my life." And with tears, the lieutenant turned again to the chaplain, "Chaplain, will you autograph this book for me now?"

"Yes, of course I will, lieutenant. Now that you can and will give God all the glory for your conversion, I will do much more than that for you."

The gospel has a message which needs no defense. Its message comes from God, from the "other side" where God is. It comes to us here, who are still held by the boundaries of time.

God tells me what I need to know. He tells me that Jesus Christ of Nazareth is His Son. He tells me that He sent His Son to accomplish my salvation. He tells me that this is His grace toward me. He tells me to believe, and the faith the Holy Ghost will generate in my heart will bring a reality to me that can only be likened to a new birth. So "The gospel . . . is *the power* of God unto salvation to every one that believeth" (Romans 1:16).

The gospel, this message from God, has a throb to it, a pulse, a surge. *It is not an argument. It is an experience.*

Everything else is a periphery. Too many come out of seminaries with everything else but the gospel. They come armed with all kinds of proofs about God—the cosmological proof, the moral proof, the historical proof, the theological proof. They come with history, philosophy, and psychology. They are convinced that these are the weapons to use against atheism, materialism, pessimism, agnosticism, and humanism. *They are ready to engage in a great polemic.* Once again they want to summon the world to Mars' Hill and engage in a debate about the Unknown God.

That is money and effort misspent, sir. No man has yet been saved by a knowledge of God gained by speculation or intellect. *Saving knowledge is revealed in Jesus alone.* "Neither is there salvation in any other: for there is none other name under heaven given among men, whereby we must be saved" (Acts 4:12). *Natural knowledge* embraces at best only the law of God. A study of physics or chemistry or biology may *imply* certain things to you. As one man put it:

"Every effect has a cause.
A series of effects and causes without a
Beginning is *impossible*.
Therefore, there must be a first cause;
That cause we call *God*."

That implication will never *save* you, mister! It will bother you. You will ask, "What is God doing about it? How do I fit in?" I do not need a chemical analysis. I do not need an explanation of gravity. *I need salvation.* Only the gospel can save. *The gospel comes only with revelation, and revelation comes through the Word.*

So the *saving* knowledge of God, through which we obtain eternal life, is revealed through the Word, in which God makes known Himself and His will. To this revelation God has bound His Church, which knows, worships, and glorifies God only as He has revealed Himself in this Word; so that in this way the true and only Church of God may be distinguished from all heathen religions. *You cannot make a mistake.*

The power, the authority, is right there. It is incorporated in the gospel. You are saved because God says so. That alone is the authority that converts a soul destined for eternity. "But as many as received him, to them gave he power to become the sons of God, even to them that believe on his name: which were born, not of blood, nor of the will of the flesh, nor of the will of man, *but of God*" (John 1:12, 13).

The gospel does not need our cleverness or our dialectics. It is not in the wisdom of man's preaching. *It is in what seems to be the utter foolishness of leaving everything to Him.* All that is needed is to give forth God's Word. We do not need to apologize for it. We do not need to prove it. It is its own defense and proof. *It is the truth.* Truth needs no defense. *It convicts.* I have seen the miracle happen again and again.

Let a service be filled with gospel—gospel songs, like:

> My soul in sad exile was out on life's sea,
> So burdened with sin, and distressed,
> Till I heard a sweet voice saying, make me your choice;
> And I entered the "Haven of Rest!"

or:

> For God so loved this sinful world,
> His Son he freely gave,
> That whosoever would believe,
> Eternal life should have.
> 'Tis true, oh, yes, 'tis true,
> God's wonderful promise is true;
> For I've trusted, and tested, and tried it,
> And I know God's promise is true.

Let those songs ring out from redeemed lives; then, follow them with a spontaneity of testimony of how Jesus saves, keeps, and satisfies. Let the sinner hear real prayer, prayer that is intercessory, and follow that with the proclamation of the gospel, *and, mister, you will be in a meeting that has authority, the power of God.* It is like full stereophonic sound. There is a sweep to it. It picks you up and carries you with it.

I pray for a class of young evangelists uncluttered by onto-logical, teleological, and philosophical, speculative dialectics. Let them go forth with the gospel which always, in and by itself, has evidences of truth *and its own power to convert a sinner's soul.*

I know this to be true. The gospel has in it the transforming power to translate itself objectively and subjectively into the lives of all those who read it and hear it. *The gospel proclaims forgiveness of sins.* Nothing else does. It is not an analysis of human conduct. It is not a predicate of hope for improvement. *It is news, blessed, heaven-sent news.* It changes direction in men.

You say this power is no longer at work in this sophisticated age? You are mistaken, sir! You can call it backwoods religion if you like, but it remains the power of God. Try it in your church!

What greater satisfaction can a human being know than to *know* his sins are forgiven? What sweeter experience can man or woman share than to realize fellowship with the Son of God? What peace can surpass this peace? What hope is stronger? Every moment this strength increases. The blessed assurance amplifies. It never diminishes. *The volume of witness within becomes more and more compulsive.* You want the whole world to hear your testimony, "Jesus saves."

I love the passage that the King of England used on the first Christmas of World War II as he sought to speak comfort and direction to the Empire. He borrowed the words of Louise Haskins:

"And I said to the man who stood at the gate of the year: Give me a light that I may tread safely into the unknown! And he replied: Go out into the darkness and put thine hand into the hand of God. That shall be to thee better than light and safer than a known way."

That is the answer to every soul who asks for a light. *Sir, put your hand in the hand of God!* His gospel will not fail you.

A LAKE OF FIRE

Texts: *"These both were cast alive into a lake of fire burning with brimstone."*
Revelation 19:20

"And the devil that deceived them was cast into the lake of fire and brimstone, where the beast and the false prophet are."
Revelation 20:10

"And death and hell were cast into the lake of fire. This is the second death."
Revelation 20:14

"And whosoever was not found written in the book of life was cast into the lake of fire."
Revelation 20:15

EVERY Bible in the world is *positive* about this. There is going to be a final repository for the refuse of the ages. *Heaven and hell equate each other.* If anything is everlasting, then damnation is eternal.

I know there are objections and denials. I simply want to point out to you what the Bible says about this matter and look at what the Bible says in the light of what we know today.

Let me bring to your mind four different passages, three plus the word from Revelation that I have used as a text. All deal with *everlasting fire*.

First, there is a passage in Matthew. "It is better for thee to enter into life halt or maimed, rather than having two hands or two feet to be cast into everlasting fire ... it is better for thee to enter into life with one eye, rather than having two eyes to be cast into hell fire" (Matthew 18:8, 9).

The original word here for "everlasting" should really be "eternal," *an endless age.* The words "hell fire" should be rendered "fire of Gehenna." Christ spoke to people who were familiar with this symbol. Gehenna, you will remember, is the valley of Hinnom's son, a deep gorge near Jerusalem where the horrid rites of Molech took place and where Israel, when disobedient, forced their sons to pass through fire. *All manner of filth was also burned there.* Later it became the open sewer for waste from Jerusalem. Keep that picture in mind!

Second, there are the passages I have pointed to in our texts for this service in Revelation. "The devil . . . was cast into the lake of fire and brimstone, where the beast and the false prophet are. . . . And death and hell were cast into the lake of fire. . . . And whosoever was not found written in the book of life was cast into the lake of fire."

This is the *exact* translation. The word "lake" must connote a body of matter having liquid form. *Therefore, if the Scripture is truth, this eternal fire must be in liquid form.* I believe modern science demonstrates this to be true.

Third, there is a passage in Mark. "Go into hell, into the fire that never shall be quenched. Where their worm dieth not, and the fire is not quenched" (Mark 9:43, 44).

From this we must gather that this is *not* a fire of combustible materials. A fire of combustible matter could be quenched and would eventually burn itself out. But here is something which cannot be quenched and, therefore, *is a fire quite different from anything we can appreciate here on earth.*

Fourth, there is another passage in Matthew. "Depart from me, ye cursed, into everlasting fire, *prepared* for the devil and his angels" (Matthew 25:41).

Great attention should be given to the past tense. In plain words, when our Lord mentioned this future place of punishment for those who would not accept the wonderful salvation provided by a loving God in Jesus, the Sacrifice on the Cross of Calvary, *this lake of fire had already been made ready.* Jesus knew about it. It is, therefore, ready at this moment.

This is the official pronouncement of Scripture. The case for the Bible rests upon the authenticity of this pronouncement. *Are there evidences that such an eternal, liquid, unquenchable, existing, and definite body is in this universe?* The skeptic will settle for nothing less.

Our need is to search for literal proof. Sinners have a right to laugh scornfully when preachers attempt to answer with figurative or spiritual interpretation. No one can get away with that kind of thing. It is foolish to interpret "the lake of fire" as a burning fever.

I believe that our quest of space will continue to unfold both mysteries of light and mysteries of heat to us. Our scientists have already discovered these "lakes of fire" in the universe. They have been known as *midget or white dwarf stars.* This means planets that are not normal size. They should be 5,000 times bigger than they are. Something has happened to shrink them. *All matter involved has been compressed into an unbelievable density.*

Let me illustrate! Look at the outer joint of your thumb. That portion of your thumb occupies about one cubic inch of space. Material of the most dense part of the earth (iron) occupying that space would weigh less than four ounces. The same size material on a midget star, however, would weigh one ton or 2,000 pounds.

Most people know that the sun, our nearest star, is hot. Estimates of temperature at or near the center of stars is between 25 million and 30 million degrees Fahrenheit. At such temperatures much can happen. *Atoms burst.* Inside their covers, atoms have electrons and positrons moving at tremendous speeds of about 10,000 miles per second. That is a lot of energy. Also, at such enormous temperatures, X-rays become active. These have the speed of light, 186,000 miles per second. Atoms become so thoroughly stripped that they become mere sluggish protons moving, in the case of hydrogen, with a speed of 300 miles per second, and in the case of iron, at the slow speed of 40 miles per second.

What effect does this tremendous explosive force of temperature have that would not show on cooler bodies?

The simple answer is this. It would cause the atoms to lose their electrons. The separated parts could then be better packed in, particularly under such great pressure. With the constant activity of X rays, atom walls could not be reformed; therefore, enormous densities, such as are found in midget stars, could be attained.

In these white dwarfs the pressure is so great that *gases become compressed to the consistency of a liquid.* Remember that!

The nearest of the midgets is the one revolving with Sirius, the nearest and brightest of the stars in the heavens, and has been the subject of careful study. I am dealing with common, scientific knowledge.

Before this "lake of fire" could cool off it would have to expand to normal proportions 5,000 times its present size. Here is the difficulty! Such expansion would cause enormous heat which would absolutely keep the star compressed; so, insofar as astronomers and physicists know, the midget stars, these lakes of fire, *can never cool off. They can never burn out.*

Locked up in the data of our great university laboratories is the knowledge of oceans of hot ice on the planet Jupiter. The heat is caused by pressure.

Mister, do not scoff at mysteries! *Every day we investigate we come closer to statements given to us in the Bible by revelation.*

I simply want to show you in this service the scientific accuracy of what the Bible calls a "lake of fire." Our astronomers and physicists know about them. *They know they are there— prepared, eternal, liquid and unquenchable.* The language is not fantasy. It is literal. I want you to see that God has these "prison houses," these "eternal penitentiaries." He has them prepared. They are escape-proof.

Do not hide in the false refuge, "These things cannot be." They can be, because they are already. This universe is God's testament. God allows man's knowledge to increase and man's investigation into the universe to continue for a very apparent reason. *It is God's further grace toward mankind.* God has graciously allowed us to see that His Word can be shown to be truth and is possible of fulfillment *with the knowledge we have now* of forces and materials in the universe. Never forget it! There are "lakes of fire" prepared—eternal, liquid, and unquenchable. Now open your Bible and read about them!

Mister, I want to fall into God's grace and not into His wrath. This God of mysteries is a mighty God to save and a Consuming Fire to punish. One man in the Bible, facing this fact, said, "It is a fearful thing to fall into the hands of the living God" (Hebrews 10:31).

There is no place in the New Jerusalem for the devil, the antichrist, or the false prophet. Jesus Christ has given written warning on a final page of your Bible that whosoever is not found written in the book of life will be cast into the same eternal sewer.

Mister, *God intended something better for you.* The proof of that is in His Son, Jesus Christ. God sent His Son to this planet in the most miraculous way ever recorded in history. That is how much God thinks of this globe. *He has sent redemption, a way of escape.* The "ladder" is there! Why perish?

Do you enjoy moral filth? Do you want to spend eternity with the incorrigibles of this universe—the devil, the antichrist, the false prophet, and demons? Are you satisfied with what they have done to this planet, the sin, the sorrow, the suffering they have caused? Do you want this "filth" to spread to the moon and poison part after part of this universe with moral trespass?

God has served warning. He has an escape-proof stockade. That is the alternative. Read your Bible again and think about it.

WHY (PART I)

Text: *"For the invisible things of him from the creation of the world are clearly seen, being understood by the things that are made, even his eternal power and Godhead; so that they are without excuse."*

Romans 1:20

RECENTLY I rode a British train from London, England, to Cardiff, Wales. A young medical student from Cambridge University rode in the same compartment. He told me he could not believe. He said one professor put it this way, "Six divided by two does not always work out evenly."

Faith in God is much easier when you view a beautiful sunrise or an orchid in full bloom. It is much more difficult when you visit a young mother dying of cancer. And what about the agony of the father and the children left behind? *Does their God plan all that, as well as the sunrises?* If He made everything and really is almighty, He *must* have so planned.

What about the atrocity camps of World War II? Why did a good, loving, kind, almighty God allow such shocking horror? Even ungodly men would have stopped it at once, had they had the power to do so. Yet their God let it go on for years. *These are facts.* I, as a believer, must face them. Is there an answer?

The answer, there is a devil, does not seem to be satisfactory. It would appear that if God were almighty and good, the devil would be neutralized immediately. And if God is not almighty with absolute power over the devil and cannot stop him, then the devil must be a god too, and we are at once reduced to primitive ideas of warring gods in heaven. We are back where Greek mythology left us. These, on the surface, are strong arguments.

Such people say to me, "Mr. Ward, if you want me to believe in your God, I shall expect Him first to make a better job of

His world! If He loves us, as you say He does, why does He not put an end to misery and set up a decent order of things? Does He no longer care for us? If He has forgotten us and no longer cares, why should we care about Him? If He is omnipotent He could, of course, change things at once. He is no longer God if He is not omnipotent, and if He is not that, why bother about him?"

If your teen-ager has not talked to you like that, he will before he is through investigating. *The direction of his life will depend upon your answer to him.*

These questions are not new. They were asked before our present universities were built. Job asked them. *Am I not faced with conflicting evidence?* Is it not unreasonable for God to ask me to close my eyes to the evil I see and believe as though it did not exist?

What does the Bible teach? The first chapter of Romans gives a bold, unqualified answer. *It says that creation shows no contradictions at all.* It states, without reservation, that God is a glorious, almighty, Creator-God and that His universe proclaims solely His glory. Here is that statement: "Because that which may be known of God is manifest in them; for God hath showed it unto them. For the invisible things of Him from the creation of the world are clearly seen, being understood by the things that are made, even His eternal power and Godhead; so that they are without excuse" (Romans 1:19, 20). *That statement has never been revised.* The Christian faith must stand or fall upon its accuracy.

So, what is the demand upon our faith? It is this. A man seeing the universe must see at the same time the eternal power of the glorious Godhead. *The visible must convince him of the invisible.* That is the premise. There is no other.

The same chapter takes a further step. It is this. A man viewing the universe and recognizing a Creator-God behind the universe, who is not thankful and worshipful, will become "vain" in his imagination, and his foolish heart will become darkened. That is what the Bible teaches.

A man who cannot reach the right conclusion with the evidence at hand will begin to add wrong conclusion to wrong conclusion, *until moral darkness will overtake him.* The Bible says that man will become intellectually dishonest. There must be a strong case from the evidence available. *Paul states a verdict of guilty will be rendered on circumstantial evidence.*

Why does the Bible take this standpoint? What is the strong evidence? The Bible says it is strong enough to make an honest investigator a worshipper. The critic says, on the other hand, it is strong enough to make a man an atheist.

Here is the conflict. It rages so that in many circles today, to be a Christian is synonymous with being intellectually third rate. It is assumed that the Christian is intellectually incapable of comprehending the contradictions and anachronisms inherent in his rather naive and intellectually impossible faith. *I disagree.*

One thing I will agree to is this. *This is a damaged planet.* I can see that as well as you can see it, Mr. Atheist. I am not blind to the shambles. I have just returned from another trip to Germany. Thank God most of the scars of war have been erased. But I saw in years previous, ugly, gaping wounds.

Any reasonable man will admire the great Gothic cathedrals of the Fatherland. I have stood reverently inside and out and soaked up a sense of beauty and strength from the great flying buttresses, the superb high-domed roofs, the medieval stained-glass windows and the organs. I have thought about the architects and masons of centuries ago. They were experts. They knew mathematics. They also knew beauty. *These cathedrals are the products of the mind and soul.*

It was a shock to see some of them again after the war. They had been terribly defaced by the bombings. The wreckage was heartbreaking, *but enough remained to direct my thoughts accurately.*

Not for one moment did I connect the debris of what was once a beautiful building with *the inefficiency or purpose* on the part of the architects or masons who constructed it. Nor did I begin to doubt the existence of the men who constructed it because of the many contradictions now evident. *There was something that showed through the wreckage.* You saw at a glance the former glory. Never forget that! The strength in the buttresses remained. Skeletons of what had been towers still reached heavenward. Bomb holes in the masonry showed how well the architects had planned and how well the masons had built even in those hidden parts.

The fact can be argued that *the ruined structure showed in some ways even better than the intact edifice, the perfection of the design and construction.* Only an insane or willful man would accuse the architects of producing and designing a ruin. Any thinking man could have stood where I stood and looked upon what I was looking upon and distinguished between what I distinguished between—*a ruin and what was planned.* That is the conclusion the Bible asks you to reach, Mr. Investigator.

I know I will get mail this week from those who will quickly and accurately point out that the architects are long since dead and therefore could not prevent the bombing of their masterpiece; while the God of the Christians is, supposedly, not dead and ought to be able to do something about preventing the evil and wreckage that are in this world today. I will get to that in the message next week, the Lord willing and sparing my life. Hold on! We are going to face your questions.

Just now I ask you to be *honest* with the evidence. Do not deny it. Do not ignore it. *Evaluate it.* Paul says that the universe, even our damaged planet, reveals enough of God to bring a responsible, thinking person to thankfulness and worship. Is this your experience?

I ask you to examine your soul. Are you fully and morally persuaded that *nothing certain* can be known from the observation of the universe about the Creator's mind because of the mixed picture of good and bad? The Bible does not deny the wreckage—illness, death, hate, ugliness. Remember that! *But the Bible asks you to look at the marks of health, life, love, and beauty that still show through.*

Can you truthfully say that the creation has no mind, no architect behind it? Can you truthfully say from examining *all* the evidence, that you cannot reach a conclusion about what kind of a mind, what kind of an architect designed the world?

Look again at this ruined planet! Look at it as a qualified surgeon would look at cancer cells. That surgeon looks from the "ruined" cells to the healthy cells. His search which leads from the damaged to the undamaged lays bare the secrets of order and design. *He knows that behind a ruined cell there is a healthy cell.* Use that same reasoning! Mister, the damage that is all around us has a story to tell. That, more than anything else, sends me out as a minister.

I have followed the ridges in Western Germany around Aachen that dip down toward Liege, Belgium. Even today there are traces of the Siegfried Line that piled up the lives of so many American soldiers. The ruins of concrete, steel-reinforced bunkers are still there, built into Roer River Valley's natural line of defense. American military cemeteries tell the story in plain and simple text.

But there are stronger evidences today. The green and the vine, the shrub and the grain, the farmer and the tourist are the stronger evidence. They prevail. They say that while war and bloodshed took advantage of the original terrain, the design in the mind of the Architect could never have been for struggle and bloodletting.

That is the way I feel when I look at a man or at a community damaged by sin. I know God intended something better. I know that the possibility there can be redeemed for something better. I know that beyond a shadow of a doubt. *That basic knowledge anchors my life.*

The mind of God toward you, sir, is for good and not for

evil. Believe that *now!* It will set your personal redemption in motion immediately. Look beyond the damage! Do not perish in your sins!

Whatever is bad in your life, whatever morals have collapsed, something that can never be silenced is speaking to you. You may be a liar, a cheat, impure, reckless, hateful, greedy. You may be all of these. There is ruin all over you. But you cannot destroy all the evidences. *You were meant for better things.* Believe that, and it will lead you straight to God.

MOTHER — A BUILDER

Text: *"And the woman took the child, and nursed it."*
Exodus 2:9

BUILDING *lives is this world's biggest business.*

I am an addict to beautiful china and pottery. I love to browse through department stores that handle it. I admire Wedgewood. It has become more meaningful to me since I learned something about the character of the man who, back in the seventeenth century, attained an excellence that has made Wedgewood a superior product. *Josiah Wedgewood was a godly man.*

The Wedgewood pottery plants have always been fascinating to visitors. On one occasion a wealthy, young nobleman was an interested visitor. A likable lad of fifteen was assigned to guide the distinguished visitor.

As the tour progressed, the nobleman was liberal with his smart wisecracks, interspersed with oaths and bad language. His young guide was shocked because Mr. Wedgewood, who was a Christian gentleman, had taken a great deal of interest and pride in tutoring him. He had taught the lad a clean tongue and correct speech. He had taught by precept and example that it was wrong to ridicule sacred things. Following the lad and the aristocrat with another group of visitors, Mr. Wedgewood was shocked at the things which he heard.

After completing his visit through the plants and seeing the pottery at its different stages, the wealthy, young visitor returned to the office. There he planned to make several choices of pieces to his liking. Pointing to one which he admired, he asked the owner something about it.

Mr. Wedgewood removed it from the shelf and began to describe its beauty as only the creator of a work of art could describe it. As the visitor put forth his hand to take it from his host, it was dropped to the floor and broken into a hundred pieces.

Angered at the apparent carelessness of his host, he expressed his feelings rather strongly because he had so much wanted that particular piece of pottery. With the patience and the consideration of a father, Mr. Wedgewood leaned forward and said in substance:

"My young friend, I can replace this piece of pottery; I can make another one just as beautiful. *But there are things in life which can never be replaced, sacred and holy things which can never be restored.* By the language you used, you have destroyed something in the life of the lad who was your guide. You have shattered ideals which I have been trying to build into his life these past few years."

A mother has only a few years in which to build an edifice that must stand for eternity.

Bill Veeck, the baseball impresario, tells this story about his upbringing. His father, Bill Veeck, Sr., was an executive for Mr. Wrigley and a man greatly respected as a gentleman.

Bill says, "Early in my life, after I had done something deserving punishment, my father told me, 'I am not going to spank you, and I am not going to go through any tiresome routine of taking things away from you or depriving you of any privileges. I'm going to do something much worse. When you do something stupid, I'm going to embarrass you. *Then it will be up to you whether you want to keep on being stupid or change.* The only thing is I hate to think of a son of mine being stupid.' "

"And," Veeck says, "he did embarrass me. The first time he caught me uttering oaths, he said, 'When people can't think of anything else to say, they fall back on swearing. If you want to show people that you are stupid, that is up to you.' "

He continues, "There is no doubt that he got to me, for I have not used profanity since."

Something has to be built into children. Jochabed built it into Moses. Her opportunity was limited. She was racing against time. The odds against her were big. The court of Egypt and the web of palace morals beckoned the boy. She made it a full-time job. The payoff came when:

"He was come to years, refused to be called the son of Pharaoh's daughter; choosing rather to suffer affliction with the people of God, than to enjoy the pleasures of sin for a season; esteeming the reproach of Christ greater riches than the treasures in Egypt: for he had respect unto the recompense of the reward. By faith he forsook Egypt, not fearing the wrath of the king: *for he endured,* as seeing him who is invisible" (Hebrews 11:24-27).

Endurance passed from mother to son. Pharaoh did not frighten the mother, nor did he frighten the son. The New Testament gives this record: "By faith Moses, when he was born, was hid three months of his parents, because they saw he was a proper child; *and they were not afraid of the king's commandment"* (Hebrews 11:23).

She built him for greatness. She knew the times. She knew the destiny of Israel. She saw the providences of God, the working together of events, and she went to work on the child. She built into Moses courage, patience and faith. *It is a full-time job for any mother.*

The famous American preacher of yesteryear, Dr. A. C. Dixon, told a story of frontier life. He said that years ago there was a certain school in the mountains of Virginia which no teacher could handle. The boys were so rough that the teachers resigned.

Then a young, gray-eyed teacher applied, and the board asked him, "Young fellow, do you know what you are asking? You are asking for an awful beating."

He replied, "I'll risk it."

Finally, he appeared for duty. One big fellow, Tom, whispered, "I won't need any help; I can lick him myself!"

The teacher said, "Good morning boys! We have come to conduct school, but I confess I do not know how unless you help me. Suppose we have a few rules. You tell me, and I will write them on the blackboard."

One fellow yelled, "No stealing!" Another called, "On time." Finally ten rules appeared.

"Now," said the teacher, "a law isn't any good unless there is a penalty attached. *What shall we do with the one who breaks them?*"

"Beat him across the back ten times without his coat on," came the answer.

Several days later "Big Tom" found his dinner stolen. Upon inquiry the thief was located, a little hungry fellow about ten. The next morning the teacher announced, "We have found the thief, and he must be punished according to your rule—ten stripes across the back. Jim, come up here!"

The little fellow came trembling. He wore a big coat fastened up to the neck, and he pleaded, "Teacher, you can lick me hard as you like, but please don't make me take my coat off."

But the teacher insisted, "Take that coat off; you helped make the rules."

"Teacher, don't make me," came the plaintive request. Then

he began to unbutton, and the reason was evident. The lad had no shirt. Strings held his pants in place.

The teacher thought, "How can I whip this child? But I must do something if I keep this school." He asked, "How come you are without a shirt, Jim?" The little fellow replied, "My father died, and Mother is very poor. I have only one shirt, and she is washing it today. I wore my brother's big coat to keep warm."

The teacher with rod in hand hesitated. Just then "Big Tom" jumped to his feet and said, "Teacher, if you don't object, I'll take Jim's licking for him."

"Very well, there is a certain law that one can become a substitute for another. Are you all agreed?"

Off came Tom's coat, and five hard strokes were laid on his back before the rod broke. The teacher bowed his head in his hands and thought, "How can I finish this awful task?"

Then he heard the entire school sobbing. Little Jim had reached up and caught Tom with both arms around his neck. "Tom, I'm sorry I stole your dinner, but I was awful hungry. Tom, I'll love you till I die for taking my licking for me. Yes, I'll love you forever!"

Moses earned that kind of respect and devotion. His mother imparted it to her son. Hear him in the moment when God says: "Now therefore let me alone, that my wrath may wax hot against them, and that I may consume them: and I will make of thee a great nation" (Exodus 32:10).

And Moses replies: "Yet now, if thou wilt forgive their sin; and if not, blot me, I pray thee, out of thy book which thou hast written" (Exodus 32:32).

The history of this world must be in the *men* it produces.

The early years count. If it is not done then, the possibility is that it never will be accomplished.

Another mother of Bible record felt this way. Hannah's son

had to face the apostasy of Eli's religious headquarters. "Moreover his mother made him a little coat, and brought it to him from year to year" (1 Samuel 2:19). That coat reminded Samuel of his mother's ideals.

While Eli's sons stole and slandered, Hannah's boy grew to manhood with high ideals. He could say in the evening of his life:

"I have walked before you from my childhood unto this day. Behold, here I am: witness against me before the Lord, and before his anointed: whose ox have I taken? or whose ass have I taken? or whom have I defrauded? whom have I oppressed? or of whose hand have I received any bribe to blind mine eyes therewith? and I will restore it you. And they said, Thou hast not defrauded us, nor oppressed us, neither hast thou taken ought of any man's hand" (1 Samuel 12:2-4).

Both Moses and Samuel spent years in public life. *Their characters were unsullied.* Trace it back, and you will find praying mothers who were concerned and who interceded for their boys. *These were boys who were given to God.* Jochebed and Hannah allowed no other possibility to enter their minds.

When Martin Luther was entering Worms to make his great stand before the emperor and the Diet, the stand that means so much to mankind today, an old knight clapped him on the shoulder and said: "My dear monk, my poor monk, thou art going to make such a stand as neither I nor any of my companions in arms have ever made in our hottest battles. If thou art sure of the justice of thy cause, go forward in God's name, and be of good courage; God will not forsake thee." So it is said of the lad, Moses, "By *faith*" he did this and he did that. And it is said of the boy, Samuel, that he "grew, and the Lord was with him, and did let none of his words fall to the ground" (1 Samuel 3:19).

Thank God for women who *nurse* their children with affection, reverence, courage, faith, and an unswerving boldness and loyalty to put God's will uppermost in life!

Mother, what are you building into your children's lives? *What are they thinking about today, as they think about you?* Mother, you have the first years—the years before school begins, the years before others claim their affections, the years before moral erosion touches their lives—*you have the first years.* What are you doing with them? Build well!

Some marriage will depend upon how you build. Some business will depend upon how you build. History may depend on how you build. One thing is certain. A boy or a girl's soul will depend upon how you build.

--------◄◆►--------

WHY (PART II)

Text: *"We love him, because he first loved us."*

1 *John* 4 :19

I READ these words in my florist's shop the other day:

'Tis well indeed to thank the Lord
　　For all of life's fair hours,
For all we have, but oh, my friend,
　　I thank Him most for flowers;
They cheer and bless when spirits droop,
　　When days are dull and gloomy,
They whisper messages of love
　　And bring God's heaven to me.
God must have loved this lovely world
　　To share with us such joy,
A foretaste of eternal bliss
　　And hope without alloy,
A symbol of the life to be
　　Through His creative powers;
And so I sing with all my soul
　　Thank God, thank God, for flowers.

In our last service I spoke to you of *damage*. In this service I will speak to you of *love*. It is in this world surviving all the brutality and horror of history. Where did it come from? What gives it such vitality?

A common question that is raised many times is, "Why does God not stop it?" We say that God is all-powerful; then why does He not use this force to make things be as they should be? Why depend upon this preaching business?

The Bible makes this direct statement, "God is love" (1 John 4:8). God allows pictures of human love to describe Him. It is the only language we can understand. The love of God's Son, Jesus Christ, to us is continually compared to the kind of love a man has for his bride.

How did love of this kind originate? The pattern is well known. A young man notices a young lady. She attracts his attention. She may, at first, not notice his interest. He must do something about it. He woos her, maybe by sending her flowers or by some other discreet method. *But, until the wooing starts, the love is usually one-sided;* and a one-sided love affair can be very painful. Love is made to be mutual, if it is to be happy and satisfying.

There is one burning question, above all others, which the young man would like answered at this stage. *Is my attraction toward her reciprocated by her toward me?* He must press for the answer through courting the young lady. One day the young lady notices his attentions and attraction toward her and has to make a decision: "Do I care for him and can I return his affection?" *She must decide if she can love him.* If the answer is in the affirmative, there is great joy in two hearts that have entrusted themselves in mutual love and faithfulness to one another.

I want you to notice this. *The moment force takes the place of wooing, both joy and love cease and are replaced by hate and misery.* Keep that in mind, because you know it to be true! There must be free, mutual consent. There must be absolute respect for the sovereignty of the partner. *There can be no love without the freedom to love.*

There is a beautiful picture of this in Genesis 24. Eliezer, Abraham's servant, asked Rebekah to become Isaac's wife. He wanted to take her with him, after an agreement with the relatives. The relatives saw immediately that this was no basis for love and marriage, and demanded that the young lady herself be publicly questioned. So they called her and asked her before the family what her will was in this matter. Only after she had given her public consent, based on her own free-will decision, did the relatives agree to the marriage. *There is no virtue in being forced.* God is not making a criminal assault upon man.

In every civilized country both parties contracting a marriage are asked whether or not they *will* enter into such a contract. The couple is required to give public, free-will consent in the "I will" of marriage ceremonies. Anything less than this is pagan and barbarian. This is the picture God sets forth of Himself in the Bible.

Will you, then, agree with me *that to have the possibility of real love there must be absolute and genuine freedom to love or not to love?* Would you want any other God? Would you serve Him gladly if you were *forced* to do so?

God seeks answering love, because love is satisfied only if it is mutual, if it returned. *Therefore, God woos us.* He does everything to show us the genuine nature of His love. Calvary is proof of this. God has gone the second mile. He became man. He lived on earth. He assumed our death. He bore our penalty. *He opened His heart to us.* Every act, every word, every provision says, "I love you." I am thankful that love has found a response in the hearts of millions, including my own heart.

Are you complaining about such love? What would happen if God had so constructed man that he could not make a true, moral decision himself, but was only capable of *automatically* doing God's will, just as a lock opens when one turns the right key in it? Would you prefer it to be that way? *Would you prefer to have your freedom removed?* Would you like to be like an automatic vending machine?

Let us assume that God, *in order to be sure of our love,* took from us the responsibility of exercising our free will to love or not to love, and made us like an automatic machine. He presses the button, and we deliver our love as a matter of course. *Could such a setup be said in any way to involve real love?* No, sir. It would not. To have our love at all, God must give us free will to love or not to love, just as we please. And that is the kind of earth-planet we have.

God took the risk. He knew what it involved. I know the question you are going to raise. *If God foreknew all that would happen, why did He not stop it before it began?* Is not God, therefore, implicated in my guilt? I will deal with those questions, God willing and sparing my life, next week in the final part of this message, Part III. So, hold on!

There is no virtue without risk. This is true in giving. When I respond to human need of my own free will, it is a virtue. If I, however, say that the indigent should be cared for from taxes, to which I am required to contribute a part, I exercise no virtue, even though the poor may receive the same amount as I would have given directly. *Any virtue, to be a virtue, involves my free will.* I am not honest because I am locked behind bars and cannot steal. I must *want* to be good and not be *made* to be good. You are talking about a different world when you complain, "Why does God not stop it?"

Jesus said something interesting about giving. He said free-will giving blesses the giver. He said that it is more blessed to give than to receive. The exercise of any virtue ennobles and enriches a person's life. I know this from personal experience. *Respond freely toward God's love to you, and you will sense immediately a redemptive lift that will warm you from head to toe.*

The best state institutions can never take the place of a real home and family. This is the blemish of the welfare state. In taking over everything to remove maybe a few abuses, the system too often kills the very virtues needed for the state to survive, by destroying personal initiative on a free-will basis. This effect on the character is surely one of the most serious difficulties faced by the modern, highly socialized and organized world. *It is a pattern that is preparing a path for the dictator of dictators to appear.*

When God made the heavenly world and the angels, He wished to construct the very best and founded, therefore, a kingdom of love and virtue. *But to do this He had to build in genuine freedom.* The angels and their chief, Lucifer, were given natures capable of genuine love to their Creator and toward their fellows. *They were given free will.* A large proportion of the angels followed their chief, Lucifer, and did, in fact, show that they really could love, in that they chose not to love and to turn their backs on their Creator's wooing. *When they freely turned from Him who is all good, they became bad.*

I say this to you. The very existence of evil on earth shows that the good and the virtue in it are genuine. It shows that the love in it is really love. *The very presence of evil in a planet that an Almighty God created is really good evidence that God is genuine love.* Only a God who is all love could permit an absolute freedom of choice—a choice which when it is negative makes Him suffer. Think about that!

God treats men in high esteem, *not as inconsequential puppets.* God takes our decisions, He takes us ourselves, He takes our love seriously. God is so serious about this that He woos us. *He respects us as eternal partners.* So He sends His messages to us through His preachers. He waits for our decisions to love Him. This explains why He does not send mighty angels or appearances of spirits from other worlds or frightful reminders of His omnipotence.

That is not the way of love. Love wins its way. Love does not physically and brutishly overpower. The young man sends flowers, cards, sentiments. He exercises patience. He does not woo with sword or ultimatum.

God's purpose is to win our trust and our love. So He deals tenderly and kindly. There is no browbeating. God will never *make* you be a Christian. He will yearn over you. You will feel it. It will distress you when you turn Him away. *You will feel ashamed when you think of His goodness toward you.* But you can say "no"—a final "no"—if that is your decision. That is the risk God has undertaken in giving us a freedom of choice and in creating a basis for virtue and character. No other way is possible.

I shudder to think what this earth-planet would be like without love. It would be a cold, mechanical, automated monster. I like it better the way it is. Risk is involved. God has taken it. You and I share it.

I am glad I have turned my heart over to Him. I feel good about it. A bad choice can only bring bad results. Make the right choice, and you will experience the right results. Use your freedom for your eternal happiness. Make the choice now!

WHY (PART III)

Text: *"According to the foreknowledge of God."*

1 *Peter* 1 :2

EVERY generation asks questions. There are no new questions. *They are only new to this generation.* I am sure that when thistles and thorns sprang up, Adam and Eve asked questions.

The Bible makes positive statements. Here is another. *It tells me that God knew in advance.* It tells me that even before the wrong choice had been taken by man or by angels, God, in perfect knowledge, knew all about it and had already made careful plans. *That is an amazing statement.*

Does this not implicate God in guilt? Does it not make Him as responsible as mankind?

Think with me! *The ability to foretell does not carry with it the responsibility of commitment.* This is evident from everyday occurrences. I may observe a person very carefully for some time. I discover certain idiosyncrasies. He may say "Ah!" for example, every time he attempts to pronounce a difficult word. He may twitch his eyebrows before he tells a good joke. So I predict. *I call it before he does it.*

Professional teams engage trained scouts to make moving pictures of their opposition and run these pictures again and again on the screen until these give-away clues are detected. They they set up their offense and defense accordingly. Many a baseball pitcher has been bombed out of the big leagues because he failed to cover his pitches sufficiently. The other team was "reading" his deliveries.

But this ability to foretell in no way makes one responsible for the other person's actions. In the same way God is not implicated in the free choice exercised by man, although He foresees what that choice will be. It is true God foresaw the "fall" of both angels and mankind. And because He did, He made preparations, long before earth was shaped, to send His Son as a sacrifice for sin. *I am thankful for that foreknowledge.* The Creator's gift to me of absolute free will makes me alone responsible. *I cannot justifiably blame God.*

The critics will raise their voices again. If God saw in advance the chaos which would follow the possibility of free choice, saw all the hate, misery and sorrow which would follow, why did He proceed to make angels, man and the universe? *Is this not the evidence of a sadistic tyrant?* Would it not have been better to have left it all undone? I suppose this kind of second guessing will always go on—certainly as long as we ask, "Why?"

If we followed the critics' reasoning we would avoid *marriage,* for instance. When we enter the contract, we know in advance we will experience the sorrows of separation by death. We make it a statement in our vows, "till death us do part." Yet the knowledge of this heartbreak and sorrow impending are not enough to deter us from entering into marriage. Why? We believe the joy of love and the ennoblement of giving ourselves to each other are better than no love at all.

In the plan of God something compensates for it all. The benefits outweigh both the risks and the costs. Love can, and does, create something that is eternal. *The final product justifies God's creative act.* Paul calls it "a far more exceeding and eternal weight of glory" (2 Corinthians 4:17).

Sin is a fact. Mankind made a wrong choice. The evidence is conclusive. *What would we expect God to do, whose nature is love?* What would you expect of a real gentleman whose love had been misunderstood and refused? Paul defines such love as that which "suffereth long, and is kind; ... is not easily provoked, thinketh no evil; ... beareth all things, ... endureth all things ... never faileth" (1 Corinthians 13:4-8).

That story is written into human history, mister! God's patience, mercy, and determination are written on every page. *Salvation is the big word.* It is the only solution. God is determined to redeem man and this planet. The story is too immense to deny. It is not preachers' talk. It is a fact.

Mankind cannot plead lack of warning. God set forth the consequences of a wrong choice. When it was made, God did not attempt to force His way back into the affections of mankind. That would have eliminated the possibility of genuine love. *Another choice on the part of man was imperative.* So God set about trying to win our hearts. He uses every advantage at His disposal to accomplish this purpose. *He has revealed His intentions toward us fully in His Son, Jesus Christ.*

How could I continue in death and trespass, continue making the wrong choice, in the light of what Jesus did for me? No earthly lover has ever wooed the object of his choice as ardently as God has searched after me. Those are the facts. I cannot deny them. The New Testament puts it this way: "Who will have all men to be saved, and to come unto the knowledge of the truth" (1 Timothy 2:4).

Who but God would have waited these long generations before bringing evildoers to judgment? "Not easily provoked"—the words stir my conscience. Would not we long ago have set up a puppet state where men would slavishly obey the dictum set forth by an all-powerful administrator? God's will is done in heaven. So said Jesus. It is not always done in earth. Sinners thwart God's will. *This is the basis of their sin.*

If for a moment you think God's will cannot be rejected upon earth, there is one way to make the matter clear. Ask yourself whether God planned a certain act of sadism in our generation. Was it God's will to gas miserably six or seven million Jews? Among them were old men, expectant mothers, and children. To say that it was anything but a thwarting of God's will is to lessen the heinous sin of it all.

What would happen if there were no real love toward God upon this earth? Ask yourself that! If all lived under a divine "police state," a puppet kingdom, forced to do His will, what would happen? So, God takes the course of patient entreaty. The thousands who turn to Him by free choice exercise a saving influence upon this planet that has kept it decent enough to live in. I thank God for His plan of salvation and for His long-suffering toward us.

A wonderful story is told about the late King George VI and the present Queen Mother. It may be apocryphal.

As a young man the future King of England fell in love with the pretty, young, Scottish lady, Elizabeth, and after a time approached her to ask for her hand. She refused. It is said that the prince was not exactly a lady's man and was maybe a little awkward in speech and manners.

The young prince was heartbroken over his setback and went to his mother, Queen Mary, for advice. Queen Mary listened to his tale of woe sympathetically. When he had finished his story, she said she wanted to ask him just one question, did he really love Elizabeth, or would anyone else do? After a moment's consideration the young prince replied that he would marry Elizabeth or no one else at all in the whole world. "Well then," said his mother, "there is only one way open to you. *Go and ask her again.*"

So the young prince put his pride in his pocket and gathered up what courage was left him and asked the charming young Scottish lady again. The story runs that he was again refused.

After recovering somewhat from the shock, he again approached his mother for advice, who again listened sympathetically. Again she inquired if he thought he really loved her after his second rebuff. Her son was quite clear that Elizabeth alone, of all the eligible young ladies, was the only one he wanted and loved.

"Then," said his mother, "in that case, there is only one way open to you. *Go and ask her again.*"

So, after a considerable period of preparation, the young prince approached the pretty, young Scottish lady for the third time. She noted, of course, how serious the young prince was, how constant his love had been, and how she was his one and all. And one thing more she noted. *His love toward her was beginning to kindle an answering fire in her own heart.* The warmth of it was beginning to return some of the love with which he loved her.

So, she felt able to say that she did love him and would become his wife. Such love led to one of the most exemplary, continuing romances in the annals of the royal family.

Love begets love, but it often has to be very patient. God knows best how to kindle that fire in the sinner's life, a life that so often seems utterly impervious to the love of God. He will come back to you again and again, sir, *because He loves you.* There is no other reason for it. God wants you for His eternal partner.

We cannot escape a finality. Even love has its bounds. There comes a moment in every affair when a final "yes" or "no" must be said. How close you are to that moment, sinner, I do not know. As an evangelist, I am glad that I do not know. It would break my heart if I thought there were those in this service for whom that final moment should come with the benediction of this meeting, now only moments away. *But it will come, if not today, some day!*

Remember, this can always be a two-way decision. The one who is being sought after can turn away the seeker for the last time, and the seeker can come to that point where he seeks no longer. If I were you, sinner, I would ask, "Will He come again? Will I ever receive another invitation? Will Jesus want me after I have rejected Him so often and trifled with His love for me so frequently?" If I were you, I would ask that question before I turned back to the card party or turned my thoughts again to make-believe.

I will tell you another thing the Bible says. "My Spirit shall not always strive with man" (Genesis 6:3). You can be lost forever. God can depart from you. *You can reject His love once too often.*

God alone knows that moment when you have given yourself completely to another. You have locked your life in an embrace with fame, money, power, distinction, with this present evil world system. You have fallen in love with material things, social ratings, and sinful ways. You will not allow anyone to reason with you. You have shut out of your life all other suitors. You have bidden your conscience to keep silent.

Then, sir, your wooing days are over! You have made a final choice. You have turned your back on God. *You have placed your own soul in judgment.* "There remaineth no more sacrifice for sins, but a certain fearful looking for of judgment" (Hebrews 10:26, 27).

RUIN

Text: *"And he awaked out of his sleep"*

Judges 16:14

THE word "Delilah" is an eternal symbol for perfidy and treachery. Mothers avoid calling their daughters by this name, as they avoid the names Jezebel, Athaliah, and Herodias.

Samson was *blinded* long before the Philistines put his eyes out. A normal man would have sensed the trap. Think of Delilah's heartlessness in pretending to respond to his love-making and at the same time having armed men in her private chamber ready to spring on her lover at a prearranged signal. *It is a rotten situation.*

Samson had accepted an outward designation to show that he had entered into a personal contract with God. It was not wishful thinking. *God kept His part of the agreement.* He made Samson unlike other men. God gave Samson unusual strength. For this gift God asked Samson to bear a testimony, to declare publicly his mission and responsibility. *His badge was his unshorn hair.* Everybody who knew him understood what it meant. *It meant that here was a man who was entirely at God's disposal.*

In the power of the Spirit, without any organization, with no army or soldiers to help him, Samson went out and won great victories. *All he needed was God's Spirit.* His strength and success depended upon this one fact alone. Evil forces found a way to rob this man. *They never stopped trying until they neutralized him.*

Mister, it always starts with *play*. The world invites you to play with it. "Join us for some fun," is the successful pitch of the ages. "You do not have to be so serious all the time," is a sugar-coated winner.

There is a *second secret* to Samson's strength that a lot of people miss when they read this story. They fail to notice where he lived in the days of his victory. Judges 15:8 says, "And he smote them hip and thigh with a great slaughter: and he went down and dwelt in the top of the rock Etam." *He found a place in the cleft of the rock.*

Sir, our security is in Jesus Christ. I know this from personal experience. When haste, worry, and the taunt of modern life move us from the Rock, we cannot expect Samson's power.

Samson formed a habit that led to failure and disaster. *He worshipped with God's people and sought his recreation with the devil's crowd.* It led to a tug-of-war, to an inner conflict. It was the beginning of the end. You must be one thing or the other. No man can serve two masters.

This does not suggest that a separated man is a *recluse.* Samson invaded enemy territory. He left Gaza without gates. He stripped this Philistine strong points so thoroughly that it was not able to defend itself.

It is comparatively easy to live a nice Christian life in Christian circles, *but a different thing altogether to be a victor in the midst of the enemy's camp,* in the midst of hatred, enmity, arguments, and dishonesty small and great. God was with Samson in these expeditions.

It is one thing to take the initiative in spiritual conquest and use the power of God in evangelism. It is quite another thing to trifle with the power of God for selfish pleasure and *presume* upon the promises of God. Nowhere in the Bible is the difference made so plain as it is here in the story of Samson.

The story of Samson is the story of a thoroughly weak man whose only strength was in the Spirit of God. *God helped a stumbling man over and over again; but He could not rescue a willful man, who against warning, persisted in sticking his head into a well-baited trap.*

There is a difference when there is premeditation. One thing God's Word warns about from Genesis to Revelation is that you can go too far. It took Samson a long time—twenty years—to reach that point.

His spiritual victories did not come as easily as we may think. *It was never a romp.* He knew what it was to sink down completely exhausted and in great lowness of spirit. *Thirst, weakness, loneliness, discouragement, and unbelief all attacked him.* His countrymen, for whom he fought, never held many parades for him. Good people seemed to have ostracized him.

Only God really understood him. He was the same breed as Elijah and John the Baptist. We sometimes forget that these men are "subject to like passions as we are."

God was near to this man. When he cried his heart out to God and intreated Him, God answered by opening the rock and slaking Samson's thirst with living water. *He drank directly from God's hand.* His spirit was quickened. He knew moments of great communion. They came too infrequently; that was the trouble. So a time came when he lost the beauty of holiness. And when he did, the skids had been placed under him that eventually led to his ruin and powerlessness. It is not a hard outline to follow.

He fell for a sworn enemy of God's people, a person as ruthlessly dedicated to evil as he had been set apart for good. *Samson underrated her from the start.* It never really dawned on this man until it was too late, how much Hell hates the testimony and the purposes of God. Samson treated it as though it were a joke until he was handcuffed.

Sin should never be taken lightly. It is not something to play with. The Bible warns: "When lust hath conceived, it bringeth forth sin: and sin, when it is finished, bringeth forth death" (James 1:15).

Sin is always reaching for your jugular. Sin will never quit until a man exposes his secret with God to the ribald gaze of the enemy. "If they bind me with seven green withs that were never dried ... If they bind me fast with new ropes that never were occupied ... If thou weavest the seven locks of my head with the webb" (Judges 16:7, 11, 13).

You cannot be a conservative sinner, mister. *There is no halfway.*

"And it came to pass, when she pressed him daily with her words, and urged him, so that his soul was vexed unto death; that he told her all his heart, and said unto her, There hath not come a razor upon mine head; for I have been a Nazarite unto God from my mother's womb: if I be shaven, then my strength will go from me, *and I shall become weak, and be like any other man.* And when Delilah saw that he had told her all his heart, she sent and called for the lords of the Philistines ... Then the lords of the Philistines came unto her, and brought money in their hand" (Judges 16:16-18).

Sold! That is the story. She plotted it from the beginning. There was no mercy. Her goal was Samson's complete ruin. He did not really think it could happen. He had always come back. God had always had mercy. He had always been able to shake off the effects of his temporary excursions into enemy territory and lapses from righteousness.

More and more a hollowness appeared where once there had been fire and purpose. He learned the hard way. You may think you are playing with the world, but be sure of this, *the world is never playing with you.*

My text says that just before final tragedy struck, "he awaked out of his sleep." His commitment to evil had drugged him. Samson was oblivious to what his enemies were doing with him. *He still thought it was a game.* He decided to increase the odds the third time, to make the game a little livelier, a little wilder. He said, "It is in my hair. Weave these seven locks of mine. You are getting warmer, Delilah." Christian boldness is never in walking the brink. *That is folly.*

The end came swiftly. It is all there in that pathetic sentence, "And he wist not that the Lord was departed from him" (Judges 16:20). Sin had deceived him. It left him numb. He kept saying, "It cannot happen to me. This is not true. I will show them."

It is a delayed shock, lady! Only the sober moment when the Philistines take you and put out your eyes and bring you down to Gaza to ridicule you, where once you have openly triumphed over them, and bind you with fetters of brass and assign you to the prison house to grind—*only then do you know how well you have been taken.*

Lose your testimony, mister, and the world will overcome you! God's power in your life depends upon your keeping His secret with you. Playing with sin leads to sleepiness. *Drop your guard and the devil will steal you blind.* Outward compromise leads to inward surrender. And when that inside dedication is gone, there is nothing left but a form of godliness, nothing but the shell of the man who used to be.

It does not take long to go bankrupt once you mortgage your soul and testimony. The enemy is "cuter" than you think he is.

POVERTY

Text: *"I know thy ... poverty."*

Revelation 2:9

PRESIDENT Johnson has boldly declared war on poverty. He has begun to mobilize for this fight. The President says we are poverty-stricken. I want to examine some of that *poverty* with you.

Most of us do not seem to realize that the same God who spoke the words of my text to the church at Smyrna in the first century is speaking to us in clarion tones today. *The great issues before us, what we shall put into our bodies, with whom we will associate and share, where we shall worship and acknowledge God, are moral questions.* They have come to the surface in a great nation.

Let us pray that God will give us wisdom to understand where our poverty lies!

This letter was made public not long ago:

"Everything was fine in our family until Dad lost a lot of money in a business my mother told him not to go into. Mom took the financial loss so hard she talked of nothing else for months. Dad began to stay out later and later. Some nights he doesn't come home at all.

"To get even, Mom has started to go out, too. I'm afraid ours is going to be a broken home if something is not done soon. My folks hardly speak to each other and we haven't had a family meal in ages. I'm 17 and will be in college soon, but my two sisters need both Mom and Dad."

I would call that *poverty*. Let us declare war on sins that are wasting our homelife in this nation!

Today a new kind of child is growing up. There are many names for him: underprivileged, handicapped, an economic minority, the less fortunate, the maladjusted. *Formerly such children grew up with a dream of getting ahead. Today they grow up with the dream of getting by.* They are fostered in an atmosphere of disrupted social order, with its corruption, fierce competitiveness, nervous instability and tremulous existence under the cloud of atomic catastrophe.

Miss Connie Francis, wealthy, young recording-success, expressed herself the other day: "Unfortunately, the songs are getting worse and worse. I think some of these barbaric things should be barred. All trace of sensitivity, sentimentality and sincerity are gone. Some of these songs are just animalistic grunts."

That is the opinion of a woman of the world. Yes, there is poverty—poverty of spirit, poverty of ideals, poverty of discipline, poverty of parenthood, poverty of respect! We should do something about it.

Many of America's colleges were originally founded by religious groups, for religious purposes. During most of the nineteenth century, they were centers of religious activity, with student conversion a major preoccupation of school leaders. *There has been a radical shift toward religious neutralism among academic leaders.*

Richard Butler, author of the penetrating book, *God on the Secular Campus,* says: "The student of traditional faith may discover that his cherished convictions are ignored, dismissed in silence, or questioned by another standard of belief.... Their decline in a secular environment (intellectually and morally) is rapid and not infrequently disastrous."

What about this present religious vacuum in higher education? *I would call it a poverty area.* We need conquest here. The alternative may well be a generation which fulfills the warning of the late philosopher, Alfred North Whitehead, "You may easily acquire knowledge and remain bare of wisdom."

There is a poverty in modesty. One of our junior high school administrators wrote the other day:

"Many of our young students come to school wearing tight skirts and sweaters, eye make-up and lacquered hair-do's. They appear in false eyelashes—girls that are 11, 12, and 13-year-olds. When I called one girl into my office she said, 'This is a free country. My mother knows I fix myself up like this, and if it's O.K. with her I don't think it is any of the school's business.'

"I phoned the girl's mother, and she supported her daughter. Her attitude was, 'She has to get it out of her system.'"

There are not many messages preached on the "flesh" any more. *There is a poverty of restraint. Time* magazine had this to say this year:

"One of the remarkable facts is that there is much less indignation in the churches today—at least as far as sexual morality goes. The watchword is to be positive, to stress the New Testament's values of faith, hope and charity rather than the prohibitions of the Commandments."

There is a poverty of sobriety. The latest Gallup Poll audit of the nation's adults found 63 per cent saying they drink alcoholic beverages. Five years ago, the proportion was 55 per cent. *Seven out of every ten men placed themselves in this category.* Seventy-seven per cent of those persons with college training today said they drink.

Let me speak to you of another source of poverty! Our citizens wager about 15 billion dollars a year, legally and otherwise, on everything from nags to numbers. This is the spawning ground for hoodlums and racketeers, the financial bloodstream for organized crime. This nation bet more on horse races last year than all of its families put together spent for bread. In one West coast city, a cigar store numbers game took in $600,000 a year; the average bet was 35 cents. In a Midwest community, a numbers game employed more than 2,000 workers to handle bets made by as many as 200,000 persons a day.

The souls of our people are starved; so they reach out for fascination, diversion, suspense, and excitement. They court personal financial disaster and corrupt law enforcement agenices. Let us declare war on this wasteland!

Justice Tom C. Clark has some private, deep-rooted convictions. He says:

"What counts in life is what a man believes. . . . If we know what a man believes, we know what manner of creature he is. *Nations, too, are judged by their religious character.* Our national history has a definite moral and religious background. The Founding Fathers knew that the depth of this foundation would be the measure of our nation's strength and the certain guaranty of its prosperity, permanence and peace. They knew further that it was not the numbers of texts one read, nor the sermons one heard, nor the religious conversations in which one participated that counted, *but the earnestness with which one accepted the truth of religion and made it a part of his life.* The Founding

Fathers believed devoutly that there was a God and that the inalienable rights of man were rooted—not in the state, nor the legislature, nor in any other human power—*but in God alone."* There is a famine for that faith today.

Many may never have noted what Justice Tom C. Clark has said about prayer. I quote:

"We read every day of polls and pollsters. The only thing I think of that they have not checked upon is the number of families that have prayer—not 'grace' at meals—*but real prayers in their homes!* It would be interesting to know just what the percentage would be. I dare say, however, that even among the churchgoers the percentage would not be very large.

"We must hold prayer in higher esteem; it is of the highest virtue and the source of the grace we need to discharge our duties and solve our problems."

What does God call *poverty?* "For ye know the grace of our Lord Jesus Christ, that, though he was rich, yet for your sakes he became poor, that ye through his poverty might be rich" (2 Corinthians 8:9).

Poverty and wealth are not always what we define them to be. A man can have a single shirt to his back and be rich in character and faith, and another man can be a modern Croesus and at the same time a useless playboy. Let us attack the "big poverty" first! That is where the gospel starts. *Salvation is bigger than socialism.*

I have never forgotten how one man described his experience of renewal in those terrifying night bombings in London during World War II. He said the center of the city was aflame and all seemed to be lost—the war, England, and civilization. He put his head in his hands and wept like a child. But then as he looked up, a gust of wind cleared the sky for a moment, and he saw the gold cross of Christ standing on the dome of St. Paul's. *Then he knew there was a Power that would see men through their chaos and which the darkness of the world could never defeat.* No nation is poverty-stricken so long as that wealth of redemption is encouraged and allowed free exercise.

Let us draw from that wealth *to defeat the anemic Sunday night attendance at our churches.* Let us go to our altars this Sunday and pray the prayer of George Washington:

"Almighty God, we make our earnest prayer that Thou wilt keep the United States in Thy holy protection; that Thou wilt incline the hearts of the citizens to cultivate a spirit of subordination and obedience to government and entertain a brotherly affection and love for one another and for their fellow-citizens of the United States at large; and finally, that Thou wilt most graciously be pleased to dispose us all to do justice, to love mercy, and to demean ourselves with that charity, humility, and pacific temper of mind which were the characteristics of the Divine Author of our blessed religion, and without a humble imitation of whose example in these things we can never hope to be a happy nation. Grant our supplication, we beseech Thee, through Jesus Christ, our Lord. Amen."

You can read that prayer for yourself in New York City. It appears on a plate in his pew in St. Paul's Church.

That is the true welfare of our nation. Without it we are all poverty-stricken. Lord Coke, as Chief Justice of England during the early part of the seventeenth century, based the limitations which he applied to the British government on the moral, sometimes called the natural law, or God's law for the human race. There was at that time and is today no written constitution in England. The moral law remains the basis of the jurisprudence of that country.

Although this nation adopted a written constitution in 1789, *the moral law was the basis thereof and remains to this day a parallel and antecedent authority to the Constitution itself.*

Anglo-Saxon law is based on the concept of right and wrong, and the best guide to making that distinction is found in the Bible. The Declaration of Independence plainly says that our rights are granted to us by God. *We are entitled to enjoy them only so long as we obey the moral law.* Disobedience to God's law deprives us of His protection, and since the common law of our country is based on the moral law, it also endangers our rights as citizens.

The speech that President Kennedy planned to deliver in Dallas on the Friday he was summoned to meet his God, was to have ended with these words:

"And the righteousness of our cause must always underlie our strength. For as was written long ago: 'Except the Lord keep the city, the watchman waketh but in vain.' "

God has given us wealth. Let us make it available! You do not need to be stripped, wounded, shamed, and feeding on husks. God has a better deal for you, sir! Get rid of that inside poverty first. That is the "big poverty."

CAMP-MEETING TIME

Text: *"We went out of the city by a river side, where prayer was wont to be made; and we sat down."*
Acts 16:13

BISHOP Francis Asbury, first bishop of the Methodist Church in America, said, "We must attend to camp meetings. They make our *harvesttimes.*"

No narrative is better known today than the story of our wild West and how it was opened and developed. The story has supported a great deal of our communications industry. *But few know how it was challenged and tamed morally.*

Ralph H. Gabriel, looking back and reflecting in 1940, made this observation: "The frontier was crude, turbulent, and godless. Evangelical protestantism, more than any other single force, tamed it."

Faith went outdoors. It rode horseback. It went where the

people were. It sought their problems. It fought their enemies. It understood their heartaches. It spoke their language. It did again what it did on the riotous streets of Jerusalem, "Now when this was *noised* abroad, the multitude came together" (Acts 2:6).

James Quinn, a circuit rider, pondered how it was being done in the nineteenth century; he reflects:

"And where did Washington and his brave fellows learn the dreadful trade of war? Where, but on the toilsome march, the tented field, or battleground? And yet were there ever better soldiers? And where and how did the Methodist preachers learn to preach? *By preaching.* The answer to these interrogatories should be clearly given by the historian. *And then it may be asked, where or when has there been a better or more successful set of truly evangelical preachers?*"

Such faith on the march knows no permanent time-niche in history. The main features of camp-meeting time are as old as evangelism itself.

Peter Cartwright, one of the most intrepid, came to this conclusion:

"The great mass of our Western people want a preacher that can mount a stump, a block, or stand in the bed of a wagon, and without a note or manuscript, quote, expound and apply the word of God to the hearts and consciences of the people."

Abraham Lincoln, against whom Cartwright ran for public office in the state of Illinois, said about the same time, "When I see a man preach I like to see him act as if he were fighting bees."

One fire-baptized preacher of the day, when he saw a seminary-trained clergyman trying to read a sermon from a carefully prepared manuscript, said it reminded him of "a gosling that had got the straddles by wading in the dew."

There was a deadly seriousness about camp-meeting time, mister. It took on evil where it found it and left a witness for

Christ. Even Bishop Asbury took off his coat and neckcloth as he preached in the open to great throngs and aroused them to repentance. *Something happens when God's people mean business.*

There was something to the common name, "the shouting Methodists." Finney came to this conclusion:

"Mankind will not act until they are excited. How many there are," he exclaimed, "who know they ought to be religious, but they are procrastinating repentance until they have secured some favorite worldly interest. Such persons never would relinquish their ambitious schemes until they were so excited that they could contain themselves no longer." That is what Charles G. Finney said.

So these camp-meeting preachers were earnest and forcible. They felt that great issues were at stake, that this was the last time they should ever have the opportunity of speaking to their audience. *The weight of souls was on them.* They felt their immediate duty, therefore, most earnestly and even passionately, to warn, to counsel, to entreat, to admonish, to reprove, and to win them by the love of Christ to be reconciled to God. *This was the burden of their preaching.* They were men of quick, intense, and profound emotions.

Nothing could stop these out-riders for God. Benjamin Lakin, one of the great ones, described his experience of crossing the Scioto River as follows:

"My horse plunged into deep water and came out the same side I went in at; and in getting up a steep bank lost my saddle bags, and it was some time before I could get them again. Just as I got my bags the fever struck me. I rode about ten miles with wet clothes on, and shaking and vomiting until I vomited blood. *On the next morning I attended the meeting and preached."*

Yes, sir, they were there along with the Indian scouts and the covered wagons and the Daniel Boones, the James Bowies and the famous woodsmen. *The circuit rider rode.* That is where the camp meeting began.

One historian describes it this way:

"The altar services were often advanced on a wave of song. When the services were at their height, every tent became a 'bethel of struggling Jacobs and prevailing Israels,' every tree 'an altar,' and every grove 'a secret closet.' Dozens of prayers were offered up simultaneously, and a stranger might infer 'that the one praying assumed that God was deaf.' Sinners and workers labored together in prayer and exhortation, and frequent were the loud shouts as penitent after penitent 'crossed over into Beulah land.' "

Thank God! How many in this audience can remember scenes like that in our time? I have witnessed them in present day camp meetings.

And the power of God attended these meetings. In one of the early Methodist camps near Liberty, Illinois, two Methodist ministers had preached and exhorted in turn. One of them began leading the hymn, and when he came to the second verse, "Soon as from earth I go, What will become of me!" the power "of the Almighty came down in such a wonderful manner as is seldom witnessed. Brother Harris fell back in the pulpit, overcome by the influence of the Holy Spirit, and called upon his fellow-minister to invite the people to the altar. The invitation was no sooner extended than the seekers came pouring forward in a body for prayer *till the altar was filled with weeping penitents.*"

Yes, sir, never forget it was that religion that moved westward with the unfolding of our ever-widening perimeter. It subdued, as no guns could ever subdue, the unbridled sin and lust of that period of our nation's history which is depicted on today's screens. Do not forget that for one moment! I am dealing with facts, not fancy.

Writing in the 1840's, Presbyterian Robert Davidson had this to say about camp meetings:

"The laborer quitted his task. Age snatched his crutch. Youth forgot his pastime. The plow was left in the furrow. The deer enjoyed a respite upon the mountains. Business of all kinds was suspended. Dwelling houses were deserted. Whole neighborhoods were emptied. Bold hunters and sober matrons, young women and maidens, and little children, flocked to the common center of attraction. Every difficulty was surmounted, every risk ventured to be present at the camp meeting."

Whole areas were stirred for God. Men, women, and even little children exhorted one another, prayed, wept, and preached. One instance is recorded of a seven-year-old child who "sat on the shoulders of a man and preached until she sank exhausted on the bearer's head."

In the Great Awakening of 1801 through 1805 there is testimony that the power of God would sweep over audiences until five hundred or more at one time would shout aloud "the high praises of God," and the "Cries of the distressed . . . the rejoicing of those that were delivered from their sins of bondage" would rend the air. John McGee, a Methodist, described it this way: "Some exhorting, some shouting, some praying, and some crying for mercy, while others lay as dead men on the ground."

The devil was stirred. In many cases toughs and scoffers fell at the services "as suddenly as if struck by lightning," sometimes at the very moment when they were cursing the revival. One unbeliever tried to prove that those prostrate under the power of God were shamming, and so he prodded them with a nail on a stick, but to no avail. He had boasted that he would not fall, and so he got liquored up, thinking that would pacify his feelings. In a short time, however, he too was struck down and when able to speak, "acknowledged himself a great sinner, and asked for pardon through Jesus Christ."

Yes, Mr. American, that was the old-time religion that moved in where the fast gun was the rule of the day, where the bawdy saloon set up for business, and where danger shadowed the primitive trails that led toward the West! *That kind of religion turned the tide.* I believe it will do the same thing today.

God supernaturally changed the life of James B. Finley, and made him one of the greatest and most fearless of frontier preachers. Here is his own testimony of what happened to him:

"The noise was like the roar of Niagara. The vast sea of human beings seemed to be agitated as if by a storm. I counted seven ministers, all preaching at one time, some on stumps, others in wagons . . . .

"Some of the people were singing, others praying, some crying for mercy, while others were shouting. *While witnessing these scenes, a peculiarly strange sensation, such as I never felt before, came over me.* My heart beat tumultuously; my knees trembled; my lip quivered, and I felt as though I must fall to the ground. A strange supernatural power seemed to pervade the entire mass of mind there collected. Soon after, I left and went into the woods, and there strove to rally and man up my courage.

"After some. time I returned to the scene. The waves, if possible, had risen higher. *The same awesomeness of feeling came over me.* I stepped up on a log, where I could have a better view of the surging sea of humanity. The scene that then presented itself to my mind was indescribable. At one time I saw at least five hundred swept down in a moment, as if a battery of a thousand guns had been opened upon them, and then immediately followed cries and shouts that rent the very heavens.

"I fled for the woods a second time, and wished I had stayed at home."

Thank God camp-meeting time is here again! *It takes bold religion to meet bold times and bold sinners.* It is recorded in the Book of Acts that when the Christians got out of jail, they had a prayer meeting, and this is what they prayed:

"Lord . . . grant unto thy servants, that with all boldness they may speak thy word, by stretching forth thine hand to heal; and that signs and wonders may be done by the name of thy holy child Jesus. And when they had prayed, the place was shaken where they were assembled together; and they were all filled with the Holy Ghost, *and they spake the word of God with boldness"* (Acts 4:29-31).

Over and over again God has counterattacked. I believe it is time again to look for a new move of camp-meeting religion.

NO FATHER HAS A RIGHT TO SEE HIS FAMILY GO TO HELL

Text: *"As for me and my house, we will serve the Lord."*
Joshua 24:15

WE usually think of Joshua as a general who wrote his name in God's Hall of Fame. We think of him, too, as a fine statesman who served a long apprenticeship under Moses. *But he was also a great husband, and a pretty good daddy.*

The government of his *family* was as important to him as the government of his *nation*. He believed in *family religion,* and he worked at it. He determined there would be more than a form of godliness in his house.

The New Testament places great emphasis on this. Paul sends greetings to one of his friends, "and the *church* which is in his house." What would the apostle find in professing Christians' homes today?

Would he say, "the *theatre* which is in his house," or "the *drive-in* which is in his house," or "the *fashion shop* which is in his house?" What would he write about your home, sir?

It starts with a man's own dedication. He has a responsibility that the Creator has put squarely in his hands. *He will answer God for it at Judgment Day.*

There is no question about this, mister. The Bible states plainly that a man who does not provide for his own house in temporal things, "has denied the faith, and is worse than an infidel" (1 Timothy 5:8). Such a man, according to the Bible, is *a lost soul.*

Spiritual things are a heap more important than temporal things. A man who neglects the salvation of his family is an apostate. Reason it out for yourself!

I will tell you this, let a preacher neglect his church family, his congregation—fail to teach them, fail to give them spiritual incentive, fail to intercede for them, let them run wild—that preacher would be the most criticized man in the community. Let him say that he is so busy looking after his own soul that he has not the time to look after the souls in his charge, and I will show you a preacher that is going to face the action of a church board.

Every household is a small congregation. Every father is a priest in God's sight, and responsible for the souls under his command. *According to the Bible, he has greater responsibilities than just the salvation of his own soul.*

Job worked at this job. He said at his family altar: "It may be that my sons have sinned, and cursed God in their hearts," and so he went to God in prayer on their behalf. And the record says: "Thus did Job continually" (Job 1:5).

Captain Cornelius took his family responsibilities seriously. Here it is. "A devout man, and one that feared God *with all his house*" (Acts 10:2).

I want to speak to you for one moment, unsaved father. Some of you are good men, kind men, but you are not serving God. On Father's Day members of your family will put fishing tackle in your hand, or a new tie and shirt, or an electric razor. They will kiss you, and you will feel like a king on a throne. But on Judgment Day I will tell you what they will do to you. *They will curse you. They will point you out as the guilty party.* Your children will say, "Our dad is to blame that we are going to hell." How much sorer will be the punishment of a man, who not only himself refuses to serve God, but makes no effort to lead his family to Calvary.

Mister, there will be no mercy for you. The Bible talks about you, about those who are not content with not entering into the kingdom of heaven themselves; but those also that are willing to enter in, *they hinder.* If a child gets any help at all to be a

Christian, a child should get that help from his or her own father.

You say, "Brother Ward, how can a man be a Joshua, a Job, a Cornelius in his own home?" I am going to suggest these things to you:

1. USE THE WORD OF GOD IN YOUR HOME. The Bible is more than a symbol of authority. *It is authority.* It subdues devils, and devils will attack your family. God told Israeli men in the Old Testament to keep His commands in their *hearts,* and then teach the same commands "diligently unto thy children" (Deuteronomy 6:7).

Mister, if God's Word is not in your heart, if you do not love it, you will never take the time to teach it to your family. That is what is happening today.

You need more than a Bible lying on some endtable in your home. *You need systematic study.* Start early. Feed it to your young like milk. They will grow up on Bible stories. I did. Later on they will reach out for the deep truths of God, as men reach for meat.

2. USE THE FAMILY ALTAR AND PRESIDE OVER IT. Bible reading and prayer go together like food and drink. How can a man go day after day without offering prayer for his family? Mister, how can you expose your wife and children to precarious world-system without making your claim upon the prevailing sacrifice of Calvary? *It is next to insanity to ignore God.*

Sir, until you can prove beyond any reasonable doubt that somewhere in this universe there is another creator, *you have an obligation to God.* The most primitive people on this globe have had that much sense. I pity a home where a man does not pray with his family.

The death angel still roams the streets of this world. Fortunate is that home where a father-priest exercises his faith in the Lamb for a household.

3. USE YOUR GOD-GIVEN PREROGATIVE FOR COR-
RECTION AND INSTRUCTION. The New Testament calls
this raising your children in the nurture and admonition of the
Lord. That means, sir, that you are to set the example, and see
to it that your family accompany you to Sunday school, the
preaching services, the Wednesday night prayer meeting, and the
special revival efforts. That is what it means.

A little while ago I was a guest, riding with our great song-
writer-pastor, Ira Stanphill, the author of our invitation song,
"There's Room at the Cross for You." We were on our way to
church, and the members of his family were with him in the car.
Mrs. Stanphill was recalling memories of her father, the late
Brother Holloway, an outstanding elder among us, and a great
soul winner. I knew him very well.

Mrs. Stanphill said, "Brother Ward, Father had a particular
way of dealing with his three daughters. He would invite one of
us at a time to take a long drive with him into the country.
Then in a quiet moment he would say softly, 'Daughter, how
are you and Jesus getting along?' He would wait until his girls
opened their hearts to him, and then counsel them and encourage
them before driving back to the house." Is it little wonder
they are serving God today, and are ministers' wives? *What
time have you taken with your children, sir?*

This world is filled with *seducing spirits*. They will attack
your home. Suddenly moral tragedies occur, and you ask yourself, "Why?" You have neglected your spiritual defenses.

Let me add this to what I have said, father! The Bible tells
me that it is God who giveth men the power to get wealth. The
Bible also says that these things shall be *added* to those who
seek the kingdom of God and His righteousness first. You
insure a *success pattern* for your children when you establish
them in the things of God. Abraham, David, Joshua were busy
men, *but they took time.*

You say to me, "Preacher, why should I burden myself with

a kind of living that seems a bit old fashioned today?" I am going to give you several reasons that I hold:

First, GRATITUDE. *God has allowed and blessed you with a position and honor among the greatest He bestows upon creation.* He puts authority in your hands. He gives you the right to command, to say to one, "Go, and he goeth; and to another, Come and he cometh; to a third, Do this, and he doeth it" (Luke 7:8).

I ask you, father, "Are you going to use this authority selfishly, *and never exercise it over your children for God's interests in their lives?"* Joshua didn't leave these matters to chance. He took command. He said, "As for me, *and my house,* WE will serve the Lord" (Joshua 24:15). He spoke for everyone under his roof.

Second, LOVE. Do you love your children, sir? You reply, "Yes, I do. Look at the toys I provide, the clothes I put on their backs, and the food I supply for the table." I appreciate that, sir. *What have you provided for their souls?* Otherwise you are doing no better than the fowl of the air do for their young and the beasts of the field do for their offspring. Otherwise you *betray* your children, sir! Delilah spoiled Samson with food and feeling, and at the same time threw him to the Philistines.

Third, HONESTY. As father and parent, you demand and receive years of service from each child's life. God confirms that right. *You take that chunk of a person's life.* What do you give in return? What rewards do you offer that your children will always think that their years at home were worthwhile? Will your son, your daughter, look back and say, "Dad showed me how to be a Christian and head toward heaven?" *They deserve more than food and raiment.* They deserve a head start toward paradise. There is one more reason that comes to my mind.

Fourth, SELF-INTEREST. A wife and children who serve God will make your life a lot easier, husband! Promote religion in your house, sir, and you will have less household problems than anyone on your street. This is what the Bible says about it, "godliness has the promise of the life that now is, as well as that which is to come." *There is your guarantee.*

You will escape a catalog of things that drive other men to either divorce or desertion. You cannot gather where you have not sown. Mister, make an investment in your own happiness!

Dad, God's Word establishes you in a place of dignity and leadership. God backs you. Accounts must be settled some day. You must answer to God for your stewardship. How did you handle your family and your home? Better think of it now!

Your own flesh will be there to face you on Judgment Day. *That will be evidence enough to either save you or damn you.*

I ask you, fellowmen in this audience, to make this year's Father's Day a day of renewed dedication to your spiritual responsibilities. I ask you, dad, to stand up and be counted for righteousness. Say for all to hear: "As for *me* and *my* house, we *will* serve the Lord" (Joshua 24:15).

God will help you make it stick. It will make the difference with the teen-agers in your household.

───────◄►►───────

IS IT POSSIBLE TO BE TOO RELIGIOUS?

Text: *"Be not righteous over much; neither make thyself over wise: why shouldest thou destroy thyself?"*
Ecclesiastes 7:16

I HAVE taken this text from a book in the Bible in which Solomon describes his experiences. The words of the text are words suggested to Solomon *by an unbeliever.*

A cliche asks, "Who needs enemies when you have friends like these?" *So many of our unsaved loved ones offer us the same advice.* They appreciate that we are not drunkards or rakes; and they are all for us keeping up appearances by attending church on Sunday mornings, receiving communion on schedule, saying prayers, and donating to the right causes.

Most family circles place great value on reputations. But they feel some of us run religion into the ground; that we overdo it. They urge us as Peter would to Christ, "Spare thyself, do thyself no harm (Acts 16:28)."

This is favorite ground for today's psychiatrist who determines so often that the knots and snarls are the result of *too much religion, and too little diversion.*

Do you take spiritual things in stride, or do you *feel* the Spirit moving in your heart? Were the Apostles and early disciples too religious? I mean, now, something deeper than so-called evangelistic activity.

King Saul received the spirit of prophesying, and had another heart, yet Saul was probably a castaway. *This question goes deeper than a busy church program.* It ties into a changed nature. Only the Holy Ghost can accomplish it. Outward ordinances only scratch the surface.

Nicodemus, a respectable, reputable church member asked, as so many of you ask, "How can these things be?" (John 3:9).

Jesus Christ gives the answer to that question, sir. "The wind bloweth where it listeth, and we hear the sound thereof, but canst not tell whence it cometh and whither it goeth" (John 3:8). In other words, *you have got to feel it, you have got to experience it.*

Mister, when a poor, lost torn-up sinner can no longer feel that he is saved, can no longer sense a complete reversal of appetite and affection within, religion has not much to offer this world. *A person who can no longer be touched by the Holy Ghost is a person with a reprobate mind, and past feeling.*

Salvation is more than doing good, being decent, and keeping away from the police blotter. Seneca, Cicero, Plato, or any of the heathen philosophers, would have given as good a definition of what it means to be religious as many of today's creeds. *It takes more than a common-sense approach.* The Spirit of God, alone, can reveal the treasures of another world.

Again I ask. Should I limit my visits to the house of God? I ask the world. Should you have ball games on week nights? Should you open the taverns daily? Should you run matinees and showings for children? But you take objection to my going to church so often! *Why?*

I must ask you again. Am I too religious when I abstain from the entertainments of the age? What advice must I follow? My Bible says: "Abstain from all *appearance* of evil" (1 Thessalonians 5:22). My Bible commands: "Whether therefore ye eat, or drink, or whatsoever ye do, do all to the glory of God" (1 Corinthians 10:31).

Those are the rules. Are they inconsiderate? Are they impractical for this era? Do they bind us too tightly? *I hope some day that some theologian will define what is meant by innocent diversions.*

What do you want to be in life—a playboy, a playgirl? What are you doing that brings you nearer to Jesus? What do you indulge that makes sinners come to the Saviour? Where do you go, and what do you do, that makes you feel the same way you did when you knelt at God's altar and received God's Christ?

Are you able to spend whole hours, right up to midnight, at games, and grumble at the preacher when the Wednesday night prayer meeting goes past a quarter to nine? *Are there no longer questions about it in your soul?*

You ask, "What harm is there in it?" The Bible says, "for whatsoever is not of faith is sin" (Romans 14:23). Do your favorite recreations build your faith and testimony? Do they ennoble your soul?

You say, "Preacher, I cannot be religious all the time." I ask, "Why not?" Must you be "earthy" part of the time? Must you be *sensual* occasionally to be normal? Why must you be "diverted" from the call of God, from the eternal importance of His mission for your life, from the work of the kingdom of heaven?

Do you mean that make-believe, pretense, nothingness, silly and futile and meaningless dialogue can replace the power of God upon your life? Do you mean that you find some kind of contentment, some kind of inward satisfaction feeding upon *husks?* What kind of professing Christian are you? You are worse than the prodigal. *What better food is there than the Bible? What better drink is there than communion with God in prayer?*

Examine yourselves! A form of godliness is never enough. You must deny the power of God to ever settle for a shallow program.

I know what a lot of polite people are saying in this audience. "Are we to be always on our knees? What are you trying to do, make *saints* out of us?" Take a look at the fashionable set of this world! Are they your envy? Are they not the dedicated ones—always partying, always riding to the hounds, always seen at the right places?

If religion is only a *duty,* you have missed it. The secret is *pleasure.* You find a *taste* for it. Something grows on you. Call it being a "saint" if you will! The answer to real Christianity is not, "I endure it," but "I enjoy it—I like it."

O yes, you can be "righteous overmuch." I will tell you how. *You can demand everyone to go to the same church or be boycotted.* Mister, there are many wonderful families in Christ. Do you feel that Christ cannot be preached in a tent or a field, a store building or on a street corner? That is bigotry, sir.

Peter had to get rid of that kind of overrighteousness. He found that God could baptize in a Roman captain's house in the same way that the Holy Spirit filled believers in the Upper Room. It took a lot of convincing to persuade the other church members at Jerusalem.

You and I are overrighteous until we can embrace our fellow believers from other folds. The worst snob of all is a spiritual snob. There is no established church other than the circle that Christ began. There is no other creed than Christ. Pentecost is not Phariseeism. It goes out into the street to preach an open door and a welcome through repentance in a Risen Christ.

When the disciples informed Jesus of some casting out devils in His name, and were for rebuking them, Christ said, "Forbid him not: for he that is not against us is for us" (Luke 9:50).

Paul said, "Some indeed preach Christ even of envy and strife; and some also of good will ... notwithstanding, ... Christ is preached, I ... rejoice, yea, and will rejoice" (Philippians 1:15, 18). You and I have got to learn to read the church ads without a feeling of censoriousness, or lack of charity.

You and I can be too religious *to the neglect of our families.* My first obligation under God is to my own home. Adam and Eve dressed the garden. They may have sung hymns all day, but they did it while they worked. God's Son toiled in a carpenter shop.

An old Hebrew proverb says: "He who brings his son up without a business, brings him up to be a thief."

Paul's post-graduate studies under Gamaliel never destroyed his respect for work. He made tents while he mailed his epistles. He was as conscientious about the one as he was about the other.

There are things to do at home, parent! Some professing wives are so religious, run around to so many conventions and doings, spend so much time exchanging greetings on the telephone, that the kitchen floor goes unscrubbed, the beds are unmade, and the family seldom sits down to a home-cooked meal. *I call that being too religious.*

There is something else in which we can be too religious. *We can afflict ourselves with corporal austerities until we become untouchables instead of witnesses.* God has placed fasting in our hands as a weapon against the flesh, where it needs to be disciplined and brought under control, and made to serve a higher purpose. *God never intended fasting to be made a badge of superior living.* Emaciation and self-destruction are not the objects of grace.

The goal of divine life is "life more abundantly." A burden can be carried graciously—"as sorrowing, yet always rejoicing." The long face, the sigh of subjection, the secret pride in self-abnegation are but a scarecrow of New Testament salvation. Jesus Christ provides a joy unspeakable and full of glory.

Salvation is not *asceticism.* The New Birth is not a still birth. It is *life.* God will not sanction any form of self-righteousness. All forms are foul in His sight. He calls them in His Word, "filthy rags." *Do not rob Jesus of His victory by trying to be your own saviour in part.*

Christ is all. He is your sufficiency for everything. Nothing is lacking in His sacrifice. *His is the finished work.* Jesus Christ must be our whole righteousness, our whole sanctification, or Jesus Christ can never be our eternal redemption and sanctification.

I plead His covering, and His alone. He alone can provide an inward holiness. It is activated in me through the exercise of faith. I have no fitness in myself—nothing that God sees and bestows His grace upon. *God sees what Jesus Christ did for me, a sinner, on the cross.* He is ready to impart that victory to me by the power and agency of the Holy Ghost. It can never be of works, lest any man should boast.

Jesus Christ hath fulfilled the law, every code, every detail. He hath made it honorable. Jesus Christ has satisfied every demand of justice. *It can make no further demands.* Remember that! You cannot prove something that Jesus failed to prove. His work on Calvary is complete. *God will never demand it again from anyone.*

Christ is your answer. You need no other, either here or in eternity. When you attempt to do it in yourself, by your own strength and willpower, you rob God of His victory.

Sinner, you must have a part in Christ, you must own Him as your Redeemer, or forever be lost. God has not published a catalog of good works for you, who have never done a good work in your lifetime, to perform in order to work your way to heaven. God says, *receive My Son and you will receive my acceptance*. There is no other way. There is no other choice.

I know this is a leveling doctrine. It brings all men through the same gate. It reduces the proud. It encourages the despairing.

How do you come to Christ? I will tell you, do not come bragging about the good you have done, the sacraments you have received, the commendations you have obtained from the clergy. Do not come like that, or you will come overreligious. Come to Christ as a guilty sinner, a sheep who has lost its way. Come without an excuse or a plan of your own. Come simply because He bids you come, *and He will receive you*.

God's terms have been stated and offered to you and to me. They are unconditional. They demand a full surrender. I must lay down my proud ways, my alibis. I must be willing to admit that Jesus died for me, and that my sins nailed Him there.

Do not flatter yourself. Do not flaunt your morality. You need God's mercy, not His admiration. Pray with me that you may feel His cleansing power on earth, and so escape His consuming wrath in eternity.

I ask you, now to taste and see! God offers Jesus Christ to every one of you.

DIVORCED

Text: *"Let the dead bury the dead."*

Matthew 8:22

THIS is another of Christ's *abrupt* statements. He did not use ambiguous language. His gospel has a clarity that no other ideology has. No one went to sleep when Christ preached.

In one public gathering Jesus gave a certain person an immediate summons to follow Him. The response was halfhearted. He said to the Christ, "Suffer me first to go and bury my father" (Matthew 8:21). *Suddenly he is concerned about business in another direction.* A common explanation of this verse is, "Let me first go and dispatch some important business I have now in hand."

Most sinners get things backwards. They think that the things of time are important, and that religion is only for dying. In God's view the things of eternity are the matters of concern, and momentary ambitions bear the kiss of death. "And the world passeth away, and the lust thereof: but he that doeth the will of God abideth for ever" (1 John 2:17).

In Christ's estimation, dead men were occupied with dead things. Salvation wills us into another world of activity. We "pass from death into life." There is no compromise. The new birth is a complete break.

In plain language, mister, *nothing—no possible business—can ever be more important than your salvation.* The very posture of Christ upon earth refused to confirm the foolish fallacy that the reason for existence is to care and toil for the uncertain riches of this life. His every day upon earth was a loud denial of what men strive for. *He declared with power and authority that we were here for nobler ends.* All else were dead issues to Jesus Christ. They did not count.

You would be surprised to know how many people on your street think that religion should be confined to the clergy, while they get on with the real business. They feel a secret comfort that in this world of buzz and babble there are a few simple-minded souls who are willing to forego the ample provisions of this life. They vicariously absorb a sense of respectability and decency from the clergy—a group that by choice of color (black), and by severity of cut (their clericals), suggest a state of joyless eternity. They are willing to extend this group certain benefits no other group in society shall enjoy, as long as they do not have to enter this undesired state of suspension.

Christ dealt with that kind of thinking point-blank. To Him it was dead, meaningless, not worth spending time on. *The real world of living was the world of living He came to reveal.*

Sinner, what do you wish to *postpone?* Why cling to corrupt passions? Why yield to bad habits? There is no possible way that you can work out a postponement of the new birth. *Christ will not make a deal with you.* You cannot say to Jesus Christ, "I like what you have to offer. I know it has value. I know I should respond. It is in my best interests. I fully intend to go Thy way ... 'but first let me. . . .'"

God has never extended any sinner an agreement on that basis. Salvation will never take a second place in your life. "Behold, now is the accepted time; behold, now is the day of salvation" (2 Corinthians 6:2). Your soul is in mortal peril.

Nothing has a greater immediacy than your new birth. According to God's way of thinking, there is not one legitimate excuse why you should not be a Christian right now—*why you should not drop everything else this very moment and follow Jesus Christ.*

What right do you have to ask God to wait? What value do you create for yourself greater than Calvary's victory? Are you saying, "Yes, I will come, *but first,* let me spend my youth in dancing, in smoking, in drinking, in gambling, in lust."

With God it is one way or the other. There can be no temporizing. Are you saying, "Yes, I will come, *but first,* let me accumulate riches and acquire properties."

"Thou shalt love the Lord thy God with all thy heart, and with all thy soul, and with all thy mind. This is the *first* and great commandment" (Matthew 22:37).

"But seek ye *first* the kingdom of God, and his righteousness; and all these things shall be added unto you" (Matthew 6:33). *Your God has a right to say what shall be first.*

Do you know what you are? You are a spiritual miser. You

deny yourself the greatest values in all this universe, and exist on the scraps of time. You are denying yourself the fellowship and benefits of the Son of God. You are hoarding mirages. Every breath brings you closer to the moment of truth. "For what shall it profit a man, if he shall gain the whole world, and lose his own soul? or what shall a man give in exchange for his soul?" (Mark 8:36, 37). Answer that question, and you have the answer to my text!

I know how busy you are. I know why you could not make it to the house of God, but you made it to the party last night. I found out during my school days that my teachers had heard all the excuses before. So has heaven! Read the record for yourself:

"A certain man made a great supper, and bade many: And sent his servant at supper time to say to them that were bidden, Come; for all things are now ready. And they all with one consent began to make excuse.

The first said unto him, I have bought a piece of ground, and I must needs go and see it: I pray thee have me excused. And another said, I have bought five yoke of oxen, and I go to prove them: I pray thee have me excused. And another said, I have married a wife, and therefore I cannot come.

"So that servant came, and showed his lord these things. Then the master of the house being angry said to his servant, Go out quickly into the streets and lanes of the city, and bring in hither the poor, and the maimed, and the halt, and the blind.

"And the servant said, Lord it is done as thou hast commanded, and yet there is room. And the lord said unto the servant, Go out into the highways and hedges, and compel them to come in, that my house may be filled. For I say unto you, *That none of those men which were bidden shall taste of my supper"* (Luke 14:16-24).

Mister, those were not bad things which demanded the attention of those men. They were investments, thrift, and industry, and homelife. What better occupations could you name?

God's solemn truth to you is this. *Lawful callings can never justify your neglect of Jesus Christ.* The warning is there, sir! You better read it before it is forever too late.

You say to me, "Preacher, I have got to earn a living. I have got to spend some time with my family. There are certain things that just have to be done." Yes, sir, God knows that.

Cornelius was a busy Roman officer, but he found time to serve God. Zenas was a lawyer, and you know how busy lawyers are, but he found time to serve God. Jesus did not condemn Martha for working hard in the kitchen. He bade her not to be cumbered or worried about many things. The fact is, *you will get more done when you put Christ first.*

Let me put it to you very simply! If you were going to stay around here forever, it would be a different matter. You and I can reasonably expect some seventy years. That is not a very great amount of time. The fact is, *you and I have no permanent address.* We were only sent into this world to have our natures changed, and to get fit for what is ahead. That is why the big business at hand is to look ahead.

One of America's great advertising executives once said, "Every business man in this nation should keep this motto before him at all times: 'This night shall thy soul be required of thee. Then whose shall those things be, which thou hast provided?'" You *must leave it all behind.*

I wonder what the speculator thought on the other side? Did he still wish he could have stayed a bit longer so that he might have pulled down his barns and built greater; or would he have liked to have returned and employed himself in pulling down every high thought that had exalted itself against his God, and building up his soul in the knowledge of Jesus Christ, the only Saviour? What do you think?

Well, sir, you will have your turn! It could come this week. How rich are you toward God? What is your heavenly balance?

I want to speak to businessmen. You have achieved a degree of distinction in the community where you serve. Let me use the words of a great and elderly preacher! Paul knew fame and fortune before he entered the ministry. He wrote to the young pastor, Timothy, that young as he was, he should charge the rich with all authority. Here are his words of counsel:

"Charge them that are rich in this world, that they be not high-minded, nor trust in uncertain riches, but in the living God, who giveth us richly all things to enjoy; that they do good, that they be rich in good works, ready to distribute, willing to communicate; laying up in store for themselves a good foundation against the time to come, that they may lay hold on eternal life" (1 Timothy 6:17-19).

That is the New Testament direction to you, Mr. Businessman! *The same rule applies for the privileged gentleman as applies for the laborer and tradesman.* That rule is the First Commandment—PUT GOD *FIRST*. My fellow human being, there is only one sacrifice for sin. That sacrifice is offered during a period of infinite importance—*between two eternities.*

Nothing can ever be more important to you than the welfare of your soul. When your few days are ended upon earth, there will remain no more sacrifice for your sin. No good work, like burying your father, can ever save you. Neglect God's Son and you are a lost soul!

What will it be in this moment? You must divorce yourself from one or the other. God has given you a hard choice to make, but Calvary was a hard death to die.

————◆————

FREE SPEECH

Text: *"And Satan came also among them to present himself before the Lord."*

Job 2:1

IN the years of my Christian testimony I have returned many times to the Book of Job. *It is an inexhaustible mine of truth.*

It provides the world's finest close-up to the inner working of the council and counsels of God.

Truth and falsehood make their claims on the highest level. Freedom of speech is the heritage of any government of free-moral agents. The God of heaven is not a tyrant. If He were, He would never permit an accusing voice to be heard.

God has nothing to fear from any gainsayer. That is why God hears sinners. If He listens to the devil, He will listen to you. All of His acts, His motives, and promises are open for examination and test. *Mister, you do not need to be afraid to put God to the test!*

The devil does not want you to believe there are multiplied thousands of free-moral beings in this world who serve God because they *want* to, and not because they *have* to. The devil does not want you to believe it, although he knows it to be a fact. *He, himself, has put it to the test.*

You are asking the same question the devil asked. "What good is faith when your health is gone, when your property is gone, when your family is gone, when your friends are gone, when your wife lets you down—*what good is faith then?*" The devil said the same thing to the Lord that he says to you, "Put forth thine hand now, and touch all that he hath, and he will curse thee to thy face" (Job 1:11).

That daring and impudent speech was made in heaven before the throne of God. *No one was arrested for making it.* God's full and free salvation was at stake. *Was it big enough, and strong enough to hold a man, and to keep a man in every possible emergency?* That test had to be made.

God never forces a man to serve Him. God never bribes a man to serve Him. The powers of darkness resort to lies and force to bring men into subjection. *Satan requested the use of every possible force short of death to bring Job to his knees.* If God had been a sentimentalist, He never would have permitted it. Nor would He have allowed the crucifixion of Jesus Christ.

God deals with facts, sir! This universe is run on law, not on feelings. You are saved because God says so, not because you feel like it. Count this to be an eternal truth. "The Lord knoweth them that are his." That is what counts, whether anyone else thinks so or not.

Remember this! God took the very worst the devil could throw at a good man and made it bring a depth and maturity to Job's character. He exposed the devil to be the liar that he is. *And God proved that He alone knows what is in the heart of man.* God has a confidence in you, sir, that neither devils nor men share. I ask you to rest upon that trust.

Any hypocrite can give lip service to God when the sun shines and when things keep going his way. *That is not faith;* that is politeness; and it takes more than politeness to save your soul. It took more than politeness for Daniel to survive in the lions' den, and for Joseph to survive in prison. Your religion has to go deeper than that, mister!

Remember! The devil is going to work on you. The Bible says, "And Satan came also among them" (Job 1:6) to present himself before the Lord.

He is there to investigate every man who makes a religious profession, and to do something about it. He is there to put it to the test, to satisfy himself how real your profession is, how long and under what conditions you will hold out. God said, "And still he holdeth fast his integrity, although thou movedst me against him, to destroy him without cause" (Job 2:3).

Faith is not something you think you have. Faith is stronger than bank accounts or credit ratings. It remains when finances disappear.

Will faith hold a man when his health is gone? "Put forth thine hand now, and touch his bone and his flesh, and he will curse thee to thy face" (Job 2:5). *The devil said this in another world where there is no sickness.* No wonder it is said of our salvation, "which things the angels desire to look into" (1 Peter 1:12).

God has confidence in it. He has risked His Word on it. You and I need have no fear. *The devil's lies about us can never change our salvation.* I will never make it as far as the devil is concerned, but God says I will.

Job was a good man. There is no question about that. *But goodness is not enough.* The devil claimed it would not stretch far enough, that every man has a breaking point. The devil claimed that away down underneath all his profession and all his good works, Job was just like himself—a devil, selfish and anti-God.

God said the heart of this man was different. He said, "There is none like him in the earth, a perfect and an upright man, one that feareth God, and escheweth evil" (Job 1:8).

Yes, sir! There is an old-fashioned faith that takes hold. It is not just skin deep. It is in the heart. It is born there of the Spirit of God. *It is an impartation of the divine nature.* You can see its beauty when you put it to the test. They saw it in Stephen.

Job was smitten with boils "from the sole of his foot unto his crown" (Job 2:7). His pain-wracked body carried him to the brink of the grave. Day and night this suffering man was held captive in a body that was loathsome even to himself. Have you noticed that *the devil left Job's tongue free to speak?* He wanted Job to have no handicap when he was ready to repudiate his faith.

The devil always offers a way out. "Curse God, and die" (Job 2:9), was the way he offered Job. That is the final trap. That is the final lie.

The Bible says, "There hath no temptation taken you but such as is common to man: but God is faithful, who will not suffer you to be tempted above that ye are able; but will with the temptation *also* MAKE A WAY TO ESCAPE, that ye may be able to bear it" (1 Corinthians 10:13). Obedience to God's will is the only true way of escape.

The devil often uses those dearest to us to transmit his voice. It is a tactic the enemy often uses in time of war. There is always a "Tokyo Rose."

There is a line in the early part of this narrative that always challenges me. The line says, "And he sat down among the *ashes*" (Job 2:8). Something must burn before there can be ashes. What had been destroyed? What treasure had he sacrificed? Heaven does not need them, *but we need to be without them*. They clutter our lives. It is easy for the heart to become attached to possessions.

Treasure on earth looks better to a man than treasure in heaven. It takes the moment of death to show us the difference. Satan uses "the care of this world and the deceitfulness of riches" to choke out the Word and make the life of a professing Christian barren. *Many an ash pile has brought a new revelation.* Here in the blackened ruin of human plans and ambitions Job could easily commit his all to the Lord.

> When storms of life are round me beating,
> When rough the path that I have trod,
> Within my closet door retreating,
> I love to be alone with God.
>
> What tho' the clouds have gathered o'er me?
> What tho' I've passed beneath the rod?
> God's perfect will there lies before me,
> When I am thus alone with God.
>
> Alone with God, the world forbidden.
> Alone with God, Oh blest retreat!
> Alone with God and in Him hidden,
> To hold with Him communion sweet.

Circumstances had alienated his friends and family from him. His flesh was so loathsome that he bitterly declared: "Even young children despise me" (Job 19:18). *Will faith sustain?* Not if it is a myth! Not if it is only a fair-weather proposition!

His closest friends misjudged his conduct. They claimed that somewhere he had sinned. *They attacked his inward assurance.* They said, "Look at yourself. A man in your condition cannot be God's child."

Job turned *introspective.* Self-condemnation is another torment of hell. Many believers are heckled with thoughts of the UN-KNOWN SIN—that somewhere and somehow, unknown to them, they have failed God.

Do not believe it! Refuse to live in this shadowland. True conviction by the Holy Spirit never leaves any man in doubt concerning what sin has been committed, and where it has been committed. The Spirit of Truth always names the sin.

One night during the chill hours of his darkest gloom this member of the human race raised an arm rotting with infection toward heaven, and cried out the message that still shatters the powers of evil: "Though he slay me, yet will I *trust* in him" (Job 13:15).

It reduces itself to this, my friend: *no faith, no salvation.* If I cannot pin my very life on God's Word, I have nothing to trust. Everything else wavers. Wealth, pleasure, health, popularity, fame, success, influence may be here and gone tomorrow. *What, and whom, can I trust?*

A few nights later, Job again strengthened himself in faith. He flung his testimony into the teeth of the enemy. He said, "I know that my redeemer liveth . . . and though after my skin worms destroy this body, yet in my flesh shall I see God" (Job 19:25, 26).

I ask you, sir, *does your life move on that conviction?* What have you got to see you through the dark days, the lonely days, the feeble days? Can you say, "I am now ready . . . the time of my departure is at hand. I have fought a good fight, I have finished my course, I have kept the faith" (2 Timothy 4:6, 7).

Without faith you are adrift. You are without defense. Right now the devil is zeroing in upon you. He aims to finish you off.

Job suffered one final attack. It came through a young, self-appointed defender-of-the-faith crusader. He allowed his wrath to be kindled against Job. He made this good man the target of his rage.

I will tell you this. As much as you may want to please everybody, you will find those in life who are impossible to please. *They are always right. You are always wrong.* You will have to rest your case in God.

God will come to you, my friend! Count on it! There is a God who reveals Himself to the believer personally. Oh, yes, there is adventure and thrill in philosophy and science. Four of the deepest chapters ever written are included in this record. There is a psychosomatic experience in learning *about* God. Religious education and the pursuit of academic mastery have their place, *but they can never substitute for personal revelation.* God came to Job. From that moment he was a changed man. Others speculated. He *knew.*

One thing further, sir! God is never in any man's debt. Let a man glorify his God, and God will set that man on high. It is not because God *has* to; it is because God *wants* to. "So the Lord blessed the latter end of Job more than his beginning" (Job 42:12).

A COLONY OF HEAVEN

Text: *"But we are a colony of heaven, and we wait for the Saviour, who comes from heaven, the Lord Jesus Christ."*
Philippians 3:20 (*Moffatt*)

THE revised version of my text has it, "For our *citizenship* is in heaven . . ." I like the picture language of Moffatt's translation, "We are a *colony* of heaven."

Every time I visit the historic beginnings of this nation (Jamestown, Plymouth, and others), I think of this text. With nationalism the word of the hour, the colorful word, "colony," will soon disappear from our language.

Anyone who has been to Hong Kong, to American Samoa, to the Azores visualizes this word picture. *The identifying marks of the Mother Country are everywhere.* Language, customs, style remind you immediately of a far-away touch. You see a little bit of Britain, a little bit of America, a little bit of Portugal, or whoever the colonizing power may be. You can tell it by the habits of the people.

Paul says it is like that on earth. He says the church he is talking about is a colony of heaven. *He says there is an eternal tie to the Mother Country.* I believe it.

Dr. H. W. Bieber of Philadelphia commented on this verse. He said, "If we are a colony of heaven, we are to live here like they live in heaven; we are to live as if we were already in heaven; we are to be like those who are now in heaven."

The strength of the meaning is there, mister! *We are representatives of heaven.* Our neighbors must see something in us that reminds them of that Other World. *Our longing and our loyalty are toward the Mother Country.*

WHAT ARE THE PEOPLE IN HEAVEN LIKE? Complete travel descriptions and arrangements are printed in every Bible. Here is what I read:

"Who shall ascend into the hill of the Lord? Or who shall stand in his holy place? He that hath clean hands and a pure heart; who hath not lifted up his soul unto vanity, nor sworn deceitfully" (Psalm 24:3).

Here is another description:
"He that walketh uprightly, and worketh righteousness, and speaketh the truth in his heart. He that backbiteth not with his tongue, nor doeth evil to his neighbor, nor taketh up a reproach against his neighbor.

"In whose eyes a vile person is contemned, but who honoreth them that fear the Lord. He that sweareth to his own hurt, and changeth not. He that putteth not out his money to usury, nor taketh reward against the innocent. He that doeth these things shall never be moved" (Psalm 15:1-5).

That gives you a little idea of heavenly citizenship. It does not include the gossiper, the perjurer or liar, the irreverent, the greedy, the treacherous, the dirty and smutty, or the hypocrite.

You cannot possibly make a mistake about this, my friend, if you will only take time to read the Bible. It says:

"There shall no wise enter into it anything that defileth, neither whatsoever worketh abomination, or maketh a lie: but they which are written in the Lamb's book of life" (Revelation 21:27).

"Without are ... sorcerers, and whoremongers, and murderers, and idolators, and whosoever loveth and maketh a lie" (Revelation 22:15).

It is a Mother Country *without pretense or sham.* There is not one thing that is immoral, indecent, or suggestive. *Abomination makers are barred.* Every business, every racket, every trust and corporation that deals in human weakness, and exploits the unregenerate nature of man is condemned. That is what heaven is like, sir! Do you want to go there?

WHAT DO PEOPLE DO IN HEAVEN? That is a good question. I am interested in that myself. People who have never been to the United States *have strange ideas about this country.* They think they will see cowboys rushing up and lassoing wild steers as soon as they arrive at the airport. Others are terrified. They think gangsters will close in and empty machine guns at everything that moves. *And lots of folk have queer ideas about heaven.* They have an idea that folk sit on clouds in long white robes and conduct religious hootenanies. Others picture heaven as a sort of super picnic grounds where folk lie around all day and stretch out under trees.

The Bible makes it plain that God's people serve Him there. As I see it, the call will come for me when God has greater use for me there than He does for me here. I receive my training here.

My father, who left for the eternal world several years ago, called it "getting accustomed to his *space suit* and conditions he expected to find above." He put his finger on it.

Our space aeronautics administration has *simulated* conditions as far as possible for our astronauts in training. These centers at Cape Kennedy and Vandenberg are small colonies of a world above us. *Our astronauts are trained to accept conditions here that they will meet there.* For instance, they know all about "weightlessness" before they enter a part of the universe where this is an everyday affair.

I believe there is work to do, and that it is creative, rewarding work. I will *serve* my God there as I have endeavored to serve Him here. Idleness could not be heaven.

Tolstoy told a story of a country where there lives an ideal czar, all-wise, kind and benevolent. A banquet is held and a soldier at the door examines the hands of everyone who seeks to enter. Those whose hands are flabby and white are turned aside, and given only the crumbs that servants bring out from the royal table. Those who have hard, worn, toil-stained hands are admitted and given seats of honor. Heaven is like that. *It is a place where honored colonists come home to greater service.*

HOW CAN YOU TELL THESE HEAVEN-ORIENTED PEOPLE? WHO ARE THEY? What does Paul mean when he says "We" are a colony of heaven? To whom was he writing?

He was writing to churches. Yes, sir, that is the purpose of your local church—*a bit of heaven in the midst of sin.*

Do the people in your town sense this when they walk into your church? Do they feel that you, and the rest of your church friends, are living like they would expect folk in heaven to live? *What is going on in your church?* Is it filled with cooking, play-acting, score-keeping, entertainment, parade, and financial drive? Is it "a colony of heaven"?

What commerce do you have between your church and the Other World? Do you receive the Holy Spirit? Do your songs have the touch of heaven upon them? Has an unction touched your preacher's lips? Are you sending saints into God's New Jerusalem?

Were some teen-ager to be suddenly called out of your group into eternity, could you say, "Father, you have called out from among us one of our number who loved Thy Word, who was not ashamed to witness for Thee at school, and whose life was always an open rebuke to those who scorned New Testament morality." *Could you say that?* You can if your citizenship is in heaven.

I think I may safely stretch this word picture to say that every *Christian home* and *marriage* is a "colony of heaven." The home came before the church. Paul talks so much about home and marriage in this letter. He compares it to the union of Christ with His bride, the Church. *That is the greatest compliment ever written to marriage.*

What is more beautiful this side of the rainbow than a lovely marriage? God planned marriage for our welfare and happiness. I will tell you this, you will never find *outside* what God put *inside*. I do not care what a world-system tries to change. It was intended to show to all of us everyday what is meant when God calls Himself our Father, and calls us His children.

Make no mistake about it! A real home, a real marriage, a real family, where Dad gives himself for the home, his wife, and the children; and where wife and the children love their husband and father, *is the best illustration of heaven around these parts.*

Can you say that about your home or about your marriage? Should I ask your neighbors? They know. What do they hear? Do they say, "Oh, oh, they are at it again," when they hear bickering and name calling? What do they see on Sunday morning? Do they see both parents and children ready for Sunday school and church? Could they set their watches by your habit and promptness?

Our homes have been planted in a pagan world. They can survive, and our marriages can endure, as we are kept by the power of God ready to be revealed on God's great day of exhibition.

And now I can say this to you without mutilating this word picture. *Every Christian heart is a small colony of heaven.* God starts something. He establishes an outreach when you come to Him, when a transaction of new birth takes place. *The Holy Spirit stakes out an area for God.* He claims a life for God. Heaven declares its intention to defend and provide for this extension of God's rule.

We live under His dominion. We acknowledge no other sovereign. We admit no other allegiance. My life, to be His colony, must bear His imprint. His will must be done. *His dominion must be seen in everything.*

Look at my money! Look at my time! Look how I dress! Listen to my language! Do you see God's possession? I must live down here as though I were already there. If I do not love Jesus supremely here, I will never put Him first in another world.

Paul says, "We wait for the Saviour who comes from heaven, the Lord Jesus Christ, you will transform the body that belongs to our colony days, till it resembles the body of his glory by the same power that enables him to make everything subject to himself."

We do not look like heavenly beings down here with our stooped shoulders, our baldness or whiteness, our cataracts and deafness, our varicose veins and stiffness. *But we have connections, mister!* Just you wait and see!

A tramp, ragged and discounted, received a letter advising him that he was the rightful heir to a large fortune, if he would come and prove his identity. He started at once. People scoffed at him. Others pitied him. It did not matter to him. His concern was for the letter he carried inside his tattered garments. What did the rest matter?

Friend, I have a witness within. Outside, I may look poor and unattractive; old and uncounted. But I, too, "wait for the

Saviour." *I am His possession.* I admit no other loyalty. *I have taken out my citizenship for heaven.*

Sometimes it seems that I am a long way from the Mother Country. There are times when I could ask, "Has God forgotten me?" Then these words reassure me: "We are a colony of heaven."

CONCERNED

Text: *"Walk in wisdom toward them that are without . . ."*
Colossians 4:5

J. B. PHILLIPS translates this text: "Be wise in your behaviour towards non-Christians."

An anonymous writer has conjectured about Lazarus:

> If it had been permitted
> Would Lazarus have gone
> With water for the thirst of one
> Who let him hunger on
> Through all his aching lifetime
> And never thought to share
> More than a meager, careless crumb
> Of all his sumptuous fare?
>
> "Send Lazarus!" The rich man
> Was most presumptuous still.
> One who had begged beside his gate
> Must surely do his will.
> And had no yawning chasm
> Forestalled the benison
> How eagerly, how quickly,
> Would Lazarus have gone.

Paul talks about two classes of people—those, who by the grace of God are "within," and those who are "without."

What are these outside people missing? Let the Bible and the Christian answer that question. The answer is clearly written in this same fourth chapter. *Paul says they are missing seven things.*

1. They are without heaven. The only heaven they can hope for is upon earth. *And earth is a difficult place upon which to find heaven.*

Where would you build it, sir? How can you guarantee safety from war, struggle, disease, want, famine, revolution, inflation, epidemic and death? I have seen many people try. I have read travel folders as avidly as anyone else.

Where is this complete paradise on earth? Where can I get away from it all? *Verse 1 of this chapter talks about a real heaven.* A lot of folk on your street, and a lot of folk in your family are without this hope.

2. *They are without God.* I would not know how that feels, sir. Tell me! You never kneel in prayer. You never read His Word. You never sense His presence. You never rely upon His guidance.

Is your life empty? Are you missing something? Verse 3 talks about God. Why do you say in your heart, "There is no God"? *How do you reconcile what you see and feel?* Are you sure you are nothing more than an animal? *Are you happy groveling, groping and grabbing?*

3. *They are without Christ.* One Member of the human race has said, "I am the way, the truth, and the life" (John 14:6). That claim was made publicly. It has been made in more languages, through more generations, before greater audiences, against greater challenges than any claim ever put forth.

If it is presumptuous, if it is false, if it has no basis of fact, *the public should be protected against it.* Authorized government agencies, whose business it is to protect the public against fraudulent claims, should put an end to this myth of Jesus

Christ, if there is nothing to His gospel. *Why deal with lesser evils when this is deceiving so many millions?*

Well, sir, the courts and communications are open. Why not undertake the task? How would you explain to sinners saved by grace that the miracle that has changed their lives is nothing more than a pitchman's cleverly stated gimmick? *Christ cannot be explained away.* It is too late to try. What a loss you suffer to be without Him.

4. *They are without fellowship.* Verses 7, 10, and 11 talk about that. There is nothing sweeter, positively nothing. No ties are closer. I have seen strong men throw their arms around each other in their mutual love for Jesus Christ. Jane Merchant describes it in the life of Pastor Ananias, the first to call upon Saul of Tarsus after his conversion:

> Old Ananias, resting in warm sun,
> Spoke softly. "You know well what Paul has done
> To win souls to our Lord from pagan ways,
> Teaching them righteousness and love and praise."
> He paused a little while. His voice was low
> When he resumed. "I didn't want to go
> And call him brother. I did all I could
> To tell myself I had misunderstood
> The thing the Master wanted me to do.
> To risk my neck and those of others too
> By seeking out someone so full of hate
> For all of us, seemed mad to contemplate.
> But I remembered how the Lord went out
> Seeking the worst and neediest ones about
> And who was worse than this fire-breathing Saul?
> And how he bore men's wrath, forgiving all
> They did to him. The message came from him.
> I could no longer doubt. The way was dim
> But I went forth. And when I found Saul, love
> And pure compassion filled me from above.
> This thought can shake me more than any other
> *What if I had not gone and called him Brother?"*

Sir, the first time a child of God calls you "brother," you will feel a rapture that nothing can ever erase.

5. *They are without the will of God.* First Timothy 2:4 declares: "Who will have all men to be saved, and to come unto the knowledge of the truth."

Second Peter 3:9 states: "The Lord is ... not willing that any should perish, but that all should come to repentance."

The outsider is on the wrong road. Paul remembers that "he trembling and astonished said, Lord, what wilt thou have me to do? And the Lord said unto him, Arise, and go into the city, and it shall be told thee what thou must do" (Acts 9:6).

It is a moment of great discovery when you find direction for your life. You embark on a sense of reality. For the first time there is meaning to existence. Paul later put it this way: "that ye may prove what is that good, and acceptable, and perfect, will of God" (Romans 12:2). *Otherwise you are facing a misspent life, sir.*

6. *They are without the Church.* This is mentioned in verses 15 and 16. But you say, "Preacher, I have joined my wife's church. I do not attend very regularly, it is true; but I am on the church roll."

What church? The gospel song says, "When the roll is called up yonder I'll be there." *What roll?* The New Testament gives the answer. "For by one Spirit are we all baptized into one body, whether we be Jews or Gentiles, whether we be bond or free; and have been all made to drink into one spirit" (1 Corinthians 12:13).

Did that happen to you when you joined your wife's church, and put your name on the church roll? What change did it make in your life? *What spiritual thirst has it awakened in your life?*

7. *They are without grace.* The last verse of the chapter mentions this. I will tell you what it means, Mister Outsider. It means that the grace of God that is offered to you is not

operative in your life. You are *lost*. You are *unsaved*. You are *unforgiven*. You are *condemned*. You are *miserable*. There is nothing ahead of you but *hell*. That is what it means to be without the grace of God.

I speak to you, fellow Christians. What are we going to do about these outsiders? *What do these benefits mean to us?* What is my responsibility to the outsider? In verses 5 and 6 of the chapter, the apostle speaks of *a threefold responsibility*.

First, *I am to live uprightly*. That is what my text says. "Walk in wisdom toward them that are without." Be mindful! *Someone is watching my life*. People are putting me to the test. They want to see if it is really true. What we *are* is far more important than anything we *do* or *say*. My daily life is still my best testimony.

Turn back one chapter in this epistle to the Colossians, and ask yourself, "Have I really 'put off' those things indicated in verses 8 and 9?" What things? There they are: anger, wrath, malice, blasphemy, filthy communication out of your mouth, and lies! *Those are the stumbling blocks to the unsaved*.

Ask yourself, "Have I really 'put on' those things listed in verses 10 and 12 through 15?" What things? There they are: bowels of mercies, kindness, humbleness of mind, meekness, long-suffering, forbearing one another, forgiving one another, charity. *Those are the things the sinner wants to see in the Christian*.

Second, *I am to work unselfishly*. The latter part of my text talks about "redeeming the time." Dr. Way translates it: "Seize every opportunity, like merchants who buy up a scarce commodity."

There are priceless opportunities. A funeral service has left lonely, perplexed neighbors. A sudden sickness has taken an employee to the hospital. A baby has arrived next door. Daughter has announced her marriage. Son wants Dad to take him fishing. Travel brings me face to face with a seat partner. *What am I doing about it?*

Third, *I must speak unceasingly*. Verse 6 tells me, "Let your speech be alway with grace, seasoned with salt, that ye may know how ye ought to answer every man." *What kind of talk is that?*

"With grace." The way I talk to my wife, the way I talk to my secretary, the way I answer the telephone is so important. Does my manner of speech, my tone of voice, my consideration of their feelings, witness to them of Christ?

"Seasoned with salt." *I can be thoughtful and strong and courageous at the same time.* Because I speak graciously I need not be two-mouthed, hesitant or backward about presenting the claims of Jesus Christ. When the occasion demands it, I must be ready to speak up.

"That (we) may know how (we) ought to answer every man." God give me the answers! I want to help men with their problems. I want to tell them there is a way, a solution for their needs. I want a man to leave my presence and be able to say, "You know, Brother Ward helped me! He said something to me that I will never forget. It has changed my way of thinking, and the course of my life." *I want my communication with others to bear fruit.*

Soul winning is my business. I must bring those who are outside, inside. I am racing against time. I will have to reach someone today before it is ever too late.

Here again is the warning of my text: "Be wise in your behaviour towards non-Christians." *Watch yourself!*

———◄•►———

BE IN HEALTH

Text: *"Beloved, I wish above all things that thou mayest prosper and be in health, even as thy soul prospereth."*
                                                        3 John 2

WE live in a day when people are more afraid of a pimple on their faces than of rottenness in their hearts. The great cry of the hour is health and prosperity. *It is a gospel that produces best-sellers.* It is a day when we lavish care on the outward man. New creams are announced. New formulas are discovered. New exercises are prescribed. New health benefits are added. *We are health conscious.*

And the healthier we become the more concerned we are to live financially secure, and in the manner to which we have grown accustomed. *The big aim is to live as long as you can and as well as you can.* We chase the calorie, and we pursue the dollar. Prosperity and physical fitness can keynote any campaign.

What about the inner man? *How important is my soul?* How well dressed am I inside? What investments have I made in the life to come? What has been my spiritual progress? What is my effort here in ratio to my efforts toward a sound body and financial guarantee? This text asks that question.

This text is part of a personal letter that John wrote to a gentleman, named Gaius, who had been his host, and who had entertained the apostle. *John had a real fondness for this liberal man.* His greetings to him are not mere courtesies. He says of Gaius, "whom I love in the truth."

What he writes to this gentleman is deep and meaningful. A friendship has been established between these two men, and they open their hearts to one another. John is concerned about his friend's physical and spiritual well-being.

Money and substance are not everything in this world. They cannot buy health, and they cannot buy salvation. John underlines this truth to his Christian friend.

I think life's greatest blessing is to enjoy *a thriving soul in a healthy body.* Radiancy and bouyancy within and without are God's greatest gifts to man. I so often remark to my friends that I thank God I am alive inside and outside.

I wonder how many people know what it is to feel healthy inside? John tells Gaius that everything that matters starts right here. It starts inside.

How can I know that my soul is prospering? Too many care little or nothing about this today. They are contented that they were converted twenty or thirty years ago. *They have taken no steps since.* They are sluggish and inept. Spiritual obesity has set in. Inward convictions have grown lax. Moral muscles have disappeared. There are evidences of spiritual deterioration.

I do not want to be like that. I am determined to do something about it. I know what it does to me when someone says, "Mr. Ward, you are looking well. I am so glad to see you enjoying the best of health. You do not look a day older."

I wish my friends could look inside as easily. I would be even more delighted to hear them say, "Mr. Ward, I certainly appreciate the development of Christian character I see in you. You seem to enjoy a richer experience in grace than when I first met you. I notice so many things about your conduct that inspire me." *Those should be the real compliments.*

If I am to prosper inwardly. I cannot neglect prayer. Bunyan put it bluntly. He said to be prayerless is to be Christless. The Bible tells me that the Spirit of grace is also the Spirit of supplication. I may not always have the same fervor. I may not always be caught up into a third heaven. I have followed this test in my own soul for many years.

Is my prayer alive, or am I only saying words? Has the Holy Spirit formed a message in my heart toward God, or am I only doing an obeisance to a Higher Power? *I know by this test the quickening or the fading of my communion life with God.* I am alarmed when there is no resurgence, when my spirit is limp. I know that I am spiritually sick.

Just as a child longs for his or her parents, so a child of God longs for communion with his or her Heavenly Father. *This is especially true as the darkness deepens.* Israel needed the same food daily until they reached Canaan.

I have a feeling that this constitutes the real secret for building a successful congregation. Too much dependence is placed upon preliminaries that entertain the outward man. *The thrill of soul-prosperity is the real growth ingredient.*

When I know that the meeting will make me husky and aggressive within, I am not so much concerned about the program. If I know that God's Spirit rests upon the meeting-house, I will not pick and choose, and say, "if such a one preaches, I am not going." I will enjoy plain, country dishes. I will not always want garnished desserts.

If our souls prosper, we will be as fond of the messengers as we are of the message. We will appreciate hearing a good ram's-horn, such as blew down the walls of Jericho, as much as we do the silver trumpets.

If I am to prosper inwardly, I will get better acquainted with myself. I will take a look within. Never a day passes that I do not examine my outward man. I am concerned about my hair, my teeth, the color of my skin, and my weight. *I could not live without a mirror.*

I must look within. What kind of man am I building for eternity? What is his appearance? How strong is he? What does he believe? What does he refuse to accept? You say, "That is introspection, preacher! That is morose. How can that express spiritual fitness?"

I know this, *if a tree is growing downward, it is growing upward at the same time.* The more I see what I am really like inside the more I appropriate Calvary.

I cry out the promise in the Word, "and the blood of Jesus Christ his Son cleanseth us from all sin" (1 John 1:7). The better I know myself the more I realize that I must depend upon a better righteousness than my own. *That knowledge invigorates me.*

If I am to prosper inwardly, I must be free from a world system. I am not suggesting negligence. I must not be harassed by the claims and demands of a system which has no place for my Saviour.

This old triumvirate—the world, the flesh, and the devil are still at work. Approved patterns of thought demand that I think in conformity with the particular craze of the hour. I must adopt the jargon. I must move with the beat. I must augment the frenzy by a personal contribution of dress and habit likeness.

This will is impressed upon me. It crushes my soul. Paul speaks out boldly about it. "And be not conformed to this world: but be ye transformed by the renewing of your mind, that ye may prove what is that good, and acceptable, and perfect, will of God" (Romans 12:2).

My well-being depends upon this step of faith. To be strong and virile I must have victory—*victory all the time.*

"They who know the Saviour shall in Him be strong,
Mighty in the conflict of the right 'gainst wrong;
This the blessed promise given in God's Word,
Doing wondrous exploits, they who know the Lord.

"Victory! victory! blessed blood-bo't victory!
Victory! victory! vict'ry all the time;
As Jehovah liveth, strength divine He giveth
Unto those who know Him, victory all the time."

My soul improves as I furnish an environment of victory.

A very old story tells of a beggar who asked a certain preacher for a donation, which the preacher refused. "Will you then, sir, give me your blessing?" asked the beggar. To which the preacher replied, "God bless you!" "O," responded the beggar, "you would not give me that, if it were worth anything."

A lot of our religious brick-a-brack is worthless. It does not put vitamins in the soul. *Victory over the world strengthens the soul.* Try it and see!

When you rise, be concerned about this one thing only. Ask yourself, "What can I do for God today? How perfectly shall

I be able to perform His will for my life during these next twenty-four hours?" *Make that your target and you will begin to live like Elijah and Paul!* One thing further.

If I am to prosper inwardly, I must grow in love. I do not want to carry around a scrawny soul. If need be, it were better to be afflicted with a club foot than a measly soul. I must reach out. Mother taught me as a lad that there were foods that were good for me. She said I would never know whether I liked them or not unless I tried them.

Life is like that. I think this is one of the most important elements in the missionary message. *There are so many who can improve my life and increase my happiness if I will give them a chance.* But if I remain picky and choosy, I will remain sickly and become the target for every attack of bias and hate.

John commends his host, Gaius, for his love, his hospitality, and his open attitude "to strangers." The little Scots woman filled with the love of Jesus put it in such a wonderful way when she said, "Come in. I have a house that will hold a hundred, and a heart that will hold ten thousand."

The New Testament says, "He that dwelleth in love dwelleth in God." I must take heed to my soul. I will look for disease there. I will search for fatigue there. I will ask for a checkup there.

More and more I am persuaded that the soul is the health-control center. A stagnant soul permeates the entire being. I am going to ask myself, as I request that you ask yourselves, "Has my soul prospered?" What conquests has it made? What new areas has it discovered? What revelations of truth has it researched? What glories has it experienced? *What pleasure does it bring me?* Am I secretly ashamed? Have I experienced moral failure too often? Have I deliberately starved my spiritual appetite? Do I have an unhealthy soul? Is it filled with infection?

Then my body is handicapped. It is conscious of an inside drag. Sleep is not what it should be. Work and employment do not have the meaning and purpose they should have. Marital relationships are unsanctified. Nerves are jangled by indecision. The mind is not at rest. Prejudices and resentments disturb the blood pressure. Hatreds and jealousies erode the heart action.

As Christ put it, I need to be made "whole." I cannot be a part of the world and a part of the kingdom of God. I cannot be concerned about my body and unconcerned about my soul. I cannot live for time and ignore eternity. *This is a sick kind of living.* God has something better for us than that.

KINDNESS

Texts: *"But thou art a God ready to pardon, gracious and merciful, slow to anger, and of great kindness."*
Nehemiah 9:17

"Be kindly affectioned one to another with brotherly love."
Romans 12:10

"That in the ages to come he might show the exceeding riches of his grace in his kindness toward us through Christ Jesus."
Ephesians 2:7

"And to godliness brotherly kindness."
2 Peter 1:7

WE have clothed the message of salvation with such masculinity and crusading fervor that, until we give it further thought, it almost seems out of character *to think of Christianity as a sense of kindness.* This planet features cold, impersonal, machine efficiency. It also incorporates brutality, vulgarity, lost souls and broken lives.

> "A little word in kindness spoken,
>   A motion, or a tear,
> Has often healed the heart that's broken,
>   And made a friend sincere!"

The gospel is kindness reaching from another world.

I am persuaded that a great deal of the tragic wreckage of

emotions and confusion of youth are originating from this age of automation. *God knows better than any other that a human being needs love.* A person needs to be needed. Without it there is no individual dignity.

Mr. Musial, now retired, but for twenty years a national baseball idol, recalls the poverty-restricted years of his youth in Donora, Pennsylvania. There were eight in the family—nine while grandmother was still living—squeezed into a small, five-room house.

He says, "My father brought home $11 every two weeks, and they paid $4 a month for rent." His father worked at the zinc mill amid fumes of sulphur. It was hard, killing, unrewarding work. He says, "Mother baked bread in an outside oven, 10 loaves at a time." Then he adds this beautiful tribute:

"Mom never failed in heat or snow to walk down the hill to the mill each morning, carrying my father his hot soup in a round lunch pail. He had a weak stomach and she felt he needed the warm lunch. And Pop would hold back a cookie or an apple so that he'd have something for me when I ran down to meet him after I heard the five o'clock whistle."

Now a man of wealth and fame, Mr. Musial looks back and says, "There were times when Mom sent my brother and me to school in canvas-top sneakers because she couldn't afford shoes for us. But there was never a time when I didn't have a baseball. My mother made many for me out of a little bit of this and that, sewn together. *We didn't have much except kindness.*"

Today, the lament of thousands is, "We have everything, except kindness." More hearts corrode away in secret anguish, for want of kindness from those who should be their comforters, than from any other calamity in life.

Salvation is an experience of kindness. Paul describes it as "the exceeding riches of his grace in his kindness toward us" (Ephesians 2:7).

If it were left to us to make Christians, too often it would be a repetition of the Crusades with force and battle. *I am afraid we do not depend upon kindness too often.* We have more faith in pressure and ultimatum.

Paul says God's kindness toward us was "through Christ Jesus." It was difficult for the early Christians to be kind toward Saul of Tarsus. He had been so unkind toward them. The brethren were loathe to admit him to fellowship.

"When Saul was come to Jerusalem, he assayed to join himself to the disciples: but they were all afraid of him, and believed not that he was a disciple" (Acts 9:26). *God was kind toward this bad man.*

God might have been *harsh* toward Saul. He deserved it. He had done his best to destroy the Church. He says in his testimony before Agrippa: "I punished them oft in every synagogue, and compelled them to blaspheme; and being exceedingly mad against them, I persecuted them even unto strange cities" (Acts 26:11).

What would we have done with a man like that? God sent the Light of the World to pierce the darkness of Saul's soul, and to speak to him with the Voice of His Word to awaken feelings that lay buried. And before the time usually taken for lunch had elapsed, in less time than a noon hour usually takes, God had taken steps to rebuild this sinner. Saul cries out and says, "Who art thou, Lord? . . . Lord, what wilt thou have me to do?" (Acts 9:5, 6).

We underestimate the power of kindness. Kindness is the link that connects earth with heaven. Paul reminds Titus that Christ's appearance on earth began a new era. "But after that the kindness and love of God our Saviour toward man appeared" (Titus 3:4).

The old-fashioned gospel song puts it well when it says:

> "More about Jesus would I know,
>   More of His grace to others show;
> More of His saving fullness see,
>   More of His love who died for me."

The gospel was never meant to be brittle, unfeeling, coldly correct and reduced to a format. The gospel is *kind*. Write your name by kindness, love and mercy on the hearts of the people you come in contact with year by year, and you will never be forgotten.

Christ moved among people who needed kindness. The invalid at the pool said, "Sir, I have no man, when the water is troubled, to put me into the pool: but while I am coming, another steppeth down before me" (John 5:7).

The woman of Samaria, with a record of marital failure said, "I have no husband." The mother, distressed over a teen-age daughter, "besought him that he would cast forth the devil out of her daughter" (Mark 7:26).

The father, exhausted in his attempts to find deliverance for his epileptic son, sobs, "Lord, have mercy on my son ... for ofttimes he falleth into the fire, and oft into the water. And I brought him to thy disciples, and they could not cure him" (Matthew 17:15, 16).

He said of a woman badly misunderstood, "Let her alone; why trouble ye her? She hath wrought a good work on me.... Wheresoever this gospel shall be preached throughout the whole world, this also that she hath done shall be spoken of for a memorial of her" (Mark 14:6, 9).

The same manner of people fill our streets today. They need the same kindness. I want you to meet your Heavenly Father, sir! He is "a God ready to pardon, gracious and merciful, slow to anger, and of a great kindness" (Nehemiah 9:17).

Western Union tells us that we will spend as a nation, before the present year shall end, a million dollars just to say words like, "thanks," "please" and "love" that express affection and courtesy. That is money well spent.

God spent a great deal more, sir, in expressing affection for this world. David, who showed anything but loving kindness for Bathsheba's husband, threw himself upon his God in the agony of his sin. He cries out, "Have mercy upon me, O God, according to thy lovingkindness: according unto the multitude of thy tender mercies blot out my transgressions" (Psalm 51:1).

Kindness is the very principle of love. *It is impossible to resist continued kindness.*

Have we not too often omitted in our picture of aggressive evangelism and soul winning the force and conquest of kindness? Life consists of little things—smiles, gestures, tones, remembrances, touches.

A housewife, who was won to Christ, said afterwards, "No, it was not the sermon. I could not forget how a woman, a perfect stranger to me, sitting next to me in the service, offered to take my restless baby to the nursery and care for the child, so that I might attend the rest of the service!" *Kindness opened her heart.*

What kind of God are we exhibiting? The sinner is looking for a Redeemer who shares a songbook, who moves over and makes room in the pew, who shakes hands and gets acquainted, who notices children, who wants him to come again.

There is so much loneliness. Zacchaeus was a lonely man. His money and real estate were poor company. He needed companionship. "And when Jesus came to the place, he looked up, and saw him, and said unto him, Zacchaeus, make haste, and come down; for today I must abide at thy house" (Luke 19:5). And the record says, "And he made haste, and came down, and received him joyfully" (Luke 19:6).

Jesus did not engage in a diatribe against greed and abuse of political advantage. He went directly to the loneliness of the man's life, to his inner need that no amount of money, legally or illegally acquired, could ever meet. The gospel is like that, sir!

Jesus Christ defined His mission to include this specific, "He hath sent me to bind up the broken hearted" (Isaiah 61:1). Think about that! *This world is full of failures, dropouts, discards and also-rans.* There is grief on every avenue.

God says through Jesus Christ His Son, "I care for you. I see the wound. I see the bleeding. I see the tear."

He does not come to censure. The condemnation is already heavy. He does not come to probe. The sentence is already passed. A thousand times the mind repeats, "I am no good. Everybody knows I am no good. It is not any use." He comes for a different purpose. "He hath sent me to bind up the broken hearted" (Isaiah 61:1). Believe it, mister!

That poor woman with cancer will always remember Jesus.

"A woman having an issue of blood twelve years, which had spent all her living upon physicians, neither could be healed of any, came behind him, and touched the border of his garment: ... And Jesus said, Somebody hath touched me: for I perceive that virtue is gone out of me.

"And when the woman saw that she was not hid, she came trembling, and falling down before him, she declared unto him before all the people for what cause she had touched him, and how she was healed immediately. And he said unto her, Daughter, be of good comfort: thy faith hath made thee whole; go in peace" (Luke 8:43, 44, 46-48).

Have no fear! Come now. God will not treat you as an untouchable. God's kindness is manifest toward you. *You need not be ashamed of your position—only of your sin and your mistaken thoughts toward God.*

Jesus was as kind toward the servant as He was toward the employer. He was as kind toward children as He was toward adults. He was as kind toward women as He was toward men; and as kind toward Greeks as He was toward His countrymen. He will receive you.

Someone said this to me when I was a young man, and I have not forgotten it. I have endeavored, not always successfully, to make it a guide in life. "Hard words are like hail stones in summer, beating down and destroying what they would nourish if they were melted into drops." I pray that the Holy Spirit will make me a kind man.

There is no gospel without kindness. Do not forget the words which Luke, the physician-evangelist places so firmly in the Book of Acts, when he describes our Saviour, who, while on earth, "went about doing good." That is God's intention toward you.

Do you know the world is dying
For a little bit of love?
Everywhere we hear the sighing
For a little bit of love;
For the love that rights a wrong,
Fills the heart with hope and song;
They have waited, oh, so long,
For a little bit of love.

From the poor of every city,
For a little bit of love,
Hands are reaching out in pity
For a little bit of love;
Some have burdens hard to bear,
Some have sorrows we should share;
Shall they falter and despair
For a little bit of love?

HOW MAY I EXPERIENCE CHRIST?

Text: *"For I have learned by experience that the Lord hath blessed me."*

Genesis 30:27

ASSEMBLIES of God people speak so often of *experience*. What is it? In common with others we have the Christ of the Creed. It will always be necessary to have a statement of fundamentals. Such a statement declares spiritual facts.

We also have the Christ of history. Millions have read the published story.

We have the Christ of ceremony and ritual. This is our use of public worship.

It cannot be all make-believe. Something real must have happened, sometime and somewhere, to make these things so positive and permanent. *But how can it become real to me?* That is what matters most.

I need something more than creed, history and ceremony. Otherwise, I grow weary and satiated. I can do all the things I am told to do. I can fulfill all the religious obligations I am expected to fulfill. *I can make contact with the externals of religion, and never once contact God.* I can live in the house of God, and never meet the Host of the house. I can sing, dress, recite, stand, sit, give and take, come and go, and finally it all becomes meaningless unless I experience the presence of God.

Every life has two aspects—*inward* and *outward*. They are what you *are,* and what you *do.* By experience, I do not mean something which you have merely done, of which you have just thought and touched at some time. It is much more than that.

In order for all these things to become parts of our experience, they must in some way get hold of our entire life. *My life must be deeply moved, stirred, gripped in some definite way, inside and out.* I must feel them so keenly that they will come out in my action and behavior. *Experience changes me.*

For example, you may be able to play a tune in a crude way on a piano or violin, or you may have a smattering of botany, or be able to put a few lines together. But as long as you only *touch* these things, as long as you *play* with these worlds of power, life and beauty, you do not have any experience of them.

At the same time, you may have a personal experience in other things like movies, jazz and the novels of the moment.

You have a burning interest in them. You live, move and have your being in them.

If I go to a river and thrust my hand into the stream, dabble in its water in a playful way, I have *contact* with that river, but I do not have *experience* of it. But if I plunge into the stream and swim across its course or drive myself against its current and measure my stroke against its force; if I submerge my whole body in the river, then I do have such experience.

When the whole of you touches the whole of anything else, then you have experience of that thing, no matter what it is, whether it be music, art, science, swimming or religion.

Have you met Christ in that fashion? Have you touched certain aspects and incidents of His story; *or have you leaped into the mainstream of His being, purpose and power, and submerged yourself in what He means and says?*

I will tell you this, unless you do, you will never make it. When the hammer-blows of modern life fall upon you; when its fierce appeal comes to your senses; when the terrible strain of modern business saps your emotional reserves; when the flaming suggestions of modern theatricals grip you, *you will never survive if your interest in Jesus Christ has been casual and trivial.* These other things will envelop you and crush you. You will find that you have built your religious profession out of pasteboards.

There is a great dark cavern of emptiness in all of us that is likely to threaten us with terror and dismay. *Be sure of this.*

Christ is striving with all His infinite power to enter into your life and take loving and compelling possession of all of its possibilities and powers. That is your first step toward peace and happiness.

Acknowledge Christ's determination toward you as a fact! Cooperate with it fairly, and you will find it to be true. *You will find that He will come into your life and that you can enter into His.*

The first step is to *receive* Christ. Christ is not a definition, a doctrine, a theory; for the Spirit of Christ is not in a dictionary or encyclopedia. If you cannot see clearly how to read an open page before you, you cannot say there is no such thing as light.

You make an adjustment. You change your position. You move. You exercise your prerogative to switch on the light. Then you see. Do not deny Jesus Christ because you have not experienced Him. Change your position! Switch on the light!

You say, "Brother Ward, how, when and where can I meet Jesus Christ? Is there a prescribed day of the week? Is there a geographical location? Is there a scheduled event?" *No.* He moves and makes Himself known along and amid the general plane of experience. I suggest these common, everyday pathways. Meet Him there! I do.

1. ALONG THE PATHWAY OF VISION

I mean people and things and places we see, and touch. Look for Christ there! Christ has something to do with all these.

Take, for instance, the Feeding of the Five Thousand. The crowd had one thought—food. Most left, aware only of Christ's ability to produce edibles.

Look at the other side! What was Jesus doing? Was He demonstrating a giant supermarket? No. *He was demonstrating God's compassion and love toward human beings like you and me.*

There is more to your day than meeting a number of people, and touching and viewing so many things. That can become dull, unless you meet Christ in these circumstances. He may be trying to come to you amid your list of appointments.

2. ALONG THE PATHWAY OF SPEECH

Life consists of interchange, of conversation and communication. We express ideas. We wish to be heard and followed. *But do we hear? Do we wish to be led?* Do we sense that Christ wants to come into our minds? His message, His will, may be clothed in some word, some conversation, some glance that is directed toward us in our communications of the day. *He is there, if I have an ear to hear.*

3. ALONG THE PATHWAY OF EVENTS

I believe that in some mysterious way, God seems to be in all the countless incidents, events and happenings which crowd themselves into my day. If God is moving upon us; if He is in a vital way trying to affect our life; if He is trying personally to reach us, *then it must be that He is moving through these events.*

There is a plot to your life whether you realize it or not. It is not a crazy hodge-podge. You must have become aware of it before this. *There is a strange unknown quality in all that is happening to you.* You sense a foreboding. You experience an escape. You change directions. You move. You make connections. It is happening everyday. It is always in the background, silent, gentle; but it is always there.

I ask you, are you aware in an intelligent way of some strange flash of light, some sudden recognition, "That just did not happen to me?" Are you sensitive to some vital, driving thought? It persists. You cannot shake it. Are you conscious of some definite, swift turn in life? What caused it? Who planned the interruption? *Who is in the shadows?*

We ought to be on the lookout for manifestations of this kind. Someone is looking over our shoulder. Jacob pondered such events. He said, "Surely the Lord is in this place; and I knew it not" (Genesis 28:16).

4. ALONG THE PATHWAY OF READING

That is another part of our every twenty-four hours—books, papers, magazines. I hold this to be true. *God is pressing into our experience through what we read. Therefore, we should be careful what we read, avoiding what is useless, vicious, sensational and sensual, and never reading merely to kill time.*

Suddenly, He is there in character and message. It may be that I am reading a book of history. It may be that I am halfway through a biography. It has happened to me over and over again. A certain beautiful Face, silent, lovely, haunting, with searching eyes, closes in upon me. *The covers of the book recede, and I see the eternal God of history; or I see the Son of Man challenging me from the pages of another man's record.*

5. ALONG THE PATHWAY OF QUIET

I mean those moments set aside. I mean the trysting place when I expect Him to come, when I have a date with Him. Those are precious moments. No existence is complete without them.

Then it is that Christ stirs within us strange heartthrobs and urges. They are like the beatings of the heart. They have nothing to do with daydreaming, or musing. *It is not nostalgia.*

I come to these moments to listen. I throw open the windows of my soul. I find great cleansing in these moments. I seek a cleansing from what is negative, critical and useless. I ask a furnishing of that which is true and abiding and generous.

I want the clutter removed from my life. I want this Friend of heaven to harmonize and rearrange my interior life, so that I may be at peace. My life, sir, would be barren without such an experience.

What I am saying in this: *I must, and thank God I do, experience Jesus Christ every day of the week, all day long.*

Life is an opportunity in which to know God. That is the big meaning of your existence, mister! God means to be entwined in every man's day. We need a personal experience of God, and we need it badly.

Breathe a prayer from your heart with me, "O, God, come to us now through Thy Son, Jesus Christ, and help us to come to Thee immediately."

Do not separate the day's events from the God of the events of the day. Do not stuff your God into a tiny compartment of a Sunday morning religious hour from eleven o'clock to ten minutes to twelve. Do not say: "After the events of the day are over, I shall return home and meet my Heavenly Father at night, when I say my prayers, in peace."

Rather say something like this: "I am going forth into the life and motion of this day, and I shall look upon all that happens as so many pathways by which God has decreed to contact me, and I, in turn, have dedicated myself to enter into Him." Then you will know the rapture of possessing, and being possessed. That is why the person who experiences Christ sings:

"To Jesus every day I find my heart is closer drawn;
He's fairer than the glory of the gold and purple dawn;
He's all my fancy pictures in its fairest dreams, and more;
Each day He grows still sweeter than He was the day before."

WHY SHOULD I LOVE JESUS?

Text: *"For the love of Christ constraineth us."*
2 *Corinthians* 5 :14

THE real wonder is not that so few love Jesus today, *but that anyone should love Him at all.* That is the miracle. Yet the multitude grows as generations increase!

The competition for that love has grown more rugged in my lifetime. So many more things fight for an entrance into my heart now than when I was a boy. They are present-day realities. They are powerful lures.

Why should I love Jesus? He lived so long ago. He lived on earth such a short time. He never adorned Himself with cultured robes of great schools. He never acquired the outward trappings of success. He died friendless, alone, broken, leaving behind no great institutions of any worldly sort. *Why should such a Man claim my life?*

I know this by personal experience. The love of Christ in the human heart is the greatest fire ever kindled on earth. I have seen humanity caught up in causes and events and enthusiasm raised to fever-pitch. Then it has burned out. Only the ashes remain.

Jesus is different. That flame is still in this world. Why?

There are times when I shudder with the impact. Sleep vanishes. For the time being I have no sense of hunger or thirst for anything or anyone else. *I am on fire.* When I yield, when I cease to trifle or coquet with it, this passion rules in my life. I am completely under its sway. *What is it that happens to me?*

It is a world of its own into which I have been brought supernaturally. It fully compensates for the loss of other possessions. It makes amends for disappointments. *It makes us live again in that great deep inside of us, where once all was dark and dead.*

I testify to the power of this flame. I have felt it challenge and conquer sin, baseness and moral rebellion. It has power. It is not a beautiful, romantic dream. It is not a theory or a pretty point of view. It crowds. It demands. It offers risk. It involves hurt. It never retires. It never offers to share its dominion in your life. It punishes you when you toy with it, or sham, or ignore it. *It explodes in a person's soul.*

It is like the sea. I am caught by its immensity. It is more than magic. It is more than spell. *It is eternity.*

The throb never lets up. There are hours when nothing else matters. I ask myself so often, "Why has this happened to me?" *I only know I would be lost without it.*

The light opera, *The Three Musketeers of Dumas,* sets forth the amazing love of these men, whose lives involved one for all and all for one. It was all they had. This blaze covered them. It controlled them. How often we see them in the tale, singing their way through the world; swinging along roads, ranging anywhere. Countless foes surround them; pain and death are everywhere. Now and then they lose each other, and all is black and hopeless. But soon they meet again, embrace and drive ahead, slashing their way through all. All they had were a trusty sword and *love*.

My salvation is something like that. It has embarked me upon adventure. It has gripped me. I have an eternal contract to fulfill and to be fulfilled—each for the other, and all for each. *Jesus Christ has gone all out for me. I must go all out for Him.*

I do not see any other way to be saved, my friend. We must have the love of Jesus within us in such magnitude and certainty that, having it, we can stand alone against the world. I have got to be captured. Nothing less will survive.

That is why the heart of man surrenders to the love of Jesus with elation and release. It enables us to face and confront the world. Look it full in the face without fear. Laugh at its threats and bribes and rejoice when it sends us away into the solitude of God.

We know that when we come back from that solitude, we come with *a sceptre of power before which the world stands in awe.* This world has always stood aghast at the flash of a face through which the light of the love of Jesus burns.

This love for Jesus brings *a transcendency*. It lifts and sustains as can nothing else in this universe.

These modern times are so brilliant, many-sided and immense, so seductive and fascinating that they sway and mold the lives of men as never before.

If you have never experienced this love of Jesus; if all He means to you is a shadow, vague and indefinite; if it is only a matter of saying a creed; attending service when convenient; this ruthless world will tear in pieces the cheap stuff, the little thread of ribbon that joins your life to Him. Soon you may find yourself parting with it all with scarcely a regret.

It is not enough, sir, to give my heart passionately to making a living and give God an occasional gesture of courtesy. *It will not work.* Somewhere there will be a crash, a collapse, a wreck.

Our love of Jesus must be our real world, our whole world. It must be to my inside, what physical air, food and light are to my body. That is why I ask you, "Do you love Him?"

To Paul it had such height, depth and breadth, that even such terrible and destructive forces as famine, sword, nakedness and death lost all reality, and their appearances became illuminated and even glorified by the consciousness of the love of Jesus. *Nothing else mattered to Paul.* It was his world.

My mother used to sing, "Jesus is *all the world* to me." I ponder that. Mother lived in His love. She visited elsewhere. She performed services elsewhere, but she resided in His love. She belonged to Him, and to Him only. She knew no other world. Nothing else really mattered.

If my real world is the front page of my daily newspaper, then the Sunday morning service is only an hour-long, filmy sense of make-believe. That is no good, mister! It is hardly a temporary relief. It certainly is not a refuge.

Our worlds are confused. We must reverse them. The world outside is the shadowy, ugly unreality. It will pass away. The love of Jesus will never pass away. It is eternal.

I say this to you. *Abandon yourself to Christ's love for you.* Love with a full thirst and a full hunger! Plunge! Cut the shoreline! Set your sails like Columbus for a new world. Leave behind you the restricted, befuddled, pasteboard grandeur of a fading, dying system. Discover for yourself what God has in store for those who love Him.

Why should I love Jesus? The plain, hard-fact answer is that I am lost without it. Every other love destroys me. Every other love encourages a selfish response. The love of Christ constrains me. *It changes my entire life.* It creates a new center of interest. It establishes a new control center.

Before, it was possessions, pleasures, activities and all the changing show of daily life. Now, it is how I think, how I feel, my motives, my aims—*what I am.*

I am awakened inwardly. A birth has taken place. Outside things have a different relationship to my life. I have destiny. It is endless. I am "a purchased possession." *I count.* That is what matters. I am no longer a scrounger, scrabbling to get bits of a small planet. *I am associated with Him.* This association is fitting me for eternity.

Do you know what it is to be penetrated by His presence? "Ye are not your own" (1 Corinthians 6:19). That is the secret.

Stop trying to own God, Jesus Christ, the Church and your soul! New Testament faith will never work on a business basis and an efficient arrangement any more than love will work on such a basis. Stop trying to tie it all into a handy package, cleverly handled and smartly marketed.

"Ye are not your own." So do not lay claim to yourself. Surrender to the love of God! Let it sweep over you. God's love is not a tidy asset that you count along with your membership in a local service club and your wedding anniversary. *It is a flame.*

Do not make the mistake of relating this love with the erection of costly buildings with enormous amounts of square footage; or with improved ceremonies; or with an endless list of things that pertain to fabric and superstructure. *Relate it to something inside of you.*

Does it do to you what it did to Francis Xavier, to David Livingstone, to Dwight L. Moody, to Billy Sunday? *Does it move you?* Are you hopelessly entwined in the throes of it?

I will say this. The very ground on which the Christian today stands is being challenged and denied.

What is that ground? It is this: *the possibility that the human spirit can really be affected by the Spirit of God*. It is denied that there is any such Spirit in God or in man.

God is presented today as a kind of mute, machine-like intelligence; a world-energy, careless of our fate and incapable of making Himself known.

Man is presented as a bundle of inherited racial instincts, a puppet of circumstances, the child of luck or accident, fated to succeed or fail, as the case may be.

I do not believe it. No, sir! God is real to me. I know a flame, a love, that has reached me from another world through Jesus Christ.

I know this. We are a part of an era that is trampling upon more spiritual ideals than ever before—ideals that have molded character, turned darkness into light and refashioned whole races.

We will either yield to the false voices that tell us to do as we please with all that we are, or become a companion of Jesus, our body ruled by His desire, our mind guided and governed by His mind, our soul in breathing from Him the life that is Life indeed.

Without Jesus Christ life is a phantom. A little while from now I will be gone. So will you. We question. *Where? What? How? Why?* If I am not wanted; if I do not mean anything to God; if I am nothing more than a little ant on a big anthill, what does anything mean?

Life is crazy. It is a jumble. But if He cares; if He loves me; if Calvary is a genuine passport, then everything has meaning.

I know this, my friend; I have personally found supreme satisfaction in constantly experiencing the love of Jesus Christ. So will you. Then you will make the big discovery. "We are not apart from God, but a part of God."

WHAT MARK BELIEVED
AND PREACHED

Text: *"The beginning of the gospel of Jesus Christ, the Son of God."*

Mark 1:1

MARK fascinates me as an evangelist. You hardly expect him to break into the company of businessmen, physicians and seniors in the company. He seems so young and "come-lately." Yet there he is forever in company with Matthew, Luke and John.

Mark's faith in Jesus is simple and direct. It is a faith that declares that a young man of his own age, and of his own time, is most unique and different to any young man who ever lived before, or who shall ever live hereafter; *that this young man is the Son of God.* He says his life proves it.

Mark designates the record of Jesus upon earth *as a new beginning.* This is the gospel that Mark believed, and which made him a great evangelist.

He believes that Jesus is begotten of God. Every other birth since Adam has followed another pattern. "That which is conceived in her is of the Holy Ghost" (Matthew 1:20).

God introduced another Adam into the human race. Mark knew Him. He personally beheld His glory, "glory as of the only begotten of the Father" (John 1:14). *This glory was for the first time set forth in humanity.*

Mark's faith and message simply say this, "Such a life as Jesus cannot be explained otherwise." No man could have produced such seed. There was no precedent for it. It began with Jesus.

When Jesus spoke of God as His Father, His countrymen

had no doubt as to His meaning. They said, "He said also that God was his Father, making Himself equal with God" (John 5:18). In Him the supernatural and the natural had been reconciled.

This conviction made Mark an evangelist. Nothing else did.

The announcement heaven made to Mary has never successfully been denied, "The Holy Ghost shall come upon thee, and the power of the Highest shall overshadow thee; therefore also that Holy thing which shall be born of thee shall be called the Son of God" (Luke 1:35). *There can be no saving gospel of Jesus Christ without this fact.*

This gospel says, *first,* THAT JESUS CHRIST IS THE PERFECT EXPRESSION IN HUMANITY, AND FOR MAN, OF THE LIFE OF GOD. Every other image is blurred and inadequate. Every other image is dim and lacks saving power. The heavens declare God's glory; but are our astronomers and space scientists evangelists?

History declares the fact of God; but are our historians and biographers evangelists? No! *These massive reflections are too imperfect, too bewildering.* Men lose their way.

My physical body declares God's glory; but are physicians and research technicians evangelists? No! Sin and generations of human failure have distorted the picture.

Only in Jesus Christ do you see the perfect likeness of God. The Word became flesh in order to dwell among men. The God-Man walked on this earth. Mark was convinced.

This gospel says, *second,* THAT JESUS CHRIST IS THE PERFECT EXPRESSION TO MEN OF THE TRUTH OF GOD. No degreed critic of any generation, from any field of knowledge, has ever proven Jesus Christ to be unscientific. He violated no known truth of healing. He set aside no principle of freedom or government. He confirmed the laws of economics.

His business with us, and ours with Him, belong to a far

more important domain. *He came to make sure of our relationship with God.*

Minds were darkened. Philosophers asked questions. The world was filled with "maybe," "perhaps," "it is reasonable to expect," "it is generally agreed," "let us suppose" and every kind of calculation.

Jesus Christ spoke directly out of the immediate knowledge of His eternity with God. *It was direct, final authority.* There was no middle man. This is why Jesus Christ cannot be superseded. All attempts to improve upon His teaching are doomed to failure. Mark was satisfied. His questions were answered.

This gospel says, *third,* THAT JESUS CHRIST IS THE PERFECT EXPRESSION OF THE LOVE OF GOD. Where else can you prove it? Nature is "too red in tooth and claw" to use an old expression.

This creation groans in travail. Our own lives are filled with fortune and misfortune. *The world is a mess, and I have been commanded to a forced residency.* No one consulted me about coming. I can do nothing to stay. It seems unfair and frustrating.

Only Jesus gives it meaning. He tells me in the language of Calvary that God loves me. He tells me in language of demonstration that God has been willing to go through hell to give me eternal life. Nothing ever again can make me incidental and impersonal.

Jesus Christ invites every member of the race to put his or her hand into His wounded side. *That relationship changes things.* I can say with blessed assurance, "My Lord and my God."

This gospel says, *fourth,* THAT JESUS CHRIST IS THE COMPLETE EXPRESSION OF GOD'S UNION AND FELLOWSHIP WITH MEN. Jesus Christ tells me in the fact of His life upon earth that God has reconciled this world unto Himself. *God has intervened.* His intents and purposes are at work.

There can be no evangelism otherwise. He has blunted evil. He has set redemption to work. He has cursed sin. He makes it possible for lives to be released.

God is active here and now. *I am a co-worker.* I want you to thrill to the meaning of these words. I want you to move in the power of these words.

Jesus says, "If a man love me, he will keep my words: *and my Father will love him,* and we will come unto him, and make our abode with him" (John 14:23).

Mister, what need you and I fear with that promise available? That puts God in business right here and now. I feel today, as Mark felt then, that I have a great gospel to preach —a gospel of action, a gospel of miracle.

All that adds up to good news. It is the big message in this world. There are other exciting things. Let us not deny it!

I enjoy favorable breaks like anyone else. I thrill to invitations. I appreciate unexpected gifts. I am glad for even a moment when earth seems a pleasant place on which to live. I love friends. I stir to challenge. I am glad to be a part of organization and fellowship. It is not all drab and routine.

It would not be true, if I gave that impression in my preaching. There is a lot to live for. *But the big news, the big thrill, the big invitation, the most wonderful Friend of all, the greatest satisfaction is Jesus Christ.*

That is Mark's conclusion. That is my testimony. Nothing on all this earth fulfills man's needs like the gospel of Jesus Christ.

The worst offender can be happy again. The greatest rebel can find clemency. The filthiest soul can be clean. The mind perforated with rot and dirty, garbage smut can be renewed. The conscience wrung in agony can be at peace. This best of all news tells me there is *forgiveness.* That is what I need before I can ask for cleansing.

There is no future for me until the past is canceled. In Jesus Christ we clearly see "the Lamb of God, which taketh away the sin of the world" (John 1:29). My sins are taken away. That is what it says, sir!

The good news also informs me that Jesus Christ reaches out and makes me a partaker of all He demonstrated. *My faith in Him releases to me a new moral power.* This is achievement, sir!

I sympathize with men who want to climb mountains. I admire men who want to overcome poverty. I congratulate those who aim for scholarships. I clap for the home-run hitter, the par-breaker and the record-smasher.

Then you know how I feel when I want to overcome a nature that would rather lie than tell the truth, that would rather covet than share, that would rather hate than love, that would rather live for time than for eternity. *Now I can do it through Jesus Christ.* I am doing it.

A guilt-consciousness has given way to a consciousness of glory. A new law is at work in the members of my body. I find that I have an urge to walk, to talk, to plan my life to His purpose for me. *Jesus Christ holds the control center of my life.*

It is true. "He that abideth in me, and I in him, the same bringeth forth much fruit" (John 15:5). You see it every day. The results overwhelm you. You look at yourself, and say, "Am I the same man I used to be? Am I that moral failure? Am I that fettered corpse? Oh, what a change! I am a new creature. Old things have passed away." That is what you will say. And it is all because of Jesus Christ.

And the good news includes not only what you have become, *but also what you can begin to do.* "Now are we the sons of God" (1 John 3:2). We are "heirs of God, and joint-heirs with Christ" (Romans 8:17). "Henceforth I call you not servants ... *but friends*" (John 15:15).

As a friend of His, I have used His Name and His authority to pray for sick people in this audience. And I have witnessed many a healing that I have reported to you. As a friend of

His, I have attempted things, and accomplished them, things I could never have attempted or accomplished by myself.

Jesus Christ encourages you to go big. It is not theory. It is action. One entire book in the New Testament is called the Book of Acts. Read it! That is the warrant God gives us for every-day living in this world—spiritual adventure, moral conquest, miracle challenge.

At first, Mark is frightened. Perhaps he feels that Paul is an unusual, singular man, one who comes along only once in a generation. He hesitates. He goes home. He thinks about it. *Then Mark throws himself completely upon Jesus.*

His convictions are crisp and clear. His evangelism is without fear. Jesus Christ is the Son of God. He never forgets that for one moment.

Time and history have changed since Jesus appeared upon earth. Mark puts it this way, "The beginning of the gospel of Jesus Christ." Calendar makers place it as the year one. *A new era began.* No other name has been so dignified in history.

Everything before His coming pointed to His coming. He said, "Your father Abraham rejoiced to see my day: and he saw it, and was glad" (John 8:56).

Mister, Jesus Christ is the answer to the dateless, meaningless existence you are checking off by days and years. *You will redate everything to the moment when He enters your program.*

Listen! There may yet appear one greater than Plato, one wiser than Shakespeare. That is quite possible. But the Christ can have no rival. He is the end, as well as the beginning. What He did for Mark He does for this generation.

Ask Jesus Christ to demonstrate in your life! Mark gives you his investigation. He writes it for all to see—the claim of the Son of God, "All power is given unto me in heaven and in earth" (Matthew 28:18). Mark says, "Put Him to the test!"

CHOICE NOT CHANCE

Text: *"I can do all things through Christ which strengtheneth me."*

Philippians 4:13

THE Gospel parts company with this world's philosophy that fate, not faith, is in ascendancy. Yes, choice involves *resignation*, but how? It never implies the negative attitude of drifting and dreaming, of saying, "What can I do about it anyhow?"

The Gospel commands me to *realization*. It demands the full use of the eternal powers within my soul. It says to me, "Be more than a conqueror!" It is not a taunting, teasing, ever-striving and never-obtaining proposition. It is simply, "I can do all things through Christ which *strengtheneth* me."

The Gospel places Jesus Christ front and center. *Unlimited* resources of resurrection victory are placed at my disposal. No longer am I confined. I am not a child of *fate*. I am an heir of *faith*. This converts impossibility into possibility. It turns a planet of obstacle, drudgery and boundary into an earth of excitement, surprise and victory.

Man's own accomplishments are vast, *but not big enough*. Man cannot find the answer to permanent peace. Man cannot banish death. He cannot compel another to be generous. He cannot insure that genius, industry and management will follow in his children. His offspring may turn out to be squanderers and pleasure-seekers.

There is always a ceiling to what man can do. "The things which are impossible with man *are possible with God*" (Luke 18:27). It is a matter of superior association. Of all possibilities opened to the human race, this is the greatest—*"with God."*

This is the remedy for frustration. It is "not my will but Thine be done." It is the joy of *trusting* instead of the weariness of *trying*. It is a baptism of divine strength. I give to get. I surrender to succeed. I let go and let God.

It changed Abram to Abraham. Only an addressee, living somewhere amid a tangle of streets in the ancient city of Ur, he became the friend of God and a pattern of righteousness. How? He made this marvelous adjustment. *Three times he relinquished the gaining of material ends by human means;* giving up his city residence; letting Lot take the best of the land; refusing the spoils of Sodom.

Was he a wishy-washy sentimentalist? Was he an ideological push-over? No. He was moved by faith. *He chose.* He put God's will and covenant for his life first. *God, not Kismet, is the ruling principle of the believer's life.*

Again he resigns the son born after the flesh—Ishmael, whom he loved. What was left? What other possible answer could there be? What lies beyond human resources? The answer is Isaac, the child of promise, God's provision. *History has not finished writing the pages of Abraham's decision to trust God, to work with God, all the way.*

Reluctance vanishes. Faith crescendos. Back in the beginning this man comes to grips with immortality. He flings asunder the fatalism of the Chaldeans. *He is decided upon a trial case.* He refuses the dogma that man ceases with the grave. Something out of this world storms in his soul. It is Columbus believing in another world, and sailing on. It is the nineteen-sixties believing in space travel. *He is willing to risk forever being tagged a murderer rather than fail in his quest for resurrection facts.*

It was not a celestial lottery that came up with the name of Moses. It is not being born under some lucky or unlucky star, mister. No, sir! It is not that at all. It is letting God put His eternal hand around yours.

There is a time, place and purpose in the will of God. The young prince of Egypt tried to ferment a national rising in his own strength. The results were disastrous.

Faith demands implicit obedience. Forty years of incognito in Midian were not wasted years. They steeled the "Lincoln of the Old Testament" in patience and singleness of purpose.

With an unshakable faith, Moses knew the day of Israel's deliverance had come. Every moment of every day in those forty years the nomad dedicated himself to one sublime passion, "I shall return to Egypt, and when I do, I shall go in the might of God to perform God's mission."

What a difference faith makes! It changes your life from lever-pulling, sweepstake chances and dependence upon the vagaries of the draw to a confidence that smiles at contradictory symptoms.

David refused twice to kill Saul when he had his hunter at his mercy. Why? Did not chance favor him? No. Luck is no foundation at all. Faith secured the promise of God to David. God had spoken. That was enough.

I do not say this life is an easy life. It is not. The desire to figure the odds for yourself is a strong pull in human beings. The temptation to place a wager is almost overwhelming. The sovereign right to figure the answers for oneself is not easy to abdicate. *The agony of human renunciation is a very real grief.* Personal hopes are crucified. Ambitions are trampled. Ego is humiliated.

Paul spoke from experience when he said, "Not I but Christ." It demands a Calvary in every life before there can be a glorious resurrection of unlimited possibility.

What is your attitude toward life, sir? Are you a take-it-as-it-comes person? Are you saying to me, "I will take my chances, Mr. Ward"? *What wheel of fortune is spinning for you?* What act of redemption depends upon capriciousness? What gate of heaven opens upon chance? What crown of righteousness is earned by luck? What have you chosen?

The Creator of us all has personalized the choice for every son of Adam. The crossroads are in Jesus Christ. Rejection or acceptance decides the issue. I either turn my back to God's will and help for my life or I submit to a Higher Power than my own and trust in His plan for me.

The contest is the most unfair proposal ever designated. *Chance cannot compete with choice*. The odds against chance make it no contest. No one has ever been saved by chance. No one has ever been honest, virtuous, loving by chance. No one has ever made paradise by chance. I am not a pawn in the Master Player's hand. *I am the player*. I make the moves.

This becomes the crowning resolution of physical life. I will make my moves *in, through* and *by* Him. It is no longer "I." It is "together."

It is as foolish for me to live without what is available to me through Christ's victory as it would be foolish for me to live without modern utilities, transportation and communication. Why should I rob myself of these facilities of electricity, automobiles and television?

Just so, why should you be without God, my friend? Why should you limit yourself? Why should your life be dormant? Why should it be insensitive to eternal possibilities like Abraham's seed of faith, a family of countless millions, the welcome of Moses into another world, the deep mysteries explored by David?

Are you going to throw your life away? Are you going to treat your destiny as though it were a toss of a coin?

No, sir, I do not have to resign myself to the inevitable, waiting for the final release of death. I have the offer to draw upon unlimited help. It is up to me. That offer is bonafide. It cannot be withdrawn without notice. It is a pledge. God has placed the words "New Testament" upon it.

He has given it a final reading. There can be no revision to this agreement. Calvary is the eternal bond that has been posted. The moment I exercise faith the contract is in force. *I can have all the help I need*.

Is my life opaque? Am I only an echo? No, sir! That is not it at all. The strength of desire is there. The will to be is strong. I am conscious of aim and conquest.

Mr. Norman Grubb pointed out on one occasion the emphasis of Psalm 37:4, "Delight thyself in the Lord, and he shall give thee the desires of *thine* heart"—*thine,* your desires, not His.

Move the control center of your life over to Jesus Christ, *and let desires come.* Let them grow big and husky! Let them reach out and almost frighten you! Let them make fantastic claims! Let them bridge continents like Paul and promote revivals that stir cities like Ephesus, Corinth and Rome!

Let them invite the sick to walk on the sunny side of the street so that a shadow of healing may fall upon them like Peter experienced! Let them know the moment of exaltation like Stephen knew when the Son of God arose to welcome him into eternity! Let them believe for miracle! Let them peer into the future like John! Let those desires pound in your soul like blood in your body when it is stirred by passion and vision!

That is life in Jesus Christ, mister. A more abundant, more satisfying life than you ever thought was possible.

Realization, not resignation, is the ultimate. *That is the story of Christian living.*

Faith is action. It is exactly what Hebrews 11:1 says it is, "Now faith is the substance of things hoped for, the evidence of things not seen." *Only faith makes the "big world" possible here and now.*

———————◆—————————

CONSCIENCE— RECORD—GOD

Text: *"For God shall bring every work into judgment, with every secret thing, whether it be good, or whether it be evil."*
Ecclesiastes 12:14

I AM going to talk to you about *eternal matters.* Conscience, record, and God are with you today, and they will be with you tomorrow.

Conscience is that inner voice you have heard a thousand times. It has made you unhappy when everyone around you has been happy. It keeps you awake at night on expensive springs topped by a foam rubber mattress. It forbids you to eat at a table loaded with tempting food. Conscience makes you ache with pain that an angel cannot relieve.

Thank God, you have a conscience! Before radar, before sonar, before compass, the Eternal provided every son of Adam with this built-in navigational direction-finder.

The pangs and pains of an outraged conscience are to the soul, what pain and suffering of the flesh are to an outraged body.

Thank God for it, mister! A pain in my lung is a warning of mercy. It says to me, "You need a physician. You need help." A pain in my head says, "Ward, you need rest." It is a voice that tells me, "Watch out! Danger!"

Yet how unwilling we are to bear pain. We shrink from it. We race for relief. God put pain in that finger, sir, to protect it. It is present at all times to say to you immediately, "This finger is too valuable, and too irreplaceable for you to trifle with. It means too much to you. Do something about it. Send for the physician!"

Your conscience is saying the same thing, mister. It says to you, "Do not trifle with your soul. Something is wrong. Send for the Great Physician."

Every human being has a *record*. You have your record; I have mine. Pontius Pilate said it for all of us, "What I have written, *I* have written." No one else writes your record for you. *You write your own.*

You and God know that record, sir. You know whether you have stolen anything. You know whether you have lied. You know whether you have been impure.

Take a good look at that record! An old American ballad

describes that record when it says, "Me and *my shadow.*" It is an inseparable part of me.

I ask you, what is your record as a church member? What is your record as a parent? What is your record as a citizen? *What is your record before God?*

What side have you chosen? What have you supported? Upon what have you placed your vote? Where does your sympathy lie? How often, and for what purpose, have you stood to be counted? What deals have you made? Whom have you betrayed?

You live with it, mister! You have a right to be uneasy. God says, "That which you have spoken in darkness . . . shall be proclaimed upon the housetops" (Luke 12:3). I am talking to you about something that is real. *You have a record.*

You snicker. You say, "Preacher, why don't you wise up? Why don't you speak about more pleasant things? There is no aftermath. The brimstone idea in preaching went out with the horse and buggy."

Auntie had the best answer for the little fellow who came to her after a service like this and asked her, "Where does God get His brimstone from?"

She replied, "Ah, honey, *every sinner takes his own brimstone to hell.*" And when you can erase the facts of conscience and record, I will quit preaching like this.

Conscience and record say to you, and they say to me, *there is a Judgment Day.* Each one of us will have his or her day in court.

Count on that, sir! *The books will be opened.* Each record will be examined. Each warning of conscience will be entered as testimony. You will be given a chance to be heard before the "Supreme Court" of the universe. It will be too late for mercy. You have demanded a fair trial, *and you will get a fair trial, sinner.*

I ask you, *who incorporated in mankind the desire and the*

ability to keep records? What is the source of this urge? Answer that, and I will tell you that the same Eternal Source is doing about you and about me what He has inserted into our lives to do about other things.

Yes, sir! There is all the evidence, meticulously gathered and unabridged. No one will cheat on you in that day. You will get exactly what you deserve under the law of God.

That is how the trial will be held, my friend! It will not be held under the constitution and bylaws of your local service club or yacht society. That makes a difference, does it not?

A copy of those rules is available now. *You should have a Bible.* You and I are going to be judged by that book of rules. Remember that!

There are only three means of acquittal under the law. You may be acquitted by:

a. force of law

b. force of testimony

c. force of pardon

First, if a man is arraigned and brought into court, and the evidence is conclusive as to his guilt, the judge may say, "Gentlemen, the crime is proven against the prisoner. But there is no law upon the statute books of this community which says it is a crime; therefore, you must acquit this man, because he has violated no law of the community." *That person is free by force of law.*

Count on it! You and I will never be punished for something that is not punishable, *regardless of what others may think.* I am answerable to God. I will be judged by His laws.

A lot of folk have their ideas about me. In their eyes I stand convicted. My life does not fit their pattern of behavior. They ask that I be prosecuted. They never let up on me. But I will never be condemned by God unless I have broken His law.

Second, if it is a crime under the statutes of the community, and the trial has progressed until the last witness has testified, the judge may say to the jury, "Ladies and gentlemen of the jury, the witnesses have not made out a reasonable case against the defendant; therefore, you must acquit him." *That person is free by force of testimony.*

Nothing will be rigged. It will not be a Nazi, Fascist, or Communist court. The state will not rule arbitrarily. You and I are not going to face a tyrant or imposter. The verdict will be rendered on complete testimony open to cross examination.

What testimony are you prepared to call? Can you prove beyond reasonable doubt that you have always told the absolute truth? Have you ever coveted? Have you ever borne false witness? That means *have you ever passed along gossip.* That means did you always come to a friend's defense when that friend was being unjustly criticized behind his back? Have you ever hated or resented? What will the testimony show?

No wonder a great many of you never open the Bible! It looks you straight in the eye. That is why. You will face the Bible at Judgment, sir. And ignorance will be no excuse.

If law and testimony cannot save you, there is only one other force which can. *That is the force of pardon.* You have the God-given right to apply for full pardon. Throw yourself upon the mercy of the court. Thank God for the altar! I have been there and it is the sweetest place on earth.

If my salvation depended upon how perfect a life I could live, then I would be a lost soul. I know, sir, that Jesus Christ is the Friend to imperfect men like myself, to sinners.

The law of God is perfect. There are no loopholes. It covers my case from cradle to coffin. *There will be no hearsay evidence.* The evidence will be written—every day, every location, every circumstance.

Mister, if we can attach telltale memories to the planes we fly and the trucks we drive that account for every mile of travel and every moment of rest, do you doubt that Almighty God can or does keep a detailed record of your life?

Everywhere in this world there are little mechanical fingers that write. We are surrounded by them. I am watched and recorded in a thousand ways every day. Bills are honored and paid because some meter says it is so. And in God's heaven of heavens there is a silent pen recording my life's story.

Would you like God to read one page of that record of yours publicly in your church next Sunday morning? Your record is as sacred and as true as the Bible you hold in your hand. *It is held inviolate.*

My mother in heaven cannot change it. My wife on her knees cannot change it. Your preacher with all his influence cannot change it. *Only God can expunge it, blot it out.*

I will tell you one thing I believe. Some of you may question me about this. *I do not believe God has ever given any man the power to be an infidel,* to be absolutely convinced without qualm of conscience, without inner questioning, without probing Holy Ghost conviction, without times of deep remorse and moral gloom, that the Bible is fiction, there is no Judgment, that God is only a convenient idea.

I have seen men who said they were infidels converted. Nothing could have reached them had they been what they claimed. No, sir, *infidelity is an act,* bravely staged, but only an act.

If your record will not stand in court, where can you regain your lost condition? What can your *scientist* do for you? He can make your laundry whiter. He can make your hair dressing a little less sticky. He can make your body odor a little less noticeable.

But what can he do for your conscience? How can he change your record? Are you any less a liar, or any less a thief because you wear whiter linen, or your hair stays in place longer, or you perspire a little less freely?

What can your *educator* do for you? He can suggest to you

that long ago you were nothing but a squirrel. He can make you wonder how you ever became a man, and in the process acquired a conscience and a sense of guilt.

Ask the educator, "Sir, what is going to become of me?" He will answer, "I do not know. I can take a breed of horses and little by little purify the bloodline until I produce a thoroughbred. I do not know why I cannot do it to men. *I do not know.*" That is what the educator will say to you.

Where can you go for cleansing and pardon? I say to you. Head for the Cross. Head for Calvary. Learn for yourself what the Blood can do for you! Know instantaneously what it is to have a free conscience and to read your record clear.

> There is a fountain filled with blood,
> Drawn from Immanuel's veins,
> And sinners, plunged beneath that flood,
> Lose all their guity stains.

That is our one hope, sir. It lies in a full pardon.

———————◄◆►———————

THOUGHTS WHILE VISITING A MUSEUM

Text: *"For love is strong as death."*

Song of Solomon 8:6

RECENTLY I spent a portion of an afternoon in the Museum of Natural History at one of our large American universities. Authorities on the campus had allegedly traced the beginnings of man back 75,000,000 years. I do not know how far back they intend to go.

I came away with the same feeling I have always had. *I am more interested in my future than I am in my past.* Where do I go from here?

If man's past has been carefully concealed, no less is his future hidden. Man has pried apart some secrets in the universe. But neither sweat, tears nor prayers have availed to wring from the lips of Nature the mystery that hangs above man's grave.

It has been said that no banker has yet devised a vault of steel that cannot be penetrated by a professional safe-cracker. But Death can build a wall that defies attack.

Death makes all of us reverent. Shallowness has no secrets. It is superficiality that tells the full story. But the *unseen forces* —the chemists in the roots, the monarchs of the clouds, the giant forces in the harvests—work in secrecy and silence.

The law of gravity does not blow a trumpet before it functions. The sunbeam does not lift up its voice and scream for attention. *Death does not debate with us.*

No one, in the museum that I visited, had delved into what might be the history of man, say, 75,000,000 years from now. Why? Has man no future? *Am I totally eliminated after a brief appearance?* Has anyone asked these questions?

I turn to the "Sage of Concord," *Ralph Waldo Emerson,* my countryman, who thought long and deeply upon this subject. His conclusion is a matter of record.

"The resurrection and the continuance of our being is granted. We carry the pledge of this in our own breast. I maintain merely that we cannot say in what form or in what manner our existence will be continued."

Later on, in his last essay, which was a study of immortality, Emerson said:

"Man is to live hereafter. That the world is for his education, is the only sane solution of the enigma. The planting of a desire indicates that the gratification of that desire is in the constitution of the creature that feels it. The Creator keeps His word with us all. *What I have seen teaches me to trust the Creator for all I have not seen.*"

Channing, the scholar, thought with disciplined mind about this matter. He noted that once the peach or pear tree had borne leaves, blossoms and fruit, *its highest end had been fulfilled.* Both root and trunk had, through ripened fruit, touched their climax. Though generations might sweep over the fragrant orchard, they could bring to the tree this alone—leaf, blossom, ripened fruit.

If a few years enable the tree to exhaust its every power and fulfill Nature's every pledge, man's fourscore years hardly avail to grow the root of possibility, much less to exhaust the latent powers of mind and spirit.

But God, who gave *the tree* time to attain its utmost perfection, will not crowd the soul with faculties that demand an eternity for their unfolding, and then cut man off with a brief handful of years. That is what Channing believed.

No inventor like *George Stephenson,* the locomotive builder, ever had time to work out a tithe of his inventive thoughts. *Coleridge* left the outlines for several hundred incompleted volumes.

Michaelangelo had to divide his life of ninety years into three periods; giving one period to architecture, one to painting and one to sculpture. In his old age, having given a lifetime to poetry, *Tennyson* expressed the desire for a like period for music, and similar epochs for science, art and history.

No man ever has enough time, except for one thing—*to get ready for eternity.*

When *Southey* knew that he must die, he asked to be carried to his library. There the old scholar went wistfully from book to book, handling each like a dear friend and bidding each a last farewell.

No man loved the outdoors more than *Wordsworth* and *Bryant.* Having observed with what skill the swallow builds its nest; with what foresight the squirrel lays up its store against the winter; with what art the spider spins its web and the wild fowl finds its way through the pathless air, these men concluded that if *the instinct* means so much to animals, *it must mean even more to man.*

Wordsworth believed the soul's birth-gifts include the instincts of God and immortality. No education, no revelation gives the instinct of immortal life, he believed; *God bequeaths it.*

That is why Bryant wrote:

"He who, from zone to zone,
    Guides through the boundless sky thy certain flight,
In the long way that I must tread alone
    Will lead my steps aright."

Bryant felt that because animals had never been deceived by instinct, God's guidebook to the art of living, it was safe for man to trust the instinct of immortality.

Science has been asked to umpire the battle between brawn and brains, body and mind.

What limitations can be placed upon the mind of man? The eye can be abetted by telescope and microscope, both fashioned from man's thought. Muscle can be increased a thousandfold by the triphammer. The footstep can be increased to stride a continent at a time by jet and rocket travel.

This inside person has invented a thousand instruments that now fulfill the duties of the body. *The body faces a boundary. The mind has no frontier.*

John Fiske affirmed that immortality is the one mighty goal toward which nature has been working from the very beginning.

Oh, yes, mister, there is something very definite out there!

Centuries ago *Plato* expressed the hope that at some future time the moral law that he recognized incorporated in the planet, *might become a person;* that, beholding, all mankind might stand amazed and entranced. He felt that *law* alone was an abstraction too cold to kindle the heart's enthusiasm.

Jesus Christ is the fulfillment of that hope. He entered the earthly scene. He came to teach the disciples of Socrates that nothing evil can befall a good man after death. He came to fulfill the thought of Cicero, that ideals are overtures of immortality. He fulfills Bryant's hope that he who notes the sparrow's fall will guard his children's graves.

I stood one day in the gallery of the Vatican in Rome. I read on one side the Christian inscriptions, copies from the catacombs. On the other side I read the inscriptions that were written on the Roman temples. Into the temples was carved a single sigh, "Farewell, farewell, *and forever farewell."* But from the catacombs were lifted these words, "He who dies in Christ dies in peace and *hope."*

I am glad that I am a creature of hope. *The certainty of immortality is the very genius of Christ's mission and message.* Paul tells Timothy that Jesus Christ has "brought life and immortality to light through the gospel."

Christ's coming has made the difference. Before He came Cicero could only say:

"There is, I know not how, in the minds of men a certain presage, as it were, of a future existence, and this takes the deepest root and is most discoverable in the greatest geniuses and most exalted souls."

That is all Cicero could say. But after Christ came, Daniel Webster on his deathbed could say:

"My general wish on earth has been to do my Master's will. That there is a God, all must acknowledge. I see Him in all these wondrous works.

"What would be the condition of any of us if we had not the hope of immortality? What ground is there to rest upon but the Gospel?

"There were scattered hopes of the immortality of the soul, especially among the Jews. The Romans never reached it; the Greeks never received it. There were intimations crepuscular twilight; but, but, but God, in the Gospel of Jesus Christ, brought life and immortality to light."

That is what Daniel Webster could say.

Think not so much of your *past,* sir! Think of your *future!*

You will find more challenge at God's altar than you will in man's museum.

In Jesus Christ you will find the fullness of argument, far, far beyond the probings of Emerson, Channing, Michaelangelo, Plato or Cicero. He who holds a bunch of crimson roses in his hand needs no botany to tell him that roses are beautiful. When the birds are in the hedges and the wheat is in the shock, no man needs an almanac to learn that it is summer.

I ask you to meet the Master, sir! To know Him is to know life eternal. Every doubt is dissolved. Every hunger is satisfied.

The poet, Browning, said it for every believer:

> "I go to prove my soul;
> I see my way as birds their trackless way.
> I shall arrive! What time, what circuit first,
> I ask not; but unless God sends his hail
> Or blinding fireballs, sleet or stifling snow,
> In good time, his good time, I shall arrive.
> He guides me and the bird. In his good time."

Do you have that faith as your hour of departure nears? Do not look *backward*. Look *forward*.

FOUR TINY MESSENGERS

Text: *"There be four things which are little upon the earth, but they are exceeding wise: The ants are a people not strong, yet they prepare their meat in the summer; The conies are but a feeble folk, yet make they their houses in the rocks; The locusts have no king, yet go they forth all of them by bands; The spider taketh hold with her hands, and is in king's palaces."*

Proverbs 30:24-28

EVANGELIST S. A. Bishop of Birmingham, Alabama, under whose ministry my life's direction was settled when I was in my late teens, and who recently was called to the other side, was fond of quoting this text. He used this passage from the Proverbs to instill guidelines into many a young life, including my own.

First, THE SPIDER.

"The spider taketh hold with her hands, and is in king's palaces." *The spider has great opposition, but it never gives up the fight.* You may sweep her web down in the morning, but she will weave it back that night with such finesse and exactness that no art can compare with it.

The Creator has given the spider a built-in, fool-proof guarantee against *discouragement.* You cannot break its spirit without first having to destroy the spider. The spider teaches us a lesson of *irresistible perseverance.*

No man is ever saved who does not *want* to be saved. "If any man *will* do his will, he shall know" (John 7:17). Put whatever will you have on God's side. That is the first step.

I know some people who are too scared to go to hell and too weak to go to heaven. God pity such miserable souls! Jesus said, "And ye shall be hated of all men for my name's sake: but he that shall *endure* unto the end, the same shall be saved" (Mark 13:13).

Every athlete is expected to absorb blows and attacks. Every soldier is trained to resist and counter-attack. Every student is taught to wrestle with examinations. The New Testament says, "Thou therefore endure hardness, as a good soldier of Jesus Christ" (2 Timothy 2:3).

I am amazed at professing Christians who will spend a good part of a day playing golf and thrill to battling par and obstacles. They want a course with bunker and sand-trap, with dog-leg fairway and water hazard. It puts zest into their game. *These same professing Christians shrink from a life of faith where God has sprinkled the course to eternity with a few obstacles.*

The spider is always preaching me a sermon. She "taketh hold with her hands." She had a lesson to teach those who grumble about how badly the world has treated them, and never think about how badly they have treated the world.

You and I owe this world something, sir! We owe our nation, our community, our family, our church something. The spider has God's message for those who are always waiting for others to do for them what they could do for themselves. There are too many looking for *a handout* instead of using their own hands. Soiled hands are no disgrace to anyone.

A passage in Hebrews recalls the stuff out of which Old Testament heroes were made, "who through faith subdued kingdoms, wrought righteousness, obtained promises, stopped the mouths of lions, quenched the violence of fire . . . out of weakness were made strong, *waxed valiant in fight*" (Hebrews 11: 33, 34).

Give God that kind of attitude, and He will crown you more than a conqueror! Remember those words the next time you see a spider. The spider never gives up the fight but repels opposition and endures tragic failure. She always fights back. She accepts the challenge to prove herself equal to the contest.

Second, THE ANT.

Here is another little thing that God has put in this world for our admonition. *The ant teaches us to make use of present opportunity.* Ants are not strong, yet they are wise and industrious in gathering proper food and doing it at the proper time. *They always keep the future in mind.*

Human instinct tells man the same thing. "Behold, now is the accepted time; behold, now is the day of salvation" (2 Corinthians 6:2).

The first clause of the verse I have just quoted, *"Now is the accepted time,"* has been on my office desk for many years. *I believe it is the secret of getting things done.* Get at them at once! Act now!

There is no sorrow or grief like the despair of lost opportunity. I wish I could recoup those losses—a paragraph I meant to clip from a newspaper or magazine, and neglected to do so—an invitation I was slow to acknowledge and suddenly it was withdrawn—a bargain I meant to investigate and thought it would last another day. *My most precious commodity is time.*

"How shall we escape, if we neglect so great salvation?" (Hebrews 2:3). *Neglect is stupidity.* The devil is making millions of otherwise good people look stupid. He tells them, "There is still time. Do not panic! Think about it a little more. God will never close the gates of mercy. You can have the best of both worlds if you play it shrewdly."

Mister, the devil is taking you. God says to you, "Go to the ant . . . consider her ways, and be wise. Which having no guide, overseer, or ruler, provideth her meat in the summer, and gathereth her food in the harvest" (Proverbs 6:6-8).

Do not trifle with your health and do not trifle with your soul. Peter says, "Wherefore the rather, brethren, give diligence to make your calling and election sure: for if ye do these things, ye shall never fall" (2 Peter 1:10).

Too many prizes have been lost by taking things for granted. *You can lose your soul that way.* More than one person has said to the evangelist, "I guess I am all right." People say the same thing about their health. They will not go to see a doctor. They will not submit to a physical checkup. Suddenly they are gone.

Face it today, mister! Get to that altar. Let the Holy Spirit check your life. *Be prepared!*

Remember this admonition the next time you see an ant. The ant teaches us the value of time, and the great necessity of that which is to come. "The night cometh, when no man can work" (John 9:4). Your quitting time, sir, may be right around the corner.

Third, THE LOCUST.

"The locusts have no king, yet go they forth all of them by bands." *This little fellow tells us what happens when there is a willingness to concentrate and unite.* A force can be set in motion that nothing can stop.

I remember the plague that swept out of our dust bowls. I drove through swarms that shut out much of the light of the sun, making it dangerous to travel. They became a slippery mass under the skid of my tires. They devoured everything. They stripped. They plundered. Their destructive power was unlimited. Every nation in this world fears a plague of locusts.

Nothing is gained by division and strife. The secret of the power and success of the Early Church is seen in Acts 2: 42-47. They were "together," and "with one accord." Paul exhorts the individualistic Colossian believers, "Forbearing one another, and forgiving one another, if any man have a quarrel against any: even as Christ forgave you, so also do ye" (Colossians 3:13).

The great Confederate general, Stonewall Jackson, ran his army on two commands (1) keep your ranks closed (2) keep moving. With these two commands uppermost he was a threat to the Union until his death.

Paul knew the power of the full church of Jesus Christ. He sets it forth in classic language when he states:

"For the body is not one member, but many. If the foot shall say, Because I am not the hand, I am not of the body; is it therefore not of the body? And if the ear shall say, Because I am not the eye, I am not of the body; is it therefore not of the body?

"If the whole body were an eye, where were the hearing? If the whole were hearing, where were the smelling?

"But now are they many members, yet but one body" (1 Corinthians 12:14-17, 20).

This little fellow, the locust, realizes he does not have much force to exert individually and alone. *So he goes forth in bands.*

It does us all good to keep in mind at all times the value of teamwork. *A massed force is a winning force.* Concentration brings realization.

Fourth, THE CONY.

Here is one more little creature on God's earth with *a big message.* "The conies are a feeble folk, yet they make their houses in the rocks." *They realize that they are an easy prey and that they need a refuge.* Would to God that everyone of us might have that much sense!

My security is in the Rock. I pray that the Holy Spirit may whisper these lines to you as I repeat them:

> "Rock of Ages cleft for me,
> Let me hide myself in Thee."

> "Other refuge have I none,
> Hangs my helpless soul on Thee."

David said, "Lead me to the rock that is higher than I. For thou hast been a shelter for me, and a strong tower from the enemy" (Psalm 61:2, 3).

I cannot tell you how often in my own life I have breathed a quick sigh, "Jesus, help me now," and I have found the same refuge. This is not poetic language. *This is reality.*

I believe with all my soul the passage which says, "The name of the Lord is a strong tower: the righteous runneth into it, and is safe" (Proverbs 18:10). *I know it works.* I cannot explain the mystery of it. I can testify to the reality of it.

All of us are like these little creatures. *We are easy prey.* The evil in this world "walketh about seeking whom it may devour." Millions of our fellow human beings are caught in the claws of intemperance, greed, revenge, perversion, folly, profanity and bitter memory. *No man is a match for evil in himself.*

The biggest lie the devil tells, he tells to the perfectly mannered young man or strictly raised young woman that he or she —depending upon breeding, culture and favorable background alone—can venture into the mainstream of society and retain such ideals untarnished. He says the world will welcome such a change; that you can mingle and be recognized and appreciated for what you are, high-class, a cut or two above the average; that extraordinary ability does not have to prostitute itself to climb the ladder of success.

I ask you to look at the human wreckage all around you. If you are going to play the world's game, you are going to have to accept the world's rules.

Call me what you want! *I need a hiding place.* The greatest sense of all is to recognize your own need in time to do something about it—in time to find *salvation.*

The Rock of Ages, Jesus Christ, the Son of God, is that hiding place.

COME UNTO ME

Text: *"For my yoke is easy, and my burden is light."*
Matthew 11:30

I COULD have selected as the title for this message, "The *Yoke* and the *Burden.*" That about describes it.

This invitation to complete rest is personal, "Come unto *me.*" It does not say, "Come unto the church, or officials, or members."

I respect organizations. I work with organizations. Yet there is something mechanical about them. I am not sure that any organization really *understands* any of us. They keep a file on us. We receive statements and reports. My logistics are on cards fed into an electronic data processor.

Does that file, or that mechanical brain, or that set of books really understand me? *I am not the same as a million other members.* I never shall be the same. I cannot be lumped together with thousands of others and put in due process. There can never be any salvation that way. Somebody has to know who I am, and why I am that way.

This might sound like egotism, a selfish demand that God take time to think about *me.* It is not that at all. It is just that I came into this world somebody, and I need help, and help from someone who cares about me.

My doctor must make an individual diagnosis. His first question to me always is, *"Where* does it hurt, or *how* were you hurt?" He wants me to tell him all about it. Often he goes deep into my past. He wants a complete case history. *He wants to be sure that he is handling my case correctly, and making the correct application of his art to me.*

Jesus says, "Come unto Me. I have never missed the diagnosis of a single case. I will treat you personally. I understand your problem. I am never misled by the symptoms. I can place My finger on the diseased spot. I know where the breakdown started. I know what must be done. Come unto *Me.*"

Follow His treatment in the New Testament. He puts His finger on the Rich Young Ruler's dilemma—the hold of wealth upon his life. He understands Nicodemus—the need of miracle life, a new birth, to satisfy where morality failed. He senses the malignancy of Simon the Pharisee—jealousy. He deals so quickly with Matthew and sees the frustration in this businessman's life.

Come to Jesus, sir, and you will feel for the first time in your life that Someone really *understands* you. It is a marvelous experience.

It is so simple! God created us, unless you want to believe

in this "monkey business." I have always thought that was a poor alternative. It is not much of a choice that the ungodly offer.

Since God created us, is it not the right thing to do, the common sense thing to do, to take yourself to the Lord and say, "Here I am. My life is not running right. I am out of order. Something is wrong. Fix my life! Set me in order so I will function in the way I was intended to function." *Can you think of anything better to do?*

Perhaps you are tempted to think that the Lord does not mean you. *The invitation is for everyone who is in trouble.* God means for you to take this invitation at face value. It is not mockery.

If you are saying, "I am wrong and I want to be right; I am stained and I want to be clean; I am guilt-ridden and I want to have peace," *this invitation is for you.*

A young, successful Christian businessman drove me to the Indianapolis Airport the other day from my hotel. He filled the conversation with his testimony.

Doyle Bryant's life was wrecked. He worked, but his real income was from gambling. He wanted money but he wanted it faster than a regular paycheck could provide it. He gambled incessantly from mid-Friday to early Monday morning every week and drove himself with liquor until his health broke.

His wife and five-year-old daughter were the victims of his obsession. His agony drew his hands until the fingers curled as though afflicted with arthritis. Time after time he writhed in pain and snaked to and fro on the floor. He lived on drug injections and nerve pills. Nothing helped.

His weight dropped from 168 pounds to 128 pounds. He chain smoked. He stood for fifteen minutes under hot and cold water showers ten and twelve times a day. Eight different physicians tried to help him. He was placed under psychiatric care.

Doyle Bryant needed this invitation, "Come unto me." It

covered his case. He decided to find out for himself. *He decided to take his case to Jesus Christ.* It worked the first time he went to the altar. Within four weeks he was a well man, sound and whole enough to hold down a full-time job.

Today the debts are liquidated. He is among the ten top salesmen for his organization. He and Mrs. Bryant own their own home. They are one of the happiest couples in the community. Doyle Bryant thinks it is high adventure today to bring others to church, and to Christ, whose lives are as tangled as his own life once was.

Somewhere, someone has told you that only certain predestined folk are to be saved. If you happen to hold a lucky number, everything will turn out all right in the end for you. If you do not hold a winning ticket there is nothing that can reach you.

Do not believe it! This invitation is for everyone. That "Come" is for *you.* I believe if you are lost, there will be a crown in heaven no one will ever wear. I believe if you are lost, you will never be able to say at the judgment throne, "I am lost because I never was meant to be saved."

Some of you are working and laboring so hard to make yourselves good men and good women. God wants you to find the easy way and the happy way through His Son, Jesus Christ. I congratualte people who want to be decent, who tell the truth, who practice honesty.

I know how desperate you feel so many times surrounded by clever deception, cheap and shoddy living and cheating. You feel like throwing away the bridle and saddle and riding unrestrained. You feel like turning your life loose and having a fling, although you know it will lead to disaster, but you say, "Who cares? What am I getting out of it? It is such a bother to try and be different."

You need Jesus Christ, my friend. That is why the invitation is to the weary, as well as the heavy laden.

Mountain climbers are not ashamed to employ the services of a guide. *Why should you be ashamed to ask Jesus to help you with your aspirations to a higher, nobler life?* People get weary. Church people get weary. Fine, honest merchants get weary. We cannot make it without Christ's help.

This is a tired world. Many of our jobs get monotonous. We want to run away. The tempter shoves at us. He whispers, "Break loose for a spell! Go out on the town once in awhile."

Calvary is for the *weary,* as well as for the heavy laden. Keep that in mind! Lots of us need this divine rest. Make no mistake about it! You get tired in this world. You get tired trying to keep yourself decent. You get tired trying to raise your children the right way. It is work, labor, to keep going to church three and four times a week for years.

God knows that, my brother! That is why this invitation is for tired people. *This is a world of struggle.* Many people do not even know what they want. They spend and are spent.

Someone is saying, "I will give *you* rest." Head toward Jesus Christ! Say to yourself right now, "If that is rest, that is what I want."

Conscious sin weighs you down. Nothing is such a drag on your life. The fact that you are breaking God's laws, and that you know you are breaking them is torment. Your life is unharnessed. It is getting away from you. You are not heading in the direction you planned to go when you were still in your early teens. It frightens you.

"Take my yoke upon you." That is the answer. Live a disciplined, directed, worthy life with Jesus Christ at your side. He can bring your life into subjection as easily and as calmly as He quieted the stormy sea.

Pride has torn you apart. Ambition has made you selfish and cruel. You have betrayed friendships. You have been a part of schemes and unprincipled acts to get ahead. You have trampled on virtue and trust to build reputation.

You wanted the front page. Now you have it; but you have something else as well—emptiness, a hollow existence without meaning.

The answer is in this text, "Learn of me; for I am meek and lowly in heart: and ye shall find rest unto your souls" (Matthew 11:29).

This Man of Calvary can build a dam across your turbulent life that is full of rapids and boiling narrows, and make the stream of your life flow quietly.

It takes submission. That is what "the yoke" means. You must let Jesus Christ be Master. You must give Him the place that belongs to Him—the control center of your life. It will mean the end of doing only what pleases you, of going only where you want to go, of saying only what you want to say. You will have company.

Sinner, you have been free too long to get drunk, free too long to tell lies, free too long to marry and divorce. *You need someone to turn you into the path of righteousness.*

Your freedom will lead you to perdition. You need an attachment stronger than your decision to turn over a new leaf, or joining the church, or helping with public charity. You need the strength of the Son of God at your side.

That does not mean idleness or the end of adventure. A "yoke" means activity, work, doing things! You will never be as busy as when you serve God. You will never go so many places and want to do so many things! *I have found the Christian life exciting.* A real Christian will never be arrested for vagrancy.

Do you remember what someone said to George Whitefield, the great preacher and companion of the Wesleys? He said, "Whitefield, you must not preach more than four hours a day, and six on Sunday." Whitefield answered, "Do you want me to rust to death?"

When you love Jesus, sir; when you are tied into His program of redemption, the more you work the better you like it. You never feel like quitting.

That is what the "yoke" does for you. It is the lightest burden you ever felt when you are with royal company. Then you will think of the burdens that weighed you down, the awful load of sin that threatened to crush you. You will think of the load of drunkenness that filled you with horrid taste and sordid memory. You will think of the load of loss that filled your gambling misery with heartache. You will think of the load of lies and subversion that burdened you and threatened at every moment to expose you.

Whatever the Lord asks you *to do* in comparison, whatever He asks you *to give;* whatever He asks you *to bear* for Him; will seem "light" in comparison.

And the best of all will be at the hour of death. You will have His company and His help. He who has yoked Himself with you in life will yoke Himself with you in death. He knows the way. Follow Him!

------◄◆►------

ONE HEART AND ONE WAY

Text: *"And I will give them one heart, and one way, that they may fear me for ever, for the good of them, and of their children after them."*

Jeremiah 32:39

GOD'S message changes the heart and nature of man. Everything is wrong until that change is made.

I think wrong. I act wrong. My values are wrong. I hate what I should love. I love what I should despise. I am headed in the wrong direction—*all because my nature is not what it should be.*

How can I possibly be happy if selfishness, malice and envy

rule my life? I need something more than education. I need regeneration. *I need a change of heart.*

I believe the heart that God creates supernaturally by His Holy Spirit is a heart of *purity.* Have you ever been shocked by the corruption you have seen in your own life?

One time God said of Israel, "My people doth not consider" (Isaiah 1:3). To "consider" means to look at something until you really see it.

A fleeting glance will not do it. A casual look will not do it. We have too much of that in our churches and preaching today. We touch problems superficially. *We refuse to allow the Holy Spirit to make a thorough examination.* We want the preacher to check us over lightly—take a pulse reading and a blood count and let us out as early as possible.

One day it will be too late for you, sir. No one will be able to reach you. No one will be able to save you. *It is better to find out now that you have heart trouble.* Pretty music, well-run services, short sermons, an atmosphere of conviviality are only postponing the evil day for you. I pray God that I may be a spiritual surgeon sent to you in this service.

What you need, lady, is a heart that has sin washed out of it *until you feel like a part of the great loving nature of God.* You feel heartsick. I know how you feel. Conviction grips you. You shrink from the darkness you feel within. You cry out in the privacy of your room against the terror and moral madness that usurp your life. *You look ahead and the end is hideous.*

Sin has carved deep crevices on your body. Lust and unbridled passion have mangled your sense of decency. Insobriety and insecurity have crushed your nerves. Your degeneracy is complete. Your foul soul writhes with hell's scum and vermin.

You need something more than a pat on the back or a handshake at the door. *You need an operation.* You need a change of nature.

God offers you a new heart, a new birth, a new start in life. That is the gospel. Anything less than that is only a clever, man-made imitation of the real thing.

You long to be *different*. On the authority of God's Word you can be different. God says, "I will give you a loving heart. I will give you a pure heart. I will give you a sympathetic heart."

Suddenly your family will realize that you *care* about them. For so long you have only cared about yourself. Your customers will discover the change. You put heart and good-will in your work. It is as though you were doing the service in your own home and for your own pleasure. In the missionary meeting you are the first to reach for your pocketbook. God does that for a man, sir!

I will tell you what happens when God gives you a new heart. *You feel religious all the time.*

It is not confined to the church auditorium for an hour on Sunday morning, and then shoved aside for the rest of the week. It is Sunday morning in your home all week long. It is Sunday morning at the office. It is Sunday morning as you take your place with the crew. *It is the new nature that is working in you. You want to be good and do good.*

I also need a change of direction. Here it is. "I will give them one heart, and one way." The tide is going in the other direction. It takes an act of God to head toward heaven. And there is only one way to get there—*God's way.*

There are many ways advertised. One man says to me, "Ward, I will show you a way to make a bit of paradise for yourself. Get yourself some quick-paying investments. *There is no heaven like a money-heaven."*

That is what he is saying to me. Ask those who have taken that way! They will tell you the misery. They will affirm the love of money is the root of all evil. They will testify that you cannot serve the demon of greed and serve God. It cannot be done.

I will tell you why the love of money hurts worse than any other sin. When a man gets drunk on whiskey, people feel sorry for him. Associations go to work for his redemption. People start praying for him. His wife requests help at the midweek service. Everybody is concerned. But let a man get drunk on money! That is a different story. The preacher will not talk to him about it for fear that the man will get angry. We would rather see him lost than stir up a row in the pews.

Let me tell you, a man can perish as easily getting drunk on money as he can getting drunk on whiskey! That is a false heaven, sir! You cannot buy happiness.

Do not misunderstand me! I do not say that a Christian cannot prosper. Abraham was very wealthy. *But he always put God first.* He started with the tithe. He saw that God got his tenth right off the top. He built bulwarks against greed and covetousness in his life. He never wanted wealth to *blind* him or *bind* him.

Everything Abraham had was at God's disposal. God always got the firstfruit of everything. *No one ever had to beg for Abraham's financial support.*

I will tell you about another way that gets a lot of publicity. Another person says to me, "Ward, I have a way that will make heaven real to you right here and now. *Step up into fashion!* Then, son, you will be living."

I hear it from every side. Heaven to this crowd is wearing better clothes, securing tickets to the biggest entertainments, driving the raciest cars, and having their pictures appear in the local social columns. Everything goes to keep in step with the pacesetters.

Ask a man like this to lead a drive for a Sunday school addition and he will tell you that all his assets are tied up at the moment. Pick up the paper and you will discover that the same man has purchased stock and a membership in the most exclusive country club in the community.

Ask a man like this to support a series of evangelistic meetings in his church by his personal presence every night for the next ten nights and he will tell you that his calendar of commitments is inflexible. Listen to the local newscast and you will hear that the same man has just accepted the chairmanship of the next tournament.

You think that man will be lost because of his *worldliness?* No, sir, that is not it. That man will be lost for *lying.* He cannot find time for God because he does not want to find time for God.

You will be a lost soul, mister, if you follow the way this fashion clique has marked out as a shortcut to glory.

God says there is *one heart* and *one way* that are acceptable to Him. Fashion momentum is a poor substitute for revival vigor. The bowling alley will never do for you what the prayer room can do for you. The church supper can never do for you what expository preaching and Bible teaching can do for you.

Sow to the flesh, my friend, and of the flesh you will reap corruption. Fill your church with entertainment and dress parades and you will live to see the day when the world, the flesh and the devil will sit on your board.

Someone else says, "I know a good way. *Everybody likes games.* There is nothing like a bit of fun."

Mister, I want to see that good man you are always talking about—that man that God uses—who plays all the games, who takes a hand at cards for low stakes, who places a small bet for fun, who can always shove aside more serious things for sport. I want to see that spiritual man of yours.

Do not take me to your local cemetery to hunt these good folk. There are no bad men in a graveyard. They are all good fathers and faithful husbands on the tombstones. Everybody, according to legends etched in marble, rests in peace.

I want to see one of your spiritual playboys alive and leading folk to Jesus Christ in your church. That is the man I want to see. I will take his testimony. I will ask his children. I want to find out about this for myself.

God says there is *one way*. That narrows the choice considerably. It will not be a prayerless way. It will not be an unrighteous way.

I have studied church history extensively, and wherever the people were, and whoever the people were, who knew God, they all preached and lived this same gospel.

There is just one way—not twenty different ways. One church says you can *dance* and get to heaven. Another church says you can *drink* and get to heaven. Another crowd says you can divorce and remarry and get to heaven, that a change of partner helps sometimes.

Do you really believe that a few dances every few days is the best way to get nearer to God? Do you really believe that? Are you willing to testify to it? If you can prove to me that these things make you more spiritual, that they build moral stature, that they bring you close to Jesus, if you can prove that by your lives, I will never say a word against them again. I am for everything that will help a man and a woman get to heaven.

I say, on the other hand, if it is not a good way, if it does not help, *then* give it up. It is better to have God's favor in our churches than the credit rating of a few folk who want to run the church their way. There is just *one way* that leads to heaven. That is God's way.

My text says "for the good of them, and of their children after them." Do you want your son and your daughter to grow up and respect you, parent?

That is the test of your training, of your religion. Will your son, your daughter say when they are living lives of their own, and presiding over homes of their own, "I want to run my home like my parents ran the home where I was raised"? *There is no greater honor in life than that.*

I want you to think about your children as I bring you to this altar. I want you to plan for their salvation. The greatest good you will ever bring into their lives is to share God's way with them.

Fill their moments with God's Word. Write into their memories your prayers for them. Lead them regularly into the house of God. Build their lives on the Ten Commandments and on John 3:16.

My father died without real estate or stock, but he died knowing that his son was following in his footsteps and serving God.

That is what will count, sir, when you come to the end and you have to leave everything else behind.

God has this great salvation for you and your family. All else is sinking sand.

IS PRAYING A WASTE OF TIME?

Text: *"Let your requests be made known."*
Philippians 4:6

ANOTHER great intercessory, worldwide, Revivaltime Prayermeeting is approaching, and I want to talk to you about these words, "Let your requests be made known."

Dwight L. Moody was conducting a great religious campaign in Chicago during the World's Fair of 1893. He had brought religious leaders from all over the world. It had been an expensive undertaking. On a certain day many bills and salaries had to be paid. *Three thousand dollars beyond what lay in the treasury balance was needed at once.*

Mr. Moody, with some other Christian workers, knelt and prayed about it. The famed evangelist prayed in his unique way:

"O Lord; I am sorely in need of money; I must have $3,000 today. I could raise it if I had time to go out after it, but, Lord, I'm booked to preach at the Great Northern Theater at noon today, and it's half past eleven now. Lord, in Thine own way, as Thou hast so often done before, please send me the needed money to carry on Thy work. Lord, I thank Thee that Thou hast heard me."

And he arose, picked up his hat, and went down to the theater to preach.

While he was on the platform waiting to preach, a lady came to one of the ushers and asked him to take her to Mr. Moody, for she had a message for him that was to be delivered in person.

The usher, naturally, refused, and said he would take it to Mr. Moody. But the persistence of the lady won out, and the usher took her to Mr. Moody to whom she handed an envelope. Thinking it was a question that someone wanted him to answer, and not having time to do it at the moment, he put the envelope in his pocket and proceeded to preach.

Later, when he came to the dinner table with his fellow workers, he remarked, "Oh, I had an envelope handed to me today; I wonder what it is about?" He then opened it, and to the surprise of all, it contained a check for $3,000, signed by Mrs. Cyrus W. McCormick, wife of the man who invented the harvester machine.

Mr. Moody went at once to see Mrs. McCormick. She told him that at about eleven-thirty a deep-seated feeling came over her and seemed to tell her that he would be needing money as he was conducting such an extensive campaign.

So she sat down and wrote a check for $1,000. Then, a second impression came strongly to her that she should enlarge the amount of the check. So she wrote a new check for $2,000.

Still, she did not feel at rest. And she wrote the third check for $3,000.

She put the final amount in an envelope, addressed and stamped it, and rang for her servant to mail it for her. *In that moment she definitely sensed that Mr. Moody needed the money that very day.*

She inquired about his schedule of services and sent her maid with the letter, instructing the maid to place it in the hand of Mr. Moody personally.

I believe in that kind of group communication. The evidence is too strong to believe otherwise.

Prayer is either a *force* or a *farce,* one or the other. If it is a force, what has it done for you, and what could it do for you?

I do not blame you if you have quit spending your time on something from which you never had any results. If you have never had one prayer answered you have a right to ask yourself, "Will I, or will I not, ever pray again?" I think I would ask myself the same question.

The pulpit needs to teach us *how* to pray. The disciples were not embarrassed to ask, "Lord, teach us to pray." *They saw results.* They wanted answers to their prayers.

Answered prayer tells me that God is at work. Of course, if I do not want anything more out of my religious life than what can be duplicated by the United Agency or a fraternal order by a charity organization, *I do not need anything more than words.*

If my church practice can be duplicated by a secular organization, all I need is a well-chosen ritual. But if I want to see the supernatural at work—the creation of new life in dead souls —I will need God's intervention. My Bible says, "This kind goeth not out but by prayer" (Matthew 17:21).

Prayerlessness *ties God's hands,* as well as our own. Electricity and water flow toward my home; but not a watt will brighten my home, not a drop will spill into my basin until the meters are turned on.

A law governs the distribution of these needs into my home. Prayer is like that. *No prayer, no power!* I must ask to receive.

Prayer is person-to-person. You will find it difficult to communicate with someone you do not know. *You communicate with a Person—not a principle.*

Prayer is not an exercise of feeding unlimited data into a supermechanical brain for machine-fed answers. *When Jesus Christ prayed, He met Somebody.*

Prayer is not a make-believe toy telephone such as a child plays with. Prayer is more than mortals receiving the reflex blessing of their own requests and petitions. *It is more than suggesting things to yourself.* Prayer is contact with God.

No Christian is self-sufficient, self-sustaining, and self-supporting. *He is not expected to be.* God is my Father, and He has arranged for me to ask for help and to present my personal needs to Him. *God expects me to do it and I do it without shame or hesitation.*

My Bible tells me, "In everything, by prayer and supplication, let your requests be made known to God" (Philippians 4:6). My fault is not that I ask too much. My fault is that I do not ask enough.

How often, when I was a boy at home, I would send my sister in to ask for me! All of us need that kind of help in the family of God.

It is interesting to note in connection with the miracles of Jesus, how many were performed because of *the intercession of others* in behalf of the sick. Perhaps two-thirds of the miracles were accomplished this way.

Nothing, for example, is said of the faith of the palsied man, whose paralyzed body was let down through a broken-up roof into the presence of Jesus; but it is recorded that when Jesus saw *their* faith (the faith of the men who bore the sick neighbor) He healed the poor, stricken fellow.

Nothing proves more to me that real Christianity is a divine family proposition than this provision. "If any man see his brother sinning a sin which is not unto death, he shall ask, and God shall give life for them that sin not unto death," (1 John 5:16).

That is something upon which all of us could work! I wonder how many of you in this audience have ever got hold of God for me or Brother Peterson or Brother McLellan? *There are tremendous provisions at the Throne!*

You ask, "How *big a request* shall I make?" I reply, "How *big a need* do you have?"

If God were not an Almighty God, prayer would be like the first homemade crystal radio sets that were all we had when I started in this business. "With God *all* things are possible" (Matthew 19:26). "Is *any thing* too hard for the Lord?" (Genesis 18:14). That is a big credit card to carry. "Hath he said, and shall he not do it? Hath he spoken, and shall he not make it good?" (Numbers 23:19).

When the angel Gabriel announced to the Virgin Mary that she would become the mother of our Lord, and that by the Holy Ghost, without the agency of a man, she asked, "How can this be?" The angel answered "For with God nothing shall be impossible" (Luke 1:37).

I say, sir, go to God on that basis! Accept the Bible verse which says "Thou hast established the earth, and it abideth. They continue this day according to thine ordinances; *for all are thy servants*" (Psalm 119:90, 91).

I believe that. Never forget for a moment that things which man's knowledge, some years ago, said were contrary to natural law and therefore impossible, are quite possible, and are everyday practices now.

Human knowledge once said that, according to natural law, nothing heavier than air could remain up and nothing heavier than water could float.

Human knowledge once said that water could not go uphill. Today water pours out of the faucets on the seventieth and eightieth floors of our modern skyscrapers. *God knows uses of natural laws that our best brains have not yet suspicioned.* God is not a prisoner in His world.

Make your requests known because God is a *Father. He expects it!* The first recorded uttered word of Jesus mentioned "Father." His closing words on the Cross included "Father." In John's Gospel Jesus calls God "Father" 140 times; in chapters 13-17, 47 times; and in chapter 14, 23 times.

Do you doubt this relationship? God can never be real to you until you know Him in the relationship Jesus Christ revealed, the "Father."

You are not coming to a laboratory technician. You are not coming to a professor. You are not coming to the chairman of the board. You are coming to our "Father." *That makes praying a comfort and a joy.*

> "Absolutely tender, absolutely true;
> Understanding all things; understanding you;
> Infinitely loving; exquisitely near;
> This is God our Father—What have we to fear?"

I ask you, will a true father turn his child away empty? You and I have *a Father* to go to. "Like as a Father pitieth his children, so the Lord pitieth them that fear him" (Psalm 103:13).

That means, mister, that God has time for me. I ask you, do you have time for Him?

There is a relationship possible for you at this altar that can change your life completely.

ESCAPE

Texts: *"Watch ye therefore, and pray always, that ye may be accounted worthy to escape all these things that shall come to pass, and to stand before the Son of man."*

Luke 21:36

"Thou sawest till that a stone was cut out without hands, which smote the image upon his feet that were of iron and clay, and brake them to pieces."

Daniel 2:34

THE giant must come down. What the *sword* cannot do the *stone* will do. We are in the revival of the Philistinian age that is prepared to say in braggart apostasy and open animosity. to every believer, "Come to me, and I will give thy flesh unto the fowls of the air, and to the beasts of the field."

There must be and there will be a final showdown between truth and error. In the meantime, where are we in God's dispensational timetable?

It seems to me we have arrived *at the very feet* of Daniel's interpretation of Nebuchadnezzar's dream.

"This image's head was of fine gold, his breast and his arms of silver, his belly and his thighs of brass, his legs of iron, *his feet part of iron and part of clay"* (Daniel 2:32, 33).

The more I have pondered this truth, the more I am convinced that these materials represent qualities of peoples or cultures. *If iron stands for nations, so does the clay.*

One hundred years ago many peoples and cultures had never reached standards higher than that of a clay pot or a mud hut. They were not strong enough to resist encroachment.

Stronger cultures with dreams of empire and profit tried to absorb them and mix their iron-clad laws and their strength of commerce with these peoples.

Inter-tribal warfare, malaria, lack of sanitation, a high rate of infant mortality decimated the ranks of the weaker groups.

The iron nations saw their opportunity and took advantage of it.

The colonizing nations banned inter-tribal warfare. They introduced education and hygiene. Missionaries brought new ideals. The death rate began to slowly recede. Numbers increased. But all of that is history.

Today there is a new mixture. Scores of colonies have been granted independence. Their new proud flags fly side by side with the flags of the older and stronger nations in front of the United Nations, New York City. They have sought and obtained equal rights in our time.

The *great cleavage* is now ready. Daily it is coming into clear perspective. The whole structure of man's present world organization stands on almost a 50-50 mixture of iron and clay.

Daniel, the statesman, told Nebuchadnezzar, the conqueror and colonizer, "They shall not cleave one to another, even as iron is not mixed with clay" (Daniel 2:43).

It is a sobering thought to realize we are so close to the end of this age.

The whole program of man is now resting on these uncertain feet. All of mankind's vaunted progress; his anthropological findings; his history and development of laws and society; his conquest—all of it—the gold, the silver, the brass, the iron of human record, *rests today on this shaky foundation.*

Is it ready to topple? God's Word says it will. Will you be caught in the crash or found worthy to escape?

The proud iron nations have not committed themselves to policies that will bring them down. The commodity that signifies their strength—basic iron ore—out of which they have built modern transportation and communication and the strength of industrial economy—*is picture language that cannot be mistaken.*

The western culture and drive that dates back to the Roman concept, and has given legs and mobility to the human race, has now been engulfed by masses and primitive hungers, thirsts, desires and claims *that cannot be controlled or satisfied.*

Nowhere is this better illustrated today than in South Viet Nam.

Large chunks of underprivileged continents have been given national status. You can weld iron. You can temper steel. You can build enormous structures that will cohere.

But this is not so with clay. Its strength dissipates quickly. It takes morality, economy, education, industry, a steady and wise government and a staple currency to build nationally. It is a long, difficult step from the tribal concept to international status. It takes more than flags and parades.

Daniel described it accurately. The Holy Spirit is the Spirit of Truth so the interpretation given by Daniel is infallible. *It has come to pass in our time.* Clay and iron have been given equal voice. Iron cannot impose upon clay. Clay will not mix with iron. Only the willful can ignore the separation.

This careening colossus is ripe for God's judgment.

"Thou sawest till that a stone was cut out without hands, which smote the image upon his feet that were iron and clay, and brake them to pieces.

"Then was the iron, the clay, the brass, the silver, the gold broken to pieces *together,* and became like the chaff of the summer threshing floors; and the wind carried them away, that no place was found for them: and *the stone* that smote the image became a great mountain and filled the whole earth" (Daniel 2:34, 35).

Daniel says it will be *a total collapse*—a shambles. The proud strength of industrial advantage will cave in with the brittle inexperience of the "have-nots."

What the great world systems have been unable to do—mingle iron with clay—diffuse strength and stability to the vast areas where primitive conditions have existed for centuries—*the miracle-message of Jesus Christ has been able to accomplish.*

The one homogeneous whole, the true testimony of our Lord

Jesus Christ, will govern. *Only the power of His blood can perform an alchemy upon customs, legends, animosities, caste, ideals so diverse as those of the human race.* Only His salvation can take the base things of this world and transform them into the likeness of Himself.

A born-again soul is a Christian wherever you meet him in this world, regardless of color, climate, continent or circumstance. *No colonizing effort, no commercial enterprise, no crusade, no conquest has ever been able to duplicate this miracle.* This new seed has been gathered from every tribe, tongue and nation to reign with Jesus Christ.

The New Testament says, and soon again every Christmas presentation of Handel's oratorio will repeat it "the kingdoms of this world are become the kingdoms of our Lord, and of his Christ; and he shall reign for ever and ever."

That is more than a song, mister! Only the Spirit of God can make mankind adhere. Nothing else can achieve it.

The *flimsy footing* of world balance today is a scaring, sobering injunction to look somewhere for a guarantee of security.

Daniel says that when the final failure starts nothing will stop it. It will be total. "No place was found for them."

Nothing will survive the practices and systems that have built the image that dominates every screen and every other medium of our world today. "And the stone that smote the image became a great mountain and filled the whole earth" (Daniel 2:35).

The return of Jesus Christ to this planet involves a mission completely different to the purpose of His birth, life, death and resurrection on earth.

He is not reappearing to save the world for either democracy or for the Atlantic Charter. He will not return as Prophet or Priest. "The government shall be upon His shoulder" (Isaiah 9:6). He will undertake the responsibility of administration.

The question your Bible poses in both Old and New Testament, is the question of *escape*. The era of frightful disintegration is just beginning. The spawn of hell that wrote into human history the blood-baths of the revolutions of France and Russia are investing themselves again with the surging masses. Sinner, where will you hide from the wrath to come?

The Son of God left word that it will be worthiness that counts. Escape will be based on that alone. *Only Jesus Christ can effect that escape.*

No international boundary can insulate you. No affiliation will cover you. No commercial connection will be strong enough to speak for you. No cave, no island, no retreat will hide you. *The escape must be upward.*

The only route open in that hour will be the miracle route of translation.

"For the Lord himself shall descend from heaven with a shout, with the voice of the arch-angel, and with the trump of God: and the dead in Christ shall rise first: then we which are alive and remain shall be caught up together with them in the clouds, to meet the Lord in the air" (1 Thessalonians 4:16, 17). *I believe that passage as I believe John 3:16.*

The Bible says, "And every man that hath this hope in him purifieth himself, even as he (Jesus) is pure" (1 John 3:3).

I know this. The Holy Spirit makes this truth known to me. *God is preparing to hurl His Rock at this tottering world-system.*

The history of this world has tried to cope with the first coming of Jesus Christ ever since Bethlehem shepherds heard the angels' serenade.

It has burned His Book. It has infiltrated His Church. It has launched invective and diatribe. It has ridiculed and persecuted. It has quoted science and philosophy. It has socialized and rationalized. But after 1,900 years, Jesus Christ is still the Name that divides and renders judgment.

If the image that mankind has built has not been able to deny

Christ's first coming, *what chance will it have against His second coming?* Answer that, sir, and you will settle the destiny of your own soul!

Make it the one purpose of your life "to stand before the Son of man." Jesus Christ continues to occupy a unique place in history. He alone is "a stone ... cut out without hands." His origin is divine, born of a virgin by the Holy Ghost.

No system can destroy Him. He is greater than all of them combined. Here and there are those He counts *worthy.* You can be among that number.

DID ADAM GO TO HEAVEN?

Texts : *"The first man Adam was made a living soul."*
1 *Corinthians* 15 :45
"And Adam was not deceived, but the woman being deceived was in the transgression."
1 *Timothy* 2 :14

ADAM is the forgotten man of Bible preaching. No one presents him. Few seem to care. He seldom keeps company in our pulpits with Moses, Daniel, Matthew or Paul. It is as though he has been reduced to an allegorical figure or a myth.

He is treated in the same manner as a society editor treats the groom in reporting a wedding. Paragraphs are written about the bride and her attendants, what they wore and the wedding arrangements. *The final line is reserved for the young man that makes the whole affair possible.* He is almost an afterthought with the editor, an uninteresting necessity.

There must be an Adam in the story. There is no narrative without him. We should present him more often than we do. "All the days that Adam lived were nine hundred and thirty years: and he died" (Genesis 5 :5).

There are no great chronicles recorded about him such as are established about David or Peter. One small community was named after him. No great city every gave him immortality such as the city of Washington.

Joshua, chapter three and verse sixteen, notes that the miraculous crossing of Israel through the Jordan took place near the community of Adam. It is not remembered for anything else.

There was an ugly, front-page murder in his household. He knew greater family sorrow, more personal tragedy, than great Biblical favorites like Abraham and Luke. He loved and lost. He knew the seductive sweetness and moral quicksand of men like Samson, Job and Ahab.

Eve "took of the fruit thereof, and did eat, and gave also unto her husband with her; and he did eat" (Genesis 3:6). *He knew a guilt-consciousness far beyond what others experience.*

Job reflected upon it. "If I covered my transgressions as Adam, by hiding mine iniquity in my bosom" (Job 31:33). He has lent his name to something that speaks of the worst in humanity, a riddle of bad in mankind that yields to no other answer than the cross, "the Adamic nature."

"For as in Adam all die, even so in Christ shall all be made alive" (1 Corinthians 15:22). *He introduced death into a planet called Earth.* He saw paradise lost. He lived in one lifetime on both sides of the Gate.

What could he ever do to atone? How did he survive the years of memory? What was his plea? What was his hope?

The New Testament gives authenticity to him. The work of the Cross is based on fact, not legend. What happened in and through this man is basic to divine revelation and provision.

A dream tumbled in Adam, if the possibility had ever existed —for Christ was the Lamb slain from the foundation of the world—*that a perfect, super race, in itself, by itself and through itself, could ever propagate and perpetuate itself.* Adam proved conclusively that there is no room for pride in God's universe.

Sin did not overtake Adam in an alley. It overtook him in a garden. Sin did not take the advantage of ignorance. It found an ally in intelligence.

"And out of the ground the Lord God formed every beast of the field, and every fowl of the air; and brought them unto Adam to see what he would call them: and whatever Adam called every living creature, that was the name thereof. And Adam gave names to all cattle, and to the fowl of the air, and to every beast of the field" (Genesis 2:19, 20).

Adam was not an automat, a visitor from outer space. *Adam was a scientist.* He was smart enough but not strong enough!

You may have high grades in zoology, mister, but what do you know about human nature? "The heart is deceitful above all things, and desperately wicked: who can know it?" (Jeremiah 17:9).

Adam was the original giant in a green valley. "God saw everything that he had made, and, behold it was very good" (Genesis 1:31).

"Thus the heavens and the earth were finished, and all the host of them. . . . And the Lord God took the man, and put him into the garden" (Genesis 2:1, 15).

Adam's seed has been trying to rebuild that garden ever since.

I think the sorrow of the human heart is best kept in the simple words that God used to describe it in the front of your Bible, "And Adam and his wife *hid* themselves from the presence of the Lord" (Genesis 3:8).

Man is born with the choice to walk with the Eternal. There are no boundaries. Today communication is instantaneous. Today transportation is faster than the speed of sound. Today we warm the winter and cool the summer by thermostatic control that we never touch.

We seem to be masters in our own garden. But there is shame, overwhelming shame! Suddenly, the race that has engineered the skyscraper, the suspension bridge, the Nautilus and the flying capsule, *hides* itself. Why? What has it done that it needs to be ashamed of itself?

Have we not built hospitals and universities? Have we not improved jungles and created new wealth? *Why are we not fit company?* Are we victims only of superstition and theological unenlightening?

No. We are lost! We have lost contact with spiritual forces. We have lost a sense of peace. *We are ashamed of ourselves.* Why?

We cover ourselves with degrees and good works, with exploit and industry. Our closets are filled with aprons. *But they cannot silence conscience!*

"Who told thee that thou was naked?" (Genesis 3:11).

Let the atheist answer that question! Mankind still repeats it in 1964, "I was afraid, because I was naked; and I hid myself" (Genesis 3:10).

Afraid of what? Uncouth? How? Ashamed? Why? You tell me, mister!

Adam knew both sides. He knew the *ecstasy* and the *agony.* He knew it was better to live among thorns and thistles, in sweat and labor with the presence of God than to live in a garden separated from the presence of God. *Adam is the irrefutable argument.*

Let every real Christian tell you, mister sinner. We talk about heaven. Heaven is our goal—not because we want fancy buildings or costly pavements. Heaven is our goal—not because we want music and pleasure. Heaven is our goal—not because we want to linger in some form of escapism.

Heaven is our goal for the same reason that compelled Adam. *We have to find God again.* In his "presence is fulness of joy," at his "right hand there are pleasures for evermore" (Psalm 16:11).

A Godless life is an empty life. A "paradise" without the Eternal Presence is only a Pandora's box. You might as well dream of castles in Spain or a great Valhalla.

Thirst mocks you. Hunger torments you until you can find unbroken fellowship with your Creator. Saint Augustine laid it down as a premise. No one has disproved it.

History has now revealed there was a day early in the postwar allied occupation of Japan when the Emperor Hirohito broke precedent and ordered his chamberlains to prepare his private Mercedes for a requested interview with General Douglas McArthur.

Speculation filled the palace. The last vestiges of the ancient and sacred system of the shoguns were about to be broken. It was proper in the traditions of the Rising Sun that the General should come to the Emperor.

Hirohito passed through the honor guard of American military police and General McArthur stood to greet the emperor. *In that moment Hirohito offered himself to go to the gallows and be publicly hanged for an atonement for his nation.*

The record says that General McArthur was so overcome by the unexpected and sincere act of Emperor Hirohito's offer that he wept on the monarch's shoulder.

Adam found there was no atonement he could make. His firstborn, Cain, tried. He "brought of the fruit of the ground." He offered his own industry. Behind the beauty which he tilled there was an unregenerated heart filled with jealousy, disobedience, brutality and murder. Nothing he could grow or produce could cover his inner nakedness.

Adam knew that. *Only God could cover him.* "Unto Adam also and to his wife did the Lord God make coats of skins, and clothe them" (Genesis 3:21).

There had to be a sacrifice first. *Another had to give his life for them.* It is the only antidote in this universe for pride.

God dwells only with a contrite, penitent heart. "For all those things had mine hand made, and all those things have been, saith the Lord: but to this man will I look, even to him that is poor and of a contrite spirit, and trembleth at my word" (Isaiah 66:2).

David said out of a full soul, "The Lord is nigh unto them that are of a broken heart; and saveth such as be of a contrite spirit" (Psalm 34:18).

When a man's garden becomes a terror of shadows and a jungle of fears, he needs a pitying eye to find him and a comforting voice to direct him.

David knew what it was to have his palace-garden turn into a shambles of sin. The serpent in every man's life will yield only to the Lamb.

Jesus, Himself, who knew no sin became sin for us and His garden of sweet communion became the battleground that led Him to the cross. There on that hill of Calvary the answer is just the same, "Father, into thy hands I commend my spirit" (Luke 23:46). *There is no other provision.*

Abraham expressed the same truth to Isaac, "My son, God will provide." I cannot atone for myself.

> "Nothing in my hand I bring,
> Simply to Thy cross I cling."

Centuries have passed. Man's efforts have expanded. *But man's experience with his God remains the same.* What Adam did he did deliberately.

The New Testament says, "Adam was not deceived." He followed suit. He allowed attraction toward and loyalty to another to come between his soul and his God. He did not want to lose Eve. He had to learn that a man's real paradise is his free and guiltless conscience.

Others may betray you. No man can find final contentment in material things.

Yes, Adam has a big place in history. His message is the message of all messages. His experience is the central experience of all experiences. Adam learned again at his family altar what he had known in the garden "in the cool of the day" that when evening comes there is one thing man needs above all, " O Lord, abide with me."

"And Adam knew his wife again; and she bare a son, and called his name Seth: for God, said she, hath appointed me another seed instead of Abel, whom Cain slew. And to Seth, to him also there was born a son: and he called his name Enos: then began men to call upon the name of the Lord" (Genesis 4:25, 26).

"This is the book of the generations of Adam. In the day that God created man, in the likeness of God made he him" (Genesis 5:1).

That is the record, sir! Yes, Adam went to heaven. Like you and me, he did not have to go. *He chose to go.* He determined that his faith should be placed on record . . . "that man should call upon the name of the Lord." That is a choice you must personally make.

TATTOOED

Text: *"Behold, I have graven thee upon the palms of my hands."*
                                          Isaiah 49:16

THIS was daring language for any Jew to use since *tattooing* was forbidden in the Old Testament. The Law, as written in the Book of Leviticus, chapter 19 and verse 28 declared, "Ye shall not make any cuttings in your flesh . . . nor print any marks upon you."

Neighboring nations practiced tattooing for religious purposes. They placed pictures of their gods on their flesh. The Hebrew was reminded by this prohibition that God is a Spirit. He cannot be reduced to image or picture.

So this is a daring simile. It is a familiar picture in our twentieth century, though men are no longer tattooed for religious purposes.

The dreaded *S. S.* under Hitler were tattooed for identification purposes. The modern practice of tattooing is usually identified with sailors. They identify themselves with some secret love or affiliate themselves with some human yearning.

I have never felt that I wanted to have my body permanently marked. Vaccination is enough for me. Yet it is more or less a worldwide practice.

Some use it in the spirit of boasting. In sign language they declare a deed of valor. In the days of long ago it publicly recorded what we now put on cards and file in steel cases. *It formed a personal history.*

Isaiah's passage deals with *the love of God.* He wants to find an expression for a deep conviction. He feels about God's love the way a sailor feels toward romance when he yields to the needles of a tattoo artist in some faraway port. The sailor wants written on his forearm for all to see his faith in something he pictures as a heart with an arrow through it.

Isaiah feels that way about God's love. He believes it is stronger than a mother's love. Isaiah believes it will never fail. He is willing to go on record before all men, "Behold, I have graven thee upon the palms of my hands."

Isaiah puts his testimony to the faithfulness of God where all may see it. He is willing to be branded. He wants the marks placed in *the palms* of his hands. The relationship is something personal and sacred between God and himself.

In all probability, Isaiah had somewhere seen a man with his tribal mark upon his hands, the sign of the folk to whom he belonged.

Our missionaries see it all the time on mission fields. Indelibly marked is the god the tribesman must worship forever. *Isaiah wants to be marked for his God.* He uses this language to say what Paul declares to be true that God is "bone of our bone and flesh of our flesh."

There is *a double application.* He believes God feels the same way toward His children. Isaiah dares to present God opening His eternal hands and showing them to the Zion which thought itself forsaken: "Behold, I have graven thee upon my palms." It is one of the most daring conceptions of God in the Old Testament.

It was colorful language that gripped the attention of Isaiah's audience. Every generation has asked, "Is there a relationship so big, so strong, so eternal that it will never let us go?"

Isaiah ministered to a ravaged land. The population was decimated. Jackals roamed through ruins which formerly had been exclusive residential areas. There were vast economically depressed areas. It was not difficult to ask, "Does God care?"

Survivors canvassed the idea whether or not there was such a God as history associated with Moses and Joshua and Samuel. Cynics were popular. There was not much material evidence to support the preacher's message.

It was a lot easier to complain, "Why doesn't God do something about it if He is so powerful?"

The always-occurring miracle is that somewhere, from someone, at some time *there is always an expression of faith.* A voice is lifted and we read:

"Why do you say, O Jacob, and speak, O Israel, My way is hid from the Lord and my judgment is passed over from my God?"

"Hast thou not known? hast thou not heard that the everlasting God, the Lord, the Creator of the ends of the earth, fainteth not, neither is weary? there is no searching of his understanding. He giveth power to the faint: and to them that have no might he increaseth strength" (Isaiah 40:27-29).

It was the voice of a man who knew God. This man was very sure. Thank God for faith!

On a steep hill just inside the western border of Austria lies the beautiful little village of Feldkirch. It was there, in 1799, that the armies of Napoleon suffered a bloodless defeat, under most unusual circumstances.

On Easter morning, the good folks of Feldkirch found themselves looking down the valley into the gunbarrels of a powerful French army which had moved up during the night. Napoleon had to take Feldkirch in order to send his legions through Arlberg Pass, the key to Austria.

The village was virtually defenseless, in military terms. It could surrender—or it could send its women and children into the hills while the men and boys died vainly in the streets.

At the hurriedly called town meeting, the dean of a church heard the panicked councilmen through, then his turn came. He said:

"This is Easter. This is the day of the Resurrection of Christ. *Let us show some of the courage that He showed, some of the faith that He had.* Let us pay tribute to His day by ringing the bells of all our churches. If we must fall prey to the enemy we will at least have paid homage to the Lord. I say ... *let the bells ring!*"

The bells rang ... from the towers of the four churches the clear silvery notes rolled down through the valley ... to the French army massed for attack.

General Massena and his staff paused. They decided that the village had learned of the approach of an Austrian army coming to the rescue ... and that would be bad news for the French forces.

Massena decided to get out of that valley before disaster overtook him. As the French forces retreated, the bells rang louder and faster—the only case in history where a great army was driven off by the ringing of church bells.

Isaiah stood up in a time of dismal doubt, *and rang the bells.*

Sinner and scoffer, will you give me a reasonable explanation as to how a long succession of men, in times of direct stress and calamity, found themselves undergirded by such assurance? These men have felt compelled to set down their faith in deathless prose. They have found words to express it. If there is no fact, no basis whatsoever for their conviction, *how do you explain it?*

Why would William Wordsworth write:

> I have felt
> A presence that disturbs me with joy
> Of elevated thoughts; *a sense sublime*
> Of something far more deeply interfused,
> Whose dwelling is the light of setting suns,
> And the round ocean and the living air,
> And the blue sky, and in the mind of man.

How would men feel this "sense sublime" if blind, mechanical forces are all that are operating in the universe? What is the basis of faith that can say "Behold, I have graven thee upon the palms of my hands?"

Are you prepared to dismiss it as mere fantasy? Why should these thoughts enter human consciousness?

Sinner, I cannot settle for the shrug of the shoulder or a snicker. I am not prepared to say that every man who has expressed faith down through the generations has been a simpleton. *They spoke and they wrote because they experienced reality.*

There is an emptiness to existence without such faith. Only in the knowledge that Someone Eternal cares about me do I find the dignity I need for survival.

In Jesus Christ, this love of God, of which Isaiah had some-how been so certain, manifested itself physically among men. It took its place in our history. It cannot be erased any more than you can erase the events of George Washington or Abraham Lincoln. *Jesus Christ fulfilled Isaiah's concept of God perfectly and completely.*

Each man, each woman who met Jesus Christ knew that He cared about them—that He would *never forget* them. None even imagined there could ever come a day when the same Christ might say, "I am sorry, forgive me. I am afraid I do not re-member you. Have we met before? Was it at Matthew's ban-quet? Or was it in the Temple? Or perhaps it was at Cana of Galilee!"

Jesus made them certain, as He has made all of us who have met Him certain, that He will never leave us *and never forget us.* He tattoos me on the palms of His hands. I am not an incident catalogued somewhere. I am His constant concern. He watches over me.

That is the faith that saves you, sir!

Calvary means to me that God cared enough about me per-sonally to write my condition, my sins and my lost way, into His very flesh. The spikes that were driven, and the thorns that pressed, and the whips that slashed, and the spear that thrust, tattooed me forever upon the Son of God.

Sometimes I wonder how Isaiah saw it all so clearly over and over again. He saw the cross when he wrote: "Behold, I have graven thee upon the palms of my hands."

I ask you, sinner, look at your Saviour's hands! Look at the marks! Ponder those scars!

Did ever a modern mariner think back upon home and a dear one with more affection, and submit himself to the needles and pricks of an engraver upon human flesh, with greater meaning and longing for reunion, than the Son of God when He laid His body bare for the indelible markings at Calvary?

Can you ever doubt again that it was for you?

SOMETHING FOR NOTHING

Text: *"And king David said to Ornan, Nay; but I will verily buy it for the full price."*
1 *Chronicles* 21 :24

IN a poignant memory of the late President Kennedy, one extremely close to him believes that the president's true conviction was inscribed on a piece of pewter the late president gave as a gift. It reads:

> There are three things which are *real*:
> God, human folly and laughter,
> The first two are beyond our comprehension
> So we must do what we can with the third.

No one at the White House knew the source of those lines. The Library of Congress has not been able to discover who wrote them. They were the expression of the man who led this nation.

David is a man of many moods, *a complex of churning contradictions*. He, too, knew the reality of God and of human folly. He had reached a crossroads where something he had done was no longer a laughing matter. He was deadly serious. "I will buy it for the full price."

All of us reach the same point sooner or later in life when we say, "I am willing to assume the full responsibility." It is the point in life when we will never again be *as big* and, at the same time, *as small* as we are at that moment.

> I counted dollars while God counted crosses,
> I counted my worth by the things gained in store.
> But He sized me up by the scars that I bore.
>
> I coveted honors and sought for degrees;
> He wept as He counted the hours on my knees.

> And I never knew till one day by a grave,
> How vain are these things that we spend life to save.
> That the richest of all in the world is God's love!

I have returned many times to this passage in my Bible because it searches me. I am that same man, standing in the same spot, reaching the same conclusions. *And in 1964 the answers are just the same.*

The son of Jesse, who had done so well in the world, wanted to build an altar. His eye fell upon the summit of a hill which at the time being was the property of Ornan. It was a site that later became the location for the great temple of Solomon. David felt a strong attraction for this hill. So he opened negotiations with the owner.

Ornan, when he learned of David's intention, made one of those unexpected and generous offers—*take the property as a free gift.* Ornan pressed him to take the oxen and implement as well. It is difficult to find a record of greater generosity in the Bible.

David objected. The gift had to be his and his alone. *It had to cost something.* He meant to be under obligation to no one. "I will verily buy it for the full price."

Many a man since has promised himself the same thing. "I want to pay for it. I must pay for it." We stand there, saying, "It is all my fault. No one else is involved. I want to be entirely responsible." It could be a moment clothed with grandeur. *Is it?*

It seems contrary to all experience in later years that it is ever possible to get something for nothing. The will-of-the-wisp of our youth has vanished. Experience has taught us sterner reality.

David had his share of bargain hunting. He had squeezed and cheated. He had taken advantage. When he wanted Bathsheba, he merely gave an order that her husband should be put in the deadliest spot of the front line.

No murder was arranged more cheaply or with less expense of effort. *So he thought!* He had not reckoned on the price to his conscience or the torment to his mind. He discovered that God is not mocked.

The full price has to be paid somehow. Confession of sin lay heavily on David's heart. "No, Ornan, no—I must pay for it. It must cost me the full price."

It is a moment when even a man's enemies respect him—no whimpering, no excuses, no begging. It appears that men stand tall in such moments.

Here is a strange direction in human nature! We are never cheap with deity. *We feel instinctively that our relationship must involve sacrifice.*

The church must rank with the best buildings on the street. The furnishings must be ornate and costly. The service must involve talent and considerable learning. It must be a personal obligation to belong.

We never think of religion on the basis of cut-rate price. We wear the best clothes. We exercise the best and most painful manners. We volunteer the best hours of the week. The very thought that there might be anything cheap about religion is vulgar.

None of us, the world over, are ignorant of what the word *sacrifice* means. Anything less, we suspicion, would offend whatever gods we serve.

Is it all a mistaken idea? What is God really like? *What is my personal obligation to Him?* What pay-off does He demand?

How big a thing must I do to merit sufficient standing? What hospital must I build? What park must I contribute to the community? What drive must I lead? What fund must I establish? *How can I earn God's mercy?*

Thousands today in every nation where this message is heard are in the same sweat as David *to pay the full price.*

It is the biggest mistake you will ever make, mister! Many centuries ago the preacher, Micah, asked:

"Wherewith shall I come before the Lord, and bow myself before the high God? shall I come before him with burnt offerings, with calves of a year old? Will the Lord be pleased with thousands of rams, or with ten thousands of rivers of oil? shall I give my firstborn for my transgression, the fruit of my body for the sin of my soul? He has showed thee, O man, what is good; and what doth the Lord require of thee, but to do justly, and to love mercy, and to walk humbly with thy God?" (Micah 6:6-8).

You had better read that again, fellow! *God's favor is not up for so many penances, so many donations, so many attendances.* God is not bribed. God is not placated with gifts.

"God is a gracious God—plenteous in mercy." "As far as the east is from the west, so far hath he removed our transgressions from us" (Psalm 103:12).

> Not the labors of my hands
> Can fulfill Thy law's demands,
> Could my zeal no respite know,
> Could my tears forever flow,
> All for sin could not atone;
> Thou must save, and Thou alone.

Let me tell you this, sir! The altar of your church is not a place where you bring your assets and bargain with God. *It is a place in your church where you humbly bow and gratefully receive God's bargain for you.* God's grace can never be deserved or earned. The "full price" is beyond any of us.

But do I owe God anything? Yes! I owe Him everything. I can never balance out my sins; but I can pour out my thanks. I can spend the rest of my life and use all of my strength in praise to Him, who alone could pay the price "in full." *There can be no haggling here, no depending upon others to do it for me.*

My body contains about 2,500,000,000 pores (about 3,000 to the square inch), and the framework of my body has over 200 bones. Every bit of blood in my body is pumped through my heart once every minute, and my normal heartbeat is 70 times to the minute, which is some 100,800 times a day.

If I am average, I can store some 230 cubic inches of air in my lungs and with each breath inhale and exhale from 25 to 30 inches.

My body has more than 500 muscles and about an equal number of nerves and blood vessels, and to counteract the daily outgoings of waste I must consume about 5½ pounds of food and drink a day, which means almost a ton annually.

My heart weighs from 8 to 12 ounces, its capacity is from four to six ounces in each ventricle, and its size is five by three and one-half inches. It is a hollow muscle organ and pumps 22 and a half pounds of blood every minute.

In 24 hours the heart pumps 16 tons. In one year it pumps approximately 11,680,000 pounds of blood.

And all of that, every muscle, every organ, every drop of blood, every heartbeat—all of it—belongs to God.

> Love so amazing, so divine,
> Demands my soul, my life, my *all*.

That must be the "full price" of my commitment to Jesus Christ.

———————◆———————

WARNING

Text: "*...And being guilty, they offered a ram of the flock for their trespass.*"

Ezra 10:19

THAT is what a sense of guilt is, sir—*a warning*. You have felt it.

Here is a minor case! You meet a person whom you have not seen for a long time. You remember you have not answered his letter, and say, "I feel so *guilty* about that."

And still scratching on the surface of this human emotion, here is another example! You promised to do something but failed to do it, and somehow or other when you get around to it, you apologize because you "feel so *guilty.*"

What I have in mind in this service goes far deeper and involves much more. *But guilt is something you can feel like forgiveness.*

"Soul guilt" is more than breaking some social custom; that may be embarrassment. It is more than an unavoidable mistake of judgment; that may be ignorance. It is more than an unresolved inhibition; that may be self-consciousness. It is more than the lack of keeping a promise; that may be forgetfulness.

It is an awareness of transgression within oneself. And the feeling is so bad that it makes you sick to your soul.

The Bible says, "Whosoever shall keep the whole law, and yet offend in one point, he is *guilty* of all" (James 2:10).

You do not have to kill or steal or lie to feel guilty. *Sin makes you feel guilty.* And we are all sinners, everyone of us.

None of us are *good enough.* "All have sinned, and come short of the glory of God" (Romans 3:23). I have not been honest *enough.* I have not been generous *enough.* I have not been pure *enough.* I have not been truthful *enough.* I have not worshiped God *enough.* That is my problem. I have fallen short of God's standard in Jesus Christ. And it is the problem of everyone in the community.

There are seven ways mankind attempts to deal with guilt.

First, SOME PEOPLE TRY TO ERASE IT BY LAUGHING IT OFF. Mister, you cannot deal with sin humorously. That is why the pulpit should be no place for jokes.
I do not want any man to trifle with my soul. You may

laugh and grow fat, but you will never laugh and grow clean.

Moral failure is not a laughing matter. No culprit with any degree of sanity laughs when he stands in court facing the judge. We may call sin a trifle. God calls it a tragedy. We may pass over it as an accident. God declares it to be an abomination.

Sin is not a toy. Sin is a terror. It is out for your life. Does a man laugh at cancer? Does a woman laugh at paralysis? *God has built into your soul, sir, a feeling of guilt for a warning.*

Second, OTHERS TRY TO DISMISS GUILT BY TALK-ING IT OVER. This is big business today. Every popular magazine on the newsstands assigns pages to this sort of thing. The big relief offered is *comparisons.*

You are urged to feel normal, to consider yourself to "be as good as most people." You are asked to do a little evaluating. "Perhaps I have some faults, and if so there are plenty of other people like me with faults similar to mine."

That is supposed to be a great comfort. Another form is this. "I am better now than I used to be," or "I hope to be better in the future than I am now."

Talking is not evidence, mister. Your case will be settled on evidence. You may think there is safety in numbers, that the crowd will save you, but God says, "the *soul* that sinneth, *it* shall die" (Ezekiel 18:4). It is not *corporate* guilt that will condemn you. It is *personal* guilt that will condemn you.

Third, SOME TRY TO ELIMINATE IT BY REASON-ING IT THROUGH. They are sure there is a *psychological explanation* for it. I know there is the subconscious, the sediment in every life that is stirred to the surface and muddied every once in awhile. *But dirtying the stream does not bring relief.*

Looking at my sin does not make it any less bothersome. David said, "Wash me thoroughly from mine iniquity, and cleanse me from my sin. Deliver me from bloodguiltiness, O God, Thou God of my salvation" (Psalm 51:4, 14).

Judas got psychological help. He saw clearly what disturbed him. He saw something surface, a sense of greed, that had been there for a long time. *It was not enough.* Filled with despair, he went out and hanged himself. You need more than *the couch,* mister. You need *the altar.*

Fourth, THERE ARE THOSE WHO TRY TO DEVIATE GUILT BY WORKING IT OFF. They throw themselves into some cause. *They recognize their guilt but they are sure it can be evaporated in service for others.* They make sure their lives are completely occupied.

This is a favorite device used when one or the other marriage partner is unfaithful. This is the method in which the guilty party seeks to become so busy that he or she does not have the time *to think.*

How easy it is to use religious observances as a cloak for our guilt and our need of repentance! *That is why Sunday morning services need to be evangelistic services with altar calls.*

Fifth, OTHERS TRY TO FIGHT IT THROUGH. They hope that by *sheer determination* they can get rid of guilt. They openly admit their past failures. *They believe that if they try hard enough in the future the past will be overcome.*

It is an admirable viewpoint if it would work. It is a lot better than the person who feels that he or she has to bear his or her guilt for a lifetime as a punishment for wrongdoing. Mister, you need a more realistic approach.

You can find that kind of help for loneliness or for worry, but guilt is another problem. It is many more times difficult.

Sixth, SOME TRY TO SOLVE GUILT BY PRAYER. It is a kind of praying with tongue in cheek. *It is a religious halloween costume effort.* This person hopes that external correctness can cover up internal disorder. It is a pretense at putting things in order—a sort of sweeping under the rug proposition.

You have a right to be suspicious of a person's prayers. Jesus said the Pharisees made long prayers as a cover-up for robbing widows' houses. Then what can avail? What can solve my guilt?

The only answer is to LET JESUS CHRIST DEAL WITH THE PROBLEM. How? He was tempted in all points "like as we are, yet without sin." He wants to share this victory with us. And multiplied thousands testify that it is a true experience.

I want you to remember a very important fact. If from this very moment you were able to live a perfect life, you would still have *your past* to consider. That's where you must find a remedy.

You need more than a clean sheet to fight smallpox. You need an internal change and a cleansing.

Christ deals with the penalty of sins—the carry-over. "He hath made him to be sin for us, who knew no sin; that we might be made the righteousness of God in Him."

Jesus Christ paid a penalty that He did not need for Himself. That stands out above everything else. Accept it. Then ask yourself the question, "Who was it for?" And say in faith and gratitude, "It was for *me*." He took what I should have taken.

You say, "Was it *enough?*" You say, "Perhaps, I will have to be punished as well." The answer is in Christ's resurrection. God raised Jesus Christ.

If Christ had failed, there never would have been an Easter. *God would have never glorified a failure.* Christ has absorbed every bit of your sin.

You say, "If only I had my life to live over again!" That is the good news. *You can have a new beginning—a new birth.* It is God's provision for you through Jesus Christ. You ask, "How is it done?" I will tell you.

First, ADMIT WHAT YOU ARE. Confess before God on your knees that you are *a* sinner—not a good, respectable sinner or a halfhearted sinner—just a sinner.

Acknowledge your guilt. Take personal responsibility for it. Do not hedge. Do not offer excuses. Come the only way a prodigal can come to his father, "I will arise and go to my

Father, and will say unto him, Father, I have sinned against heaven, and before thee, and am no more worthy to be called thy son" (Luke 15:18, 19).

Shame will keep you in the pigpen. *Faith* will lead you to repentance. Do not let an evil spirit frighten you by telling you that God is interested only in getting his pound of flesh.

"If we confess our sins, he is faithful and just to forgive us our sins, and to cleanse us from all unrighteousness" (1 John 1:9). That is the deal. You can count on it.

Second, ACCEPT WHAT HE OFFERS. He offers you a permanent standing—eternal life. That means the life of the contract; and you have personally agreed to His terms whereby an Almighty God *contracts* to save your soul and preserve your identity. And it is on *a gift basis*.

You have one responsibility. You must act in faith. You must reach out for yourself and *receive*.

Third, ACKNOWLEDGE WHO HE IS. You and I can never make it by ourselves. Our lives prove it. *I must be identified with Him.*

It is the same moment as when a soldier, sailor, marine or airman accepts the articles of war and is sworn in. He then becomes subject to another. Any other course will lead to confusion and trouble.

I must acknowledge Jesus Christ as Lord and Master of my life. The responsibility becomes His. He crowds out all sense of guilt. His presence fills my life. Say these words with me now:

> "Naked, come to Thee for dress,
> Helpless, look to Thee for grace.
> Vile, I to the Fountain fly!
> Wash me, Saviour, or I die."

Jesus Christ alone can satisfy your sense of guilt. The proof is in recorded history.

IN THE PRESENCE OF MINE ENEMIES

Text: *"Thou preparest a table before me in the presence of mine enemies."*

Psalm 23:5

MY *faith* and my *victory* revolve around that table. It is the central fact in a surging, threatening world.

Recently a mother in this radio audience wrote:
"We have a severely afflicted 14-year-old son. He has convulsions and is very retarded. He has never qualified for any schooling. His seizures usually come in the night, and I so often sense the presence of Satan. I come into the church with a heavy burden, and try to take care of infants and crying babies in the nursery. My heart breaks in the midst of all the announcements of showers, parties, and banquets scheduled for the week. *My faith has dropped to a new low.*
"Where shall I look for victory? Can I find it in programs, concerts, recreations, and entertainments of our church?" *How would you answer?*

This psalm is more than a shepherd's psalm. It is that. It tells about the shepherd, the pasture, the water, the protection by day and night. *But it is more than that!* It is a psalm of victory.

The table of our Lord is far beyond the Board tables of the money marts of this world, where decisions of high finance are made. It is superior to the round-table discussions of the world's statesmen, where communiques are issued. It is more powerful and more effective than the gatherings of scholars, soldiers or scientists.

Upon His table are the symbols and fruits of Calvary. In that "banquet" alone is there victory over our enemies. That is what I must tell that mother.

I have enemies. I must live with that fact. *Death is an enemy.* I am conscious of it every waking moment. I am conscious of it as I step into my car. I am conscious of it as I fasten the seatbelt in the airplane. I am conscious of it in the midst of epidemic. Every birthday reminds me. Every death notice in the newspaper warns me. Every ache alerts me.

The presence of death is everywhere. What shall I do? Shall I run? Shall I hide in the midst of jokes and masks? Shall I pretend and cover my fears with cosmetics and dyes? Shall I quiver and bolster my courage with intoxicants and drugs?

Shall I whimper and whine and demand assurance again and again from pulse and blood count? Shall I become the easy prey of every elixir and magic wand? Shall I cringe and surrender to the shadows?

No! The answer is in this text. "Thou preparest a table before me in the presence of mine enemies."

That table asks, "O death, where is thy sting? O grave, where is thy victory?" (1 Corinthians 15:55).

That table says: "For this corruptible must put on incorruption, and this mortal must put on immortality. So when this corruptible shall have put on incorruption, and this mortal shall have put on immortality, then shall be brought to pass the saying that is written, Death is swallowed up in victory" (1 Corinthians 15:53, 54).

Only the Lord's table dares to make that claim. His table makes it possible for me to live in the presence of that "final enemy." I thank God for such confidence.

Satan is my enemy. He dogs my feet. He is "the accuser of the brethren." He is a liar and a murderer.

How can I live a moral and victorious life in the midst of smear, invective and threat from such an adversary? The answer is in this text: "Thou preparest a table before me in the presence of mine enemies."

Satan cannot touch you at that table. The shed Blood and the broken body are my sanctuary. No evil can penetrate. "No weapon that is formed against thee shall prosper; and every tongue that shall rise against thee in judgment thou shalt condemn. This is the heritage of the servants of the Lord, and their righteousness is of me, saith the Lord" (Isaiah 54:17).

I look at the devastation. I know the power of the devil. He has possessed lives and made men and women habitations of demons. He has taught them to mock and to jeer.

No form of religion, no Sunday morning dress parade, can frighten the devil. The record of Paul the apostle sets this forth:

"And God wrought special miracles by the hands of Paul: So that from his body were brought unto the sick handkerchiefs or aprons, and the diseases departed from them, and the evil spirits went out of them.

"Then certain of the vagabond . . . took upon them to call over them which had evil spirits the name of the Lord Jesus, saying, We adjure you by Jesus whom Paul preacheth.

"And there were seven . . . which did so. And the evil spirit answered and said, Jesus I know, and Paul I know; but who are ye?

"And the man in whom the evil spirit was leaped on them, and overcame them, and prevailed against them, so that they fled out of that house naked and wounded" (Acts 19:11-16).

Mister, do not attempt to joust with the devil unless you know the victory of this table!

There were three children in our family, two sisters and myself. I recall how my father, full of faith and power, *sat at that table and claimed the lives of each one of us as sickness and disease threatened.* My own life hung on a thread during the first onslaught of influenza. A worldwide ministry teetered in the balance.

Neighbors were dying on both sides of the house. Father

invited a missionary couple to spend the day at our home. He was not afraid. He was confident. The missionary couple were Dr. and Mrs. Slocum, early Pentecostal missionaries to India.

Dr. Slocum had built a fine medical and surgical practice in New York City when the Holy Spirit crossed his path with the truth of divine healing and resurrection life through our risen Lord. The doctor closed his clinic and like Luke, gave his full time and service to the Great Physician.

My father brought Dr. and Mrs. Slocum to my bedside. *The doctor decided that I should partake of communion, not as the last rites of the church, but as the victory of our Lord and Saviour.*

My father acquiesced. A biscuit was broken. A tumbler was filled with grape juice. Dr. Slocum offered thanks. My father served me communion as meaningfully as though it were the first Sunday morning of the month at church.

As bread and drink touched my lips, the Lord of life touched my body. *And I was instantly healed.*

"Your adversary the devil, as a roaring lion, walketh about, seeking whom he may devour" (1 Peter 5:8).

"For this purpose the Son of God was manifested, that he might destroy the works of the devil" (1 John 3:8).

Sin is my enemy. A troubled conscience proves it. *What part of me is invulnerable to attack?*

My tongue lends itself more easily to sin than to righteousness. My falsehoods trail me like Treasury Agents track the counterfeiter. My eyes long to misbehave. John named it, "the lust of the eyes." My hands trigger to strike and snatch.

What will the records show? Will they show speed limits exceeded and driving to the common danger? Will they show books borrowed and never returned? Will they show wrong change accepted and never corrected? Will they show indecent approaches made and never confessed?

My feet betray me. "When I would do good, evil is present with me" (Romans 7:21). When I should be present, I am absent; and when I should absent myself for conscience's sake, I am a partaker. "O wretched man that I am! Who shall deliver me?" (Romans 7:24). Yes, sir, sin is my enemy.

I find safety at the table. "The blood of Jesus Christ his Son cleanseth us from all sin" (1 John 1:7).

No table of the world can do that for you, my friend. *You will be a hostage at those tables.* The dirty and smutty story will impose upon you and scratch itself upon your imagination. The affair that affronts your conscience will demand your participation. You will sit at those tables handcuffed to the enemies of your soul.

Calvary is God's provision for me. "Thou preparest a table before me in the presence of mine enemies."

Many centuries before Gethsemane and Golgotha, God prepared deliverance for Israel. Generations of bondage had enslaved the seed of Jacob under the whiplash of the Pharaohs.

God, Himself, broke the bondage. *He left the mark of the blood for all the world to remember.* He convoyed every believer with His visible presence, the cloud by day and the pillar of fire by night.

I, too, am assured of His presence. It is in the present tense, "Thou *preparest* (constantly the atonement speaks for me) a table before me." "Lo, I am with you alway" (Matthew 28:20). He is my defense. No hostility can reach me.

This experience is *personal.* No song of David is as personal as this song. How prominent are the personal pronouns *I, my* and *me!* "The Lord is *my* shepherd. *I* shall not want. He maketh *me* to lie down in green pastures" (Psalm 23:1, 2). It is just as true in this text. "Thou preparest a table before *me* in the presence of *mine* enemies."

This victory of the ages is for you, sir. This thrilling deliverance is for *you*. "Take, eat: this is my body which is broken for *you*" (1 Corinthians 11:24).

Face your enemies in the power of Christ's triumph! God does not propose to allow your enemy to have the last word.

Mister, you must move where there is power. "Ye cannot drink the cup of the Lord, and the cup of devils: ye cannot be partakers of the Lord's table, and of the table of devils" (1 Corinthians 10:21).

You cannot arrange what God has cursed. No ping-pong table in the basement of the church; no church supper-table loaded with fried chicken, hot biscuits and ice cream; no billiard table for the older men of the congregation; no rummage table for the support of evangelism; no card table for the pleasure of young couples—none of these tables in your church, sir, will ever heal the sick, redeem the sinner or baptize the believer. There is no power, no sanctuary in them. *His table alone can paralyze the enemy.*

THERE IS NO TOMORROW

Text: *"Behold, now is the accepted time; behold, now is the day of salvation."*
2 Corinthians 6:2

THIS is the element that makes the seventh game of a World Series a dramatic, nerve-tingling moment. *There is no tomorrow.*

John Wesley made it a rule for his class meetings that no testimony should be given that was more than a week old. What a difference this would make in our witness today.

There is no salvation *in tradition,* sir, in something you *were* forty-five years ago. What are you *now?*

There is no time for the past. Time has moved on. The past is only a memory. Memories will not save you any more than memories can feed you or clothe you.

You and I are always living in the "now"—that fluid instant that keeps stretching and stretching. It moves with us. *It is the only segment of security that I can cash in on.*

I cannot relive my yesterdays. I will never be eighteen again. I cannot borrow on tomorrow. I may not be given another birthday.

That is the sense in which John so often speaks of us "having" eternal life. Paul means the same thing when he says, "There is therefore *now* no condemnation" (Romans 8:1).

Do not overlook that important word "now." Salvation is always in the present tense. Are you free from condemnation now?

O, yes, a religious experience has its memories and hopes. I indulge them. I think back to my years when I did street-meeting evangelism and drew large crowds in the open air. I recall the power and thrill of my soul as I stood in downtown avenues.

I dream at times of what I may do when later and easier years are upon me. *These become escapes from reality if made substitutes for the salvation that is now.*

I believe there must be a moment pegged to a date when you *became* a Christian. But what have you *become?*

Yes, the date of birth does have significance. Yet it is relative. Conception and gestation preceded birth. Schooling followed birth. Birth is related to these and other events. *Why should it be different with the new birth?*

That event in my life that I designate as the date of my salvation is related to other events—victories won, prayers answered, guidance received, the Word illuminated and witness given. They are the manna of yesterdays. The "now" is upon me. The test is *immediate.*

There is something to be said for *hope.* It can keep a man going. But it can also be a trap.

A crowd of folk subterfuge their lives of defeat with a

camouflage of promises to themselves that *someday* they will come to grips with sin and bad habits. They convince themselves that heaven pays off on good intentions. Mister, you need to remember that salvation is *now*.

There is something in the future for the Christian. "If in this life only we have hope in Christ, we are of all men most miserable" (1 Corinthians 15:19).

I love prophecy. I preach prophecy. To me it is an exact science. Nevertheless, the millennium is *tomorrow* not *today*. Now is my challenge. What I will do under future circumstances is yet to be determined. *What I am doing now is a matter of record.*

Today's religion is filled with decorative crosses, stained glass windows and architectural shadows. We are surrounded by beautiful crosses of sentiment. Our churches are filled with *memories.* Some family has donated the communion table in memory of a good husband and father. Another family has given the organ in memory of a sainted wife and mother. *We sing our hymns and say our prayers in a living graveyard.*

That kind of religion may preserve, but it cannot save. I need the action of the Cross moving across the platform, marching in the gospel song, tugging in the message and demanding in the invitation. It is not my business to impress God. It is my business to yield to His presence.

How is it with you, my friend? Is there a throb in your soul? What happened to you today? Would the net result have been the same had you spent the same time in some art gallery?

Where is the radiance? Where is the sense of exploit? Where is your destiny with the miraculous? Are you merely religious?

I do not discount it for what it is worth, but will the Judgment Day of God settle for that? *If you have tasted reality, can you ever be content with less?*

Last year's victories will not save you today. An athlete knows this. He cannot win on his record. *He wins on present effort.*

You say, "Preacher, what can I do when I feel myself slipping toward a humdrum level?" You have a right to ask that question. It is encouraging that you should ask.

Perhaps there has been no conscious break in your fellowship with God. You have not yielded to sin. *The symptoms alarm you.* There is less joy. You no longer contemplate adventure. You punch the time clock of religious appearance and that is about all.

I suggest you check your relationship with others. *Have you wronged another and attempted no redress?* That is a dead giveaway. Your present moment of now will be a vacuum until there is a right relationship.

I do not believe an unforgiving person can get to heaven. You may have other thoughts. That is what I believe. You will continue to live in the negative until you return the property that belongs to someone else. There can be no present tense salvation for you until that is done.

What about the promise you made and never kept? Someone built on that. Someone's life was affected.

What about that wrong impression you left? Someone's life has been marred. Someone is laboring under an unnecessary handicap.

What salvation you may have enjoyed in the past or may again enjoy in the future is in God's hands. That is not for me to say. I only say this. *You are not enjoying it now.* And now is what counts. God says so.

What if death were to overtake you in this hour? If these things were not remedied, would memories of better days save you? Would hope of happier relationships redeem you? *Now* is the accepted time. Vital salvation must be based on righteousness.

Something all of us should remember is this. *It is not the size of the matter that counts.* It is little foxes that spoil the vine of a clear conscience.

I suggest you check *your victory over temptation.*

You experience lifelessness when you walk in the path of defeat. How long has your losing streak lasted? When did you last taste victory?

How can you thrill to the testimony meeting and know that once again you lost your temper a few hours before? How can you get meat out of the gospel song, "There's Power in the Blood" and know that very day lust ruled in your breast? How can you respond to the missionary convention and realize that your life is selfishly sheltered? Must we tell of being saved ten years ago and harbor up-to-date memories of defeat?

When the Cross becomes real enough in our own hearts to become the crucifixion spot for those very sins which defeat us, we shall experience the resurrection power of the living Christ in a salvation which is *now. Salvation means present victory.* There are no saved "has-beens."

I suggest that you check *the regularity of your devotional life.* There has been established between Washington and Moscow a hot line. This means instant communication between the capitals.

Thank God, I have enjoyed a line like that years before it was establisl d between the two nations. It is a glorious privilege in an stant to be able to lift one's heart heavenward in the midst of a noisy crowd with the assurance that God hears. But this can never substitute for those longer periods of communion in which the soul finds dimensions.

"Hop, skip and jump" devotions produce trifling character. It produces an up-and-down life. Satan can strike when you are in the trough. Death does not wait until you are at the crest of some revival meeting.

We are bombarded today with shallow and shifting philosophies. *Meaning and depth come through a study of God's Word.* It is still true that prayer changes things.

You say to me, "Brother Ward, I have such difficulty when I pray to keep my thoughts from wandering. What can I do?" Your problem is the same problem you face when you try to study.

First, discipline yourself to concentrate. Second, open your devotional period with Bible reading. The Word will sanctify your mind. Third, *pray definitely.* Indefinite praying receives indefinite answers. *Even righteous men and women must pray fervently and with faith.*

Finally, I suggest that you check your *witnessing.* Witnessing is not debating. No one gets converted as the result of evangelical arguing. That is true of academic preaching. The "letter" killeth. *It is a sign that spiritual life has evaporated.*

The glorious, bubbling "now" of salvation has subsided in your soul. You are going through the motions—grinding out Sunday school lessons in your class, mouthing anthems in your choir, listing approved conduct in your sermons—but something living and vital is missing.

Does the emptiness and hollowness of your profession frighten you? Does it sicken you?

You and I need something more than words, mister! We need the experience Jesus talked about. "Out of your innermost being *shall flow*" (John 7:38).

I am lost when that *flow* ceases. I have no defense for a barren life. I can only share what I have and if I have nothing then I can share nothing. If I am not sharing, it is because I have no *"now"* of Christian experience.

I ask you to face the words of this text: "Behold, now is the accepted time; behold, now is the day of salvation." Your business and your destiny is with this moment.

Neither history nor imagination can save you. A living Christ victorious in a living soul alone is salvation.

SHAME

Text: *"What fruit had ye then in those things whereof ye are now ashamed? for the end of those things is death."*
Romans 6:21.

THE dictionary defines *shame* as:

"Painful emotion excited by a consciousness of guilt, shortcoming or impropriety. It is disgrace or dishonor. It is that which brings discredit or reproach. It involves indecency, scandal, lack of modesty and impudency."

Today's engineers of human conduct are trying to eliminate this emotion. They are working on the blush, the sensitive conscience and the tear. They are busy building a brazen attitude by every means available from the abbreviated bathing suit to a new theology.

The preacher, Hosea, faced this problem. He said, "As they were increased, so they sinned against me: therefore will I change their glory into shame" (Hosea 4:7).

God built this reflection into man. It cannot be exercised like a diseased appendix or pair of tonsils. Shame is always there like hunger, thirst and weariness. *It is a part of sin that is seldom mentioned.* Misery and shame go together.

I want to direct this service toward those who say, "I feel so *miserable"* and to those who say, "I feel so *ashamed."*

Paul declares, "Godliness is *profitable* unto all things, having promise of the life that now is, and of that which is to come" (1 Timothy 4:8).

Like the Ark of the Covenant before the fish-gods of Philistia, *an Almighty God is willing for you to put Him to the test.* "Godliness is profitable." In any legitimate walk of life you are a better man, a better woman.

"Godliness is profitable unto all things." *Such a testimony will never prove to be a handicap.*

On the other hand James declares, "When lust hath conceived, it bringeth forth sin: and sin, when it is finished, bringeth forth death" (James 1:15).

You cannot make sin pay. It is impossible. It is the parent of misery, and the forerunner of destruction.

Paul asks the Romans, "What *fruit* had ye then in those things whereof ye are now ashamed?" In today's language he asks, "What was the *profit?*"

It seems insane to invest in something that never shows a profit. This is exactly what you do when you sin. Let me spell it out for you! "Whosoever committeth sin transgresseth also the law: for sin is the transgression of the law" (1 John 3:4).

Mister, you cannot snub God's laws of honesty, purity, sanctity and truthfulness without wallowing in disgrace and reproach. You cannot violate the rules of this universe without experiencing torture and disappointment in your soul.

Why? Part of the answer is this: *you will be embarrassed.* The kick you get out of rebellion, out of doing wrong, is short-lived. *It fades quicker than anything you have ever experienced.*

There is an inner part of you, your soul, that wants a better deal. There is a part of you that never subsides. It repudiates vanities. It chokes on husks. *It retaliates.*

When you abuse your body your head aches, your stomach retches, your pulse writes the record. When you abuse your soul, you experience misery and shame.

Haman lived only long enough to enjoy his own gallows. The thrill he felt in plotting the destruction of the Jews was short-lived. He went from the head of the parade to the hangman's noose within 72 hours.

Belshazzar did not live long enough to enjoy his own nightclub. He perished in a shambles of wine, women and song with God's verdict of his empty life written for all to see. *Sin's price tag is disgrace, dishonor, discredit.*

"There is no peace, saith my God, to the wicked" (Isaiah 57:21).

The same condition prevails at this moment. You cannot subjugate an immortal spirit. *Try it, and you experience an aching void!*

The record is there to see. In what form of covetousness, lying, sensuality would you like to indulge? The price tags go with the goods.

Does violence entice you? It attracted Cain. He paid for it. He became a fugitive and vagabond.

Does perversion interest you? It built the great white way in the cities of Sodom and Gomorrah. They paid the price for it. A holocaust of judgment leveled their playgrounds of indulgence.

Does some dramatic sense of deceit appeal to you? It attracted Ananias and Sapphira and wrote a chapter into the Book of Acts that sizzles with action.

Sin is a chamber of horrors, mister! It is not preacher's talk when Paul asks, "What fruit had ye then in those things whereof ye are now ashamed?"

What have you *accomplished?* What *influence* have you spread upon your street, upon your community, upon your generation? "Wisdom is better than weapons of war: but one sinner destroyeth much good" (Ecclesiastes 9:18).

Paul states a moral fact when he says, "Evil communications corrupt good manners" (1 Corinthians 15:33). The word evil is simply the word live spelled backwards. It is going the wrong way. It is doing the wrong thing.

What *profit* is there to show in a life rotted by unprincipled action, by prodigality, by seduction, by rioting, by smear, by falsehood?

Job asked the same question, "He looketh upon men, and if any say, I have sinned, and perverted that which was right, *and it profited me not*" (Job 33:27).

Mister, the life of sin is a life of shame from start to finish.

Are you ashamed? Am I speaking to you? Look at your God-given talents! What have you done with them? Have you allowed your gift for speech to be laced with oaths and vulgarities? Do you regret the hours you have spent in folly and lust?

That time can never be retrieved. God gave you one youth. How have you spent it? Would you repeat your mistake?

Look at yourself! What have you done to degrade your own body? You have sported with eternal things. You have trifled with divine grace. That is a sense of shame you feel, my friend!

Over and over you have told yourself, "I am not hurting anybody but myself." That is not how David felt. He came face to face with it. He said, "Against thee, thee *only,* have I sinned" (Psalm 51:4).

You have a God to reckon with. Another man of record said, "O my God, I am ashamed, and blush to lift up my face to thee, my God" (Ezra 9:6).

Your sin is hurting the heart of God. Your sin nailed Jesus Christ to a timber. Your sin is the talk of heaven. You have a right to feel ashamed.

You knew better! Parents brought you up right. They set an example for you. Good people in your community let their lights shine. Your conscience checked you over and over again. Every day there were cautions, warnings and admonitions. *What excuse can you possibly have?* That is why you are ashamed.

Who can be proud of moral ruin? Can you gloat because you have poisoned your friends with skepticism? You can tell big stories in the barracks, mister, but you cannot erase the inner shame of betraying innocence under a pretense of affection.

Where has sin brought you? You never intended to be an embezzler. Your intention was to borrow and to put it back. You felt you could make it big on the race track. You had a hot tip.

Dishonesty has forced you to wear the stripes of disgrace. You never intended it to be any more than an occasional night out on the town. Now a dissolute life has unstrung every nerve in your body.

God started you out with a constitution as magnificent as the one our forefathers hammered together at Philadelphia. Sin has shattered it. You stand there ashamed of the waste.

But in the midst of your sin you have the right to be thankful. *God has not cut you down.* You are alive. Let tears moisten your cheeks! Drop to your knees! Look toward the Cross as you think that the end of sin is death. Paul reminds the Romans, "For the end of those things is death" (Romans 6:21).

Mister, it has not fully dawned upon you what it means when God passes final judgment, "Depart from me." You have never lived in that condition. You have drawn upon God's benefits. You have mingled with God's people.

There have been churches and believers and Bibles in your world. You have met decency and honesty and purity. In a moment you are going to step out of that world into an eternal prison house of unmitigated filth. You will have an eternity to wail, "when ye shall see Abraham, and Isaac, and Jacob, and all the prophets, in the kingdom of God, *and you yourselves thrust out*" (Luke 13:28).

The shame you feel now is only a prelude, a heaven-produced warning of the eternal guilt that acts as a worm "that never dieth," always crawling, always festering your consciousness with a sense of failure.

Make no mistake about it, sir, the mortification you feel now, the repellent inside you at this moment, is God's promise to you that there is more to come.

The gnawing will never cease. The anguish will never be relieved. The gloom will never lift. *You will eternally feel unwashed, indecent impoverished, unwanted, condemned.*

Your rage will know no bounds. You will hate the devil and sinners who greased your way to perdition.

That is the big death. Sin will never finish with your life until it has locked forever the doors of this big death upon you.

Heed your shame in this moment! Ask yourself a reasonable question, "Why should I feel this ·way? What repeated irritation is this that I am suffering? What does it mean? Why can I not dismiss it?"

Get down on your knees and cry out to God and thank Him for a human emotion on this side of the grave that is designed to flash a warning that there is a point of no return where "the smoke of their *torment* ascendeth up for ever and ever" (Revelation 14:11).

Sin will take you there, unless—unless you can turn toward Jesus Christ who took our shame upon Himself.

Daniel, the statesman, saw it all at close range—the banquets, great military victories, the move of God upon the genius and talent of his day, history's parade, political events of the highest significance. Daniel who saw it all put it this way:

"And many of them that sleep in the dust of the earth shall awake, some to everlasting life, *and some to shame and everlasting contempt*" (Daniel 12:2).

Sinner, it is up to you to prove personally in the one life given to you on this earth that you have the right to live again in God's "bigger world." Your shame will guide you.

THE BABY

Texts: *"Ye shall find the babe ..."*
Luke 2:12
"By stretching forth thine hand to heal; and that signs and wonders may be done by the name of thy holy child Jesus."
Acts 4:30

THE miracle of birth far outweighs the jingle and jangle of:

"Hark! the tinselled fairies sing,
Santa Claus will come to bring
Lighted trees with presents piled,
Rocket ships for every child;
Gleeful, all the space kids rise,
Join the sputniks in the skies,
With the missile men exclaim,
'Christmas sure is getting tame!'"

Birth never loses its wonder. Christ, the Saviour was born. The great joy and excitement of Christmas is the fascination of a baby.

One thing is certain. *Heaven participated in this birth.* I believe that heaven participates in every birth.

Human offspring are not two-legged animals without souls or destiny. *Every birth is a message.* Every baby comes with privilege and power to change this world either for better or for worse.

Your baby boy can become a bloody Stalin or a blessed Stephen. Your baby girl can become a murderous Jezebel or a mother like Jochebed who brought Moses into the world. *Look at that baby in your arms and ponder!*

I have long considered the prodigal's words, "I have sinned *against heaven.*" Another world is interested in people. It has an investment in us. There is a "great . . . cloud of witnesses."

A multitude of the heavenly host could sing about the birth of the Babe of Bethlehem, "Glory to God in the highest, and on earth peace, good will toward men" (Luke 2:14), *because they knew the mission of this child,* "Lo, I come . . . to do thy will, O God" (Hebrews 10:9).

What does heaven expect of your child, parent? What is heaven prepared to do for your child? It is said of Mary that she "kept all these things, and *pondered* them in her heart" (Luke 2:19). Every mother in this audience has shared that experience.

God gave His Son to earth in the form of a baby to dignify every human being. It is His affirmation that mankind is "created . . . in His own image."

Every birth challenges the *science* of men. It cannot be fathomed. The intricate blending of body, soul and mind is beyond any research laboratory.

I have sometimes wondered what might have happened had

the three scholars come from the Western world instead of from the Orient.

What search in the heart would there have been for the *big industrialist?* Would his concern have been for untapped markets and new resources of raw materials? Would he have carried an order book with him?

What thrill, what discovery in the soul would there have been for *a Madison Avenue advertising executive?* Would he have exploded with ideas?

"This finding of a new king will be a tremendously big thing! It has great publicity possibilities, and must be handled in a big way.". Would he have carried press releases with him and entertained local journalists?

Smart people can be wrong about Christmas. Christmas is not in the wrappings, the ribbons, the decorations, the cash register. Christmas is in that Baby.

The men out of the East allowed their intellect to be guided by God. "We...are come to worship Him" (Matthew 2:2).

God can make any man "wise unto salvation." Birth means death, mister. A beginning implies an ending. When you ask, "Where did I come from?" you are also asking, "Where am I going?"

Face eternity, sir! Look at a baby! You were like that. Now look at yourself. What is happening to you? Can you stop it? Where will it end? Your answer is found where the Wise Men found it, in the stable by Bethlehem's Inn.

A baby is a mirror into which we look to discover that "all have sinned, and come short of the glory of God" (Romans 3:23).

That look turned loose demons in Herod. The Scriptures tell us that Herod was "troubled" when he heard that Jesus was born. He had grown an ugly soul. Always he was threatened by real or imaginary enemies. So low had Herod sunk that he slew his own mother and murdered his wife and children, fearing they should rob him of his throne.

The Emperor Augustus made this statement: "It were better to be one of Herod's swine than one of his children!"

Take a look, drunkard! Take a look, thief! Take a look, killer! *Look at a baby.* Then ask yourself and your God, "What has become of me?" Where did the innocence go? Where did the love and affection go? Where did the joy and sparkle go? Look and weep!

Turn now to the Child, Jesus! Let God's Christmas come into your heart! Pray the words of my text over your rotten, twisted, wasted life: "Stretch forth thine hand to heal," O God, "that signs and wonders may be done by the name of thy holy child Jesus." Thank God! There is a new beginning possible for you.

Do not go on trampling lives. The world has had enough Herods. One day Christians will turn from you as they turned from Herod. They brought him the Word. They left their testimony, but it only infuriated this man. He decided to root out and destroy the cause of Christ before it destroyed him. He failed. You will fail. God has a separate way for His people.

It is beyond your power to prevent, sinner. God's Child is set for "the fall and rising again of many." Jesus will *madden* you or *gladden* you, sir.

Every baby seems too helpless, *but birth is also a moment of triumph.* The mother beams. The father struts. It is the accomplishment of accomplishments.

Only a mother can describe the utter joy which comes into her whole being when she realizes that she is handling that which is of herself. The maternity ward is the "holy of holies" in every hospital, and rightly so. Here is the shrine of mystery.

God wants to share such a moment with you. *You can experience the birth of Christ personally.* You can share Mary's joy. You can know a peace that passeth all understanding; a peace that comes from the knowledge that you have given the Son of God a place in your life, a place that the crowd and man's agenda withhold from Him.

The first moment you embrace Him and sense His closeness you will feel exactly like Mary who knew the exhilaration of God's promise fulfilled in her life. She sang:

"My soul doth magnify the Lord, and my spirit hath rejoiced in God my Saviour .... For he that is mighty hath done to me great things; and holy is his name" (Luke 1:46, 47, 49).

Have you ever received *a birth announcement?* They always stand out in the mail we receive at our house. We read them first—before bills or advertisements or even other first-class mail.

The arrival of a new person upon earth is an exceedingly important event. The announcements reach our house in novel, arresting, compelling form. And our first reaction is always, "We must send a gift."

God has sent a birth announcement to all of us. "For unto us a child is born, unto us a son is given" (Isaiah 9:6). *Your response to that announcement is important to God.* It demands a gift. Give yourself to Him!

There are those who shut Christ out of their lives as the innkeeper did because they fear that Christ may interfere with their conduct. There are things in their lives which they know to be wrong. Christ's presence is embarrassing.

I have been a minister for a good many years. I have seen babies change the attitude and conduct in many marriages and homes. *And I have seen this Babe of Bethlehem, this "holy child" change a crowd of lives in these years of evangelistic preaching.* God gives you the good sense to acknowledge this greatest of all birth announcements!

You say to me, "Preacher, is this not all tradition and happy myth like May Day and Halloween?" Well, sir, the trees and yule logs, the mistletoe and lights may all be tradition; *but Jesus Christ is a reality.*

There are more documents available for us today which confirm the Word of God than there are for the fact that Julius Caesar went to Britain in 55 B.C. We have contemporary historians who witness to the birth of Jesus Christ, to His life and to His death—like the Jewish historian, Josephus. Are you asking for proof? Library shelves are filled with it today.

I do not bring you an *obituary.* I bring you a *birth announcement.* This service is not for observing a moment of silence. I am reading to you again the announcement of One who is *still making* history. And He can make history in your life right now.

Your Christmas lights will go out. Your Christmas tree will fade. Your Christmas ribbons will be forgotten. Your Christmas cards will be packed away. *But the Christmas Child will remain.*

He will comfort you when you are sorrowful. He will provide meaning and fullness for your life when it seems useless and empty. He will bring light when the way seems dark. He will provide joy when circumstances are grim.

Long after the plum pudding is eaten; long after the gift certificate has been cashed; long after the carols have hushed; long after these things, the presence of Jesus Christ in your life and home will continue to bring happiness and satisfaction.

I have had a lot of happy and notable things happen to me during the Christmas season over the years.

I was married on Christmas Day. I was ordained to the ministry during a Christmas week. I began this network broadcast eleven years ago on a Christmas Sunday.

These events have brought a wonderful sense of fulfillment into my life. But none can compare to the wealth and attainment I have reached in the personal knowledge of Jesus Christ as my very own Saviour—the Babe of Bethlehem.

ADOPTION

Texts: *"When the fulness of the time was come, God sent forth his Son made of a woman, made under the law, To redeem them that were under the law, that we might receive the adoption of sons. Wherefore thou art no more a servant, but a son; and if a son, then an heir of God through Christ."*
Galatians 4:4, 5, 7

"Having predestinated us unto the adoption of children by Jesus Christ to himself."
Ephesians 1:5

For a very brief series of two or three messages, I want to share with you from the Bible *the truth of a new relationship.*

In the natural this is a thrilling experience which may occur through means of marriage, application of citizenship or business commitments. In the spiritual the possibilities are unlimited.

The convincing answer to the inquiring mind of an adopted child from a parent is this, "We *chose* you."

Every real Christian is adopted. No one comes into this world a Christian. We do not *adopt* ourselves. We are *adopted.* Someone who wants us reaches out toward us. There is no other way.

God's purpose in giving the law has been sadly misunderstood. It was given to Israel on tables of stone and copied in their sacred writings. The rest of mankind had it written in their hearts. The one class had more light than the other, and therefore will be judged differently.

"As many as have sinned without law shall also perish without law; and as many as have sinned in the law shall be judged by the law" (Romans 2:12).

That is what the Bible says. Here is more of the same: "For when the Gentiles, which have not the law, do by nature the things contained in the law, these, having not the law, *are a law unto themselves*: which show the work of the law written in their hearts, their conscience also bearing witness, and their thoughts the meanwhile accusing or else excusing one another" (Romans 2:14, 15).

God had one purpose for everybody. It is plainly stated. Read it from your own Bible! "That *every* mouth may be stopped, and *all the world* may become guilty before God" (Romans 3:19).

God never intended that the law should *save* anybody. God had other intentions. God intended that the law should *apprehend* a person.

"All have sinned and come short of the glory of God" (Romans 3:23). All means everyone who has appeared on earth. *No one was saved by keeping the law.*

There can be no mistake about this. Read it for yourself!

"The Scripture hath concluded *all* under sin, (everybody), that the promise *by faith* of Jesus Christ might be given to them that believe. But before faith came, we were kept under the law, shut up unto the faith which should afterwards be revealed. Wherefore the law was our schoolmaster to bring us unto Christ, *that we might be justified by faith.* But after that faith is come, we are no longer under a schoolmaster" (Galatians 3:22-25).

The law was given for one purpose only—that mankind might be convinced of their need of a Saviour, *one to redeem them from the arrest of the law.* God's intention is much more. His intention is adoption.

I trust that the Holy Spirit will make this real to you. *God's plan with men is not simply to save them, but to put them above all other created beings.*

"For ye are all sons of God through faith in Christ Jesus." This privilege can be attained only by men coming out from under the law.

Mister, the only way you can come out from under the law is by redemption. There is no alternative.

"God's word teaches clearly, then, that when a man is redeemed, he is no longer under the law. Let me read it to you from your own Bible! "Ye are not under the law" (Romans 6: 14).

"What things soever the law saith, it saith to *those who are under the law*" (Romans 3:19).

The deduction is simple. Some are under the law. Some are not under the law.

What is your category? My full and complete freedom and exoneration is in Jesus Christ. He fulfulls my every obligation to the law. "Sin is not imputed when there is no law" (Romans 5:13).

I will be perfectly frank with you. Yes, it is true! I am hiding in Jesus Christ. I have a complete legal standing in Him. I intend to maintain that standing.

You ask me, "Then, why serve God?" I am not trying to earn my way. I am not frightened. *I do it from love.* Jesus Christ lifted me. He gave me status.

I want to read to you what every Bible in the world says. Here it is! "Wherefore, thou art no more a *servant,* but a *son*" (Galatians 4:7).

I am delivered from bondage forever. I have the assurance of heaven, not when I die; not when I unite with some church; not when I receive baptism; but the very moment I repent from sin and accept Jesus Christ as my personal and present Saviour.

"He that believeth on the son *hath* everlasting life" (John 3:36).

Salvation is not a promissory note. *It is an outright gift.*

My entire life is motivated differently. I am absolutely free of a guilt complex. Fear is eliminated.

The Bible puts it this way. "Ye have not received the spirit of bondage again to fear; but ye have received the spirit of adoption, whereby we cry, Abba Father" (Romans 8:15).

That is what this new birth does for me. *God is truly, and in an eternal sense, my Father.* That makes all the difference.

Paul says:

"For the love of Christ (not fear of the law, nor the fear of hell) constraineth us; because we thus judge, that if one died for all, then were all dead: And that he died for all, that they which live should not henceforth live unto themselves, but unto him which died for them, and rose again" (2 Corinthians 5: 14, 15).

This becomes my everyday working principle. I have stopped living for myself. My life is God's property to be used when and where and how as He sees fit. I had forfeited any personal life and choice I might have claimed under the law. I was a moral failure. I have been redeemed. God reached out and adopted me.

Jesus said, "If you love me, keep my commandments;" not, "if ye are afraid of the law, keep my commandments;" not, "if ye are afraid of going to hell, keep my commandments;" not, "if ye wish to make sure of going to heaven, keep my commandments;" but, "if ye *love* me."

But why love Jesus? Why not love Abraham Lincoln or Louis Pasteur or Martin Luther?

The answer is this. "This is *my blood* of the new testament which is shed for many for the remission of sins" (Matthew 26:28). His sacrifice has canceled my sin-debt.

Jesus illustrated it this way.

"There was a certain creditor which had two debtors; the one owed five hundred pence, and the other fifty. And when they had nothing to pay, he frankly forgave them both. *Tell me, therefore, which of them will love him most?* Simon answered and said, I suppose that he, to whom he forgave most. And he said unto him, Thou hast rightly judged" (Luke 7:41-43).

So it is not a theory, mister. Love is the controlling motive. I live this way because I *want* to live this way. No one on earth is making me.

Let me say this to you, face to face! One may be moral, have an excellent reputation and standing in the community. Yet if the motive power in that person's life is not this love, that person is *lost. That person is not a real Christian.*

You say, "That is strong preaching, Brother Ward." It is not one bit stronger than the Word of God puts it.

"Though I speak with the tongues of men and of angels, and have not charity, I am become as sounding brass, or a tinkling cymbal. And though I have the gift of prophecy, and understand all mysteries, and all knowledge; and though I have all faith, so that I could remove mountains, *and have not charity,* I AM NOTHING. And though I bestow all my goods to feed the poor, and though I give my body to be burned, and have not charity, IT PROFITETH ME NOTHING" (1 Corinthians 13:1-3).

You say, "Did it happen?" Yes, it has happened. It is on record.

Two of the mightiest preachers of all times, Chalmers and Wesley, men whose tongues were those nearest to angels in preaching, *stated that during all those years of powerful preaching they were lost.* Why? They had not been really redeemed from all iniquity. Their subsequent experience revealed this to them. They both testified later to personal salvation.

Eloquent, powerful preaching cannot redeem from sin. God says plainly, "Without shedding of blood is no remission" (Hebrews 9:22).

Men may write great books explaining the Bible. They can print commentaries, Sunday school lesson helps or instructions on church membership—*yet if the motive power of their lives is not based on a love through a personal sense of forgiveness, they remain lost men writing those helps and quarterlies for you.*

Why? Because there is nothing in understanding all mysteries, and all knowledge, in writing religious books, to redeem from sin. Writing a book about the Bible can never substitute for Calvary.

Mister, you have to be adopted into this family. You cannot earn your way in.

You can turn philanthropist and live here on in for charity, for the poor, feeding them, clothing them, housing them. The world will build you a monument.

God will not change His opinion about you. You are still a lost man. Why? Because there is nothing in giving away money to care for the poor, nor in giving up life for a cause, that can redeem from sin. Building a hospital can never be a substitute for that middle cross. *You love because you are forgiven.*

It is as simple and as unchangeable as that. And you receive forgiveness when you throw yourself upon the mercy of the one big Creditor of this universe who holds all the I.O.U.'s of mankind.

Whatever your list of sins may be, whether how long or how short, it must become evident that "when you have nothing to pay" there is only one solution for your obligation to God. It is expressed in the story Jesus told. *"He frankly forgave."*

If you have never experienced God's forgiveness, sir, you have never experienced God's love. You may be a member of some of the best societies in town, but you are not a member of God's family. You may have joined some church. Take what pride you can in that! But you cannot join the kingdom of God.

There is only one way into that family. You have to be adopted. Let me ask you, mister! "What has God done for you?"

God has determined that He alone may "be just *and* the *justifier* of him which believeth in Jesus" (Romans 3:26).

Man must not, from intellectual pride, religious prejudice, family or race, nor any other motive, trifle with God *and presume to dictate terms.* Earth's respectability does not legislate God's mercy. The wisdom of this world is foolishness with God.

God will not allow any man or any religious denomination to tell Him how they can escape from their sins and how their sins can be taken away. God is too big to be *used.* He will use you.

"Who hath measured the waters in the hollow of his hand, and meted out heaven with the span, and comprehended the dust of the earth in a measure, and weighed the mountains in scales, and the hills in a balance?

"Who hath directed the Spirit of the Lord, or being his counselor hath taught him? With whom took he counsel, and who instructed him, and taught him in the path of judgment and taught him knowledge, and showed to him the way of understanding?

"Behold, the nations are as a drop of a bucket, and are counted as the small dust of the balance: behold, he taketh up the isles as a very little thing" (Isaiah 40:12-15).

"All nations before him are as nothing; *and they are counted to him less than nothing, and vanity*" (Isaiah 40:17).

"It is he that sitteth upon the circle of the earth, and the inhabitants thereof are as grasshoppers; that stretcheth out the heavens as a curtain, and spreadeth them out as a tent to dwell in: that bringeth the princes to nothing; *he maketh the judges of the earth as vanity*" (Isaiah 40:22, 23).

That is how *big* God is, and He wants you, a lost sinner and totally without credit, to be His child.

Come to Calvary and experience divine adoption!

———————◄◆►———————

THE PURIFIED

Text: *"Behold what manner of love the Father hath bestowed upon us, that we should be called the sons of God: therefore the world knoweth us not, because it knew him not. Beloved, now are we the sons of God, and it doth not yet appear what we shall be: but we know that, when he shall appear, we shall be like him; for we shall see him as he is. And every man that hath this hope in him purifieth himself, even as he is pure."*

1 *John* 3:1-3

A MISSIONARY, after laboring for some time among the people, employed a national to help him translate portions of the Word into the local tongue. They finally came to the First Epistle· of John.

One morning as they began their work, having finished the second chapter, the missionary read, "Behold what manner of love the Father hath bestowed upon us." The national translated and it was recorded.

The missionary continued, "that we should be called the children of God." The national bowed his head and wept.

After a while, he said, "Teacher, do not make me put it that way; I know our people; that is too good for us; we do not deserve it. Put it this way, 'That we may be allowed to kiss his feet.' That is good enough for our people."

The thought that beyond forgiveness of sin God provides *a new relationship* for redeemed sinners was too much for him.

Years ago, when I was a teen-ager, we had a camp-meeting gospel song that said, "I sometimes think it is almost too good to be true that I am saved and on my way to glory."

Even in nature, God has two grades of existence—a lower and a higher, *even for some insects*. The mosquito, by beginning, is a water larvae, but by a process known only to God, rises into a higher kingdom. The caterpillar, a creeping worm, sheds its humiliation, and becomes a butterfly.

And, mister, our God has revealed that *there is a higher relationship for those who are redeemed from the curse of the law.*

I will read it to you again from your own Bible:

"God sent forth his Son, made of a woman, made under the law, to redeem them that were under the law, that we might receive *the adoption of sons*" (Galatians 4:4, 5).

That is something, sir, that the angels of heaven can never be, and can never know anything about. "Unto which of the angels said he at any time, Thou art my son?" (Hebrews 1:5).

In my work as an evangelist I have seen *this miracle of moral revolution* happen to scores and scores of individuals. Science cannot explain it. But God's Word proclaims it. *It is the new birth.*

There are always cheap copies of the real thing. The New Testament acknowledges this.

"They went out from us, but they were *not of us;* for if they had been of us, they would no doubt have continued with us: but they went out, that they might be made manifest that they were *not all of us*" (1 John 2:19).

Do not let the hypocrite and the pretender blind you!

It is one thing to *say* "Our Father," but it is something quite different to *be* "a son of God." It is not something you *try* to do.

If you have been *trying* to do good, doing your so-called Christian duty, fearing that if you failed in your performance you would not be *saved*—that your existence would be counted unworthy—then your motive has not been a love relationship between yourself and your Heavenly Father.

There is no umbilical cord between God and yourself. You are a lost soul. You are a nice person, no doubt, but you are a lost soul. Your pride and your prejudice can keep you out of heaven.

Listen to what Paul said!

"My heart's desire and prayer to God for Israel is, that they might be *saved.* For I bear them record that *they have a zeal of God,* but not according to knowledge. For being *ignorant of God's righteousness,* and going about to establish their own righteousness, they have not submitted themselves unto the righteousness of God. For Christ is the end of the law for righteousness to every one that believeth" (Romans 10:2-4).

Those words can fit you, mister, and all your church activity and your program of social service. Your relationship to God depends upon Jesus Christ alone.

If you are going to work your own way toward moral health and toward heaven, you are off on another road. There is no doubt about it! If a man keeps the law from birth to death he will go to heaven *without any redemption.* That man would not need redemption.

Paul puts it this way. "Moses describeth the righteousness which is of the law, that the man that doeth those things shall live *by them*" (Romans 10:5).

Yes, sir, you can go that way, *if you can make it.* But you better make the study of your life the Pentateuch, the first five books of the Bible.

The law that Moses put in writing *is a complicated code.* One slip, one tumble, one error and you are out of the race. But you can go that way!

Galatians 3:12 says, "And the law is not of faith; but the man that doeth them shall live in them."

Your destiny will depend upon perfect action, without one slip, one omission, one mistake.

You are welcome to try, mister! God gives you that opportunity, that fair chance. *You will not need any middle cross because a perfect record needs no redemption, no faith.*

I am telling you the truth. Look at it in your own Bible. This is what it says in the New Testament, "The doers of the law *shall be justified*" (Romans 2:13). That man does not need Jesus Christ. That man has never sinned.

Let me make this clear to you, sir! Keep the right law. It is not the fine creed of your service club that meets every Tuesday noon at the local hotel.

Let me ask you, "Have you kept those simple objectives perfectly? Have you attended every meeting? Have you served on every committee? Have you done your part in every project? *Have you?*"

No, the code, the charter, the constitution, the bill-of-rights you have to keep perfectly in order to avoid Calvary and Jesus Christ, is the law recorded in detail by Moses. It is written out. It is still a part of every Bible.

God gives every person a chance at it. You have the God-given right to try your fortune. Try it without the shedding of blood! Try it without redemption! Try it without coming to the altar! *It beckons you but it laughs at you.*

This is your curse, your nightmare, your sting. And no one can remove it from your life except Jesus Christ. "Christ hath redeemed us from the curse of law, being made a curse for us" (Galatians 3:13).

Jesus Christ taught these two ways:

"One came and said unto him, Good Master, *what good thing* shall I do that I may have eternal life? And he said unto him, Why callest thou me good? There is none good but one, that is God: *but if thou wilt enter into life,* keep the commandments" (Matthew 19:16, 17).

There you have it! You are welcome to try.

On the other hand, to the penitent woman in Simon's house the Saviour said, "Thy faith hath *saved* thee; go in peace" (Luke 8:50). That offer still stands. But it must be one road or the other.

Do not try to mix them! They will not mix. You must depend absolutely and finally upon Jesus or depend absolutely and finally upon yourself. Read it for yourself. "If by grace, then it is no more of works: otherwise grace is no more grace. But if it be of works, then it is no more grace: otherwise work is no more work."

God has raised up this service to tell you with the anointing of the Holy Ghost upon it that "to him that worketh not, but believeth on him that *justifieth* the ungodly, his faith is counted for righteousness" (Romans 4:5). That is the greatest news that will ever reach you this side of the coffin.

Salvation is not by character. Salvation is by Jesus Christ. Salvation will produce character. *But character will not produce salvation.* Jesus told men of so-called character, "The publicans and the harlots go into the kingdom of God before you" (Matthew 21:31).

Mister, God looks at the heart, *the motive.*

Two young men are trying to win a young woman in marriage. Their deeds, *outwardly,* are the same. One is prompted by pure, manly love for the young woman. The other has his eye on her father's bank account.

You drop your handkerchief on the street. One man from pure kindness will pick it up and return it to you. Another man will do the same, but his intention is to win your confidence and pick your pocket.

Four sons are equally dutiful, *in outward deed,* toward their fathers. One does it to get all the money he wishes. Another does it from a cold sense of duty. Still another is moved by fear of his father. A fourth does it from a compulsion of tender love.

This world is full of religion, sir. It is full of good effort. You have to look deeper for judgment. Ask, "Why?"

Only the man who lives a response because One died for him is the truly saved man.

Did you repeat the Lord's Prayer today? A sinner cannot pray this prayer. The Bible says, "They which are the children of the flesh, these are not the children of God" (Romans 9:8). This prayer was given to *disciples.* Are you a disciple?

Thomas Paine in, "The Age of Reason" said, "He (Jesus) was the Son of God in like manner that every person is; for the Creator is the father of all."

That is where the issue is joined, sir! It is between Thomas Paine and others on the one side and Jesus Christ and Paul on the other. You must decide whether or not Jesus told the truth when he said, "Ye are of your father, the devil."

I know that does not sound like refined language, *but it was the language Jesus used.* Better to have your feelings hurt than to have your soul lost!

How can you stand in your church and call God the Father of the drunkard, of the thief, of the pervert, of the swindler? *Even angels do not call Him Father.* This is the privilege of the redeemed.

What right has any man living in sin and in open enmity

with God, to lift up his voice and say, "Our Father"? He is acting a lie.

Jesus faced this attitude. He judged it very explicitly. He said:

"Ye do the deeds of your father. Then said they to him, We are not born of fornication; we have one Father, even God. Jesus said unto them, If God were your Father, ye would love me; for I proceeded forth and came from God; neither came I of myself, but he sent me. Why do ye not understand my speech? Even because ye cannot hear my word. Ye are of your father the devil" (John 8:41-44).

Here is a case right in your Bible where the unredeemed were calling God their Father. And thousands are doing the same thing today, and being encouraged to do it by their religious leaders.

Mister, *I do not want the devil for any relative at all.* I would be ashamed of any association. I do not want anybody to point at me and say, "He belongs to the devil."

Sinner, you can have a new relationship through the person of Jesus Christ. This is what the Man of Calvary has accomplished. God has testified to it.

"For the Father judgeth no man, but hath committed all judgment unto the Son, that all men should honor the Son, even as they honor the Father. He that honoreth not the Son honoreth not the Father which hath sent him" (John 5:22, 23).

I want you to read these solemn words found in your Bible. You will find them in Acts 10:42.

"And he commanded us to preach unto the people, and to testify that it is he who hath been ordained of God to be the judge of living and dead."

Sinner, you need help! You need redemption. You need a heavenly adoption. You need to know what it is to be a son of God.

You can have this help. You can know. "As many as received him to them gave he power to become the sons of God, even to them that believe on his name" (John 1:12). That offer stands good.

FOR NOTES